T0305142

Economic Theory and Competition Law

Economic Theory and Competition Law

Edited by

Josef Drexl

Director of Max Planck Institute for Intellectual Property, Competition and Tax Law, Munich, Germany

Laurence Idot

Professor of Law, University of Paris II Panthéon-Assas, France

Joël Monéger

Professor of Law, University of Paris Dauphine, France

ASCOLA COMPETITION LAW
The Second ASCOLA Workshop on Comparative Competition Law

Edward Elgar

Cheltenham, UK • Northampton, MA, USA

Published by
Edward Elgar Publishing Limited
The Lypiatts
15 Lansdown Road
Cheltenham
Glos GL50 2JA
UK

Edward Elgar Publishing, Inc.
William Pratt House
9 Dewey Court
Northampton
Massachusetts 01060
USA

A catalogue record for this book
is available from the British Library

Library of Congress Control Number: 2008939748

MIX
Paper | Supporting
responsible forestry
FSC
www.fsc.org   FSC® C013604

ISBN 978 1 84720 631 2

Printed and bound by CPI Group (UK) Ltd, Croydon, CR0 4YY

Contents

Preface

This book brings together the 17 contributions to the second conference of the Academic Society for Competition Law (ASCOLA) which was held at the University of Paris Dauphine and the University of Paris I-Panthéon Sorbonne on 8 to 9 December 2006.

Economic theory has always been the basis of competition law. No competition law can be applied without a clear understanding by the enforcer or the judge of the economics of the market. Yet, economic theory is winning even more ground in competition law. In the European Union, this is mostly due to the policy decision of the Commission, taken under former Competition Commissioner Mario Monti, to implement the so-called 'more economic approach'. This approach abandons the form-based approach and advocates an assessment of the legality of certain behaviour in the light of its impact on the relevant market. The more economic approach has so far been implemented by a new generation of block-exemption regulations, a fundamental reform of the Merger Control Regulation and is planned to be continued for the control of abuses of market dominance. Even control of State aid is not immune from economic reconsideration. In this brave new world, competition lawyers often have to cooperate with economists, for instance with regard to defining the relevant market and assessing market shares. Apart from a different approach to the application of competition law, the question is also whether the more economic approach changes the goals of competition law.

Given this development, it is no wonder that ASCOLA has chosen the topic of economic theory for its second conference. The ASCOLA conference differed from a conference that concentrates on how the application of the law changes in times of a more economic approach in two respects. First, as a truly international association, ASCOLA took a global and comparative approach by investigating the status of economic reasoning in different jurisdictions. Second, the conference followed a critical approach. It did not take the soundness of the current move towards 'more economics' for granted, but discussed the role economic theory should play in competition law more fundamentally.

In conformity with the structure of the conference, this book is divided into three main parts: the first part brings together five contributions written against the background of different jurisdictions. In the second part, the book confronts the tricky questions of whether economic efficiency should be recognized as the ultimate goal of competition law, whether on the contrary economic analysis should only serve as a tool to better promote legal objectives and whether additional goals in conflict with efficiency should be accepted in competition law. In the third part, the book finally addresses more concrete issues of competition law application concerning restrictive agreements, mergers and finally enforcement.

The first part starts with a contribution from European practice. *Hans Friederiszick*, who worked on the staff of the European Commission's Chief Economist for some years, provides insights into how the Commission uses economics to improve existing rules, to analyse individual cases and for ex-post analysis of the effectiveness of its enforcement policies. *David J Gerber* enriches the debate by questioning the assumption that the economic approach to competition law will bring Europe closer to the US. He argues that the economic approach may well play out differently in different institutional settings. Therefore he warns policy makers in Europe against simply transferring economic concepts used under US law without taking into account the specific embeddedness of economics in US institutions. *Shuya Hayashi* provides a very rich account of the Japanese development of competition policy and the goals it pursues. Japan, a country which has only recently attained significant levels of enforcement, has been successful in implementing a competition culture based on a concept of 'fair' competition and the conviction that protecting the competitive process is the best device for promoting prosperity. In this regard, he takes Japan as an example for the newly globalized world and explains that an approach to competition law like the one in Japan does not at all exclude taking into account modern economic reasoning for better identifying procompetitive, efficiency-enhancing conduct. *Luboš Tichý* looks at the experience of former socialist countries in Central Europe, which have become EU Member States only recently, in introducing competition law and adjusting to a more economic approach. Finally, more and more developing countries are managing to establish robust competition law systems, but have to face specific economic, social and cultural challenges. Mostly in the form of a case study, *Geoff Parr* analyses how merger control practice in South Africa is dealing with a conflict between efficiency and the interest in maintaining jobs.

Most economists would agree that efficiency should be recognized as the ultimate goal of competition policy. In the second part of the book, *Wolfgang Kerber* questions this assumption – most interestingly – from within economic theory. His starting point is that the neoclassical price theory of industrial organisation economics is not able to integrate normative values like economic freedom, legal certainty or distributive justice.

In order to build a bridge between economists and lawyers, he proposes to include other disciplines of economics, in particular constitutional economics. In what was initially meant as a comment on Wolfgang Kerber, *Roger Zäch* makes a strong statement against accepting consumer welfare and efficiency as the ultimate goals of competition law. Since competition lawyers cannot predict future economic outcomes, protecting the competitive process and the freedom to compete should remain the very purpose of competition law. Yet nobody will doubt that, for instance in the framework of Article 81(3) EC and other competition law provisions, the pro-competitive effects of certain behaviour have to be taken into account. *Anne Perrot* defends a clear-cut economic assessment of such behaviour that focuses on short-term consumer surplus, including innovation, and excludes conflicting goals like saving jobs or protecting the environment. On the same topic, *Heike Schweitze*r discusses the possibilities to consider conflicting goals in the legal framework of the EC Treaty. Here, obviously, arguments will need to be reconsidered after the coming into force of the Lisbonne Reform Treaty that moves the protection of undistorted competition – current Article 3(1)(g) EC – from the introductory list of objectives of the Community (Union) to a mere protocol annexed to the Treaty. Most importantly, however, the author reviews and discusses the possibilities for an exemption under Article 81(3) EC in view of public interest arguments as they are known from the case-law on the fundamental freedoms.

In the third part, *Thomas Eilmansberger* discusses whether an increased role for economic analysis would lead to a convergence of the application of Articles 81 and 82 EC. In so doing, he makes an assessment of a number of specific forms of conduct at the interface of the two provisions and comes up with highly differentiated results. In her comments, *Michal Gal* goes far beyond a reaction to Thomas Eilmansberger by making a strong statement that the concept of fairness has always been and remains a part of Community competition law. *Thomas L Greaney* then turns our attention to the assessment of efficiencies in US merger control law. The efficiency defence in US merger control law has undeniably been one of the first big successes of economic theory in modern competition law. However, it is also the field where we best see that making assumptions about future economic outcomes can be most difficult. This is why the author advocates very cautious legal rules on the efficiency defence. *Daniel Zimmer*, in his comments, defends a concept of protecting the competitive market structure against the efficiency defence. The last three contributions deal with enforcement issues. *Marie-Anne Frison-Roche* analyses the recent trend to more private enforcement of EC competition law as an expression of a more economic approach to the enforcement system, which transcends the traditional borderline between public and private law. *Antoine Louvaris* takes a look at the relationship between the competition law goal of promoting efficient economic outcomes, the effectiveness of the procedural arrangements and the 'efficacy' of such arrangements in the sense of the fitness of legal process to promote efficiency. Of course, procedural rules are based on many normative considerations that diverge from the efficiency goal. Such divergence may lead, as the author explains, to two types of conflicts, namely failure conflicts – that is, when the procedure is effective but conflicts with the efficiency goal – and structural conflicts – when procedural rules 'efficaciously' promote goals other than efficiency. Finally, *Muriel Chagny* picks up the distinction introduced by Antoine Louvaris and provides interesting insights into the practice of for the most part, the French jurisdiction regarding these two types of errors.

The book closes with the guest speech delivered by *Bruno Lasserre*, the president of the French *Conseil de la concurrence*, on efficiency in the agency's enforcement policy.

Many other people were involved in the preparation of this book. A number of students helped to organise the conference in Paris. Jessica Ploß and Lorenz Marx ensured that the incoming contributions conformed to the style of the book. Delia Zirilli and Dr Rupprecht Podszun played an essential role in managing the constantly changing versions sent around the digital world. Most important and time consuming was the work done by Allison Felmy. She reviewed all the contributions, especially those of the non-native speakers, from a linguistic point of view. Last but not least, the editors are very grateful to the staff of Edward Elgar, especially to Luke Adams and Nep Elverd, who strongly supported the book throughout the time of its coming into existence.

Josef Drexl, Laurence Idot, Joël Monéger

Munich and Paris, April 2008

Abbreviations

AG	Advocate General
Am Econ Rev	American Economics Review
Am J Comp L	American Journal of Comparative Law
Am J Int'l L	American Journal of International Law
AMC	Antitrust Modernization Commission
Antitrust Bull	Antitrust Bulletin
Antitrust LJ	Antitrust Law Journal
Can J Econ	Canadian Journal of Economics
Cass. com.	Cour de cassation: Arrêt de la Chambre commerciale
C. com.	Code de commerce (France)
Cir	Circuit (US Court of Appeals)
CLP	Current Legal Problems
CLS	Current Legal Studies
CML Rev	Common Market Law Review
Coll	Sbírka zákonů České republiky (Collections of Laws of the Czech Republic)
Comp Pol'y Int'l	Competition Policy International
Comp Pol'y Newsletter	Competition Policy Newsletter
Const Pol Econ	Constitutional Political Economy
DG COMP	Directorate General for Competition
DGCCRF	Direction générale de la concurrence, de la consommation et de la répression des fraudes (France)
EAGCP	Economic Advisory Group for Competition Policy
ECJ	European Court of Justice
ECLR	European Competition Law Review
Econ J	The Economic Journal
Econ Pol'y	Economic Policy
ed(s)	editor(s)
edn	edition
EL Rev	European Law Review
ERPL	European Review of Private Law
Eur Comp J	European Competition Journal

EuZW	Europäische Zeitschrift für Wirtschaftsrecht
F Supp	Federal Supplement
GATT	General Agreement on Tariffs and Trade
George Mason U L Rev	George Mason University Law Review
Hofstra L Rev	Hofstra Law Review
id	idem
ie	id est
Int J Ind Org	International Journal of Industrial Organization
IP	intellectual property
JASSS	Journal of Artificial Societies and Social Simulation
J Comp L & Econ	Journal of Competition Law and Economics
J Econ Iss	Journal of Economic Issues
J Econ Lit	Journal of Economic Literature
J Econ Hist	Journal of Economic History
J Econ Persp	Journal of Economic Perspectives
JFTC	Japan Fair Trade Commission
J Inst Econ	Journal of Institutional Economics
J L Econ & Org	Journal of Law, Economics and Organization
J Leg Stud	Journal of Legal Studies
JO	Journal Officiel (France)
J Pol Econ	Journal of Political Economy
L Ed	Lawyers' Edition
Loy U Chi L J	Loyola University Chicago Law Journal
Md L Rev	Maryland Law Review
Mich J Int'l L	Michigan Journal of International Law
MITI	Ministry of International Trade and Industry (Japan)
No	number(s)
OJ	Official Journal (EU)
OJLS	Oxford Journal of Legal Studies
ORDO	Jahrbuch für die Ordnung von Wirtschaft und Gesellschaft
Pac Rim L & Pol'y J	Pacific Rim Law and Policy Journal
para(s)	paragraph(s)
Qu J Econ	Quarterly Journal of Economics
Reg	Regulation
Rev Econ Stud	Review of Economic Studies
RIDE	Revue Internationale de Droit Economique
S Ct	Supreme Court Reporter

T. Com.	Tribunal de Commerce (France)
TEU	Treaty on the European Union
Trade Cas (CCH)	CCH Trade Cases
Trade Reg Rept (CCH)	CCH Trade Regulation Reporter
Tulane L Rev	Tulane Law Review
U Chi L Rev	University of Chicago Law Review
US	United States Supreme Court Reporter
USTR	United States Trade Representative
World Comp	World Competition
WRP	Wettbewerb in Recht und Praxis
WTO	World Trade Organization
WuW	Wirtschaft und Wettbewerb
ZHR	Zeitschrift für das gesamte Handelsrecht
ZWeR	Zeitschrift für Wettbewerbsrecht (Journal of Competition Law)

PART I

The goals of competition law – a comparative perspective

1. Economic analysis in EU competition cases

Hans W Friederiszick*

1 INTRODUCTION

Economic analysis has become an integral part of EU competition policy. Competition policy focuses on the negative effects of a measure on competition and trade and balances these with potential positive effects. In this way, counterfactual analysis, market definition and an effects-based analysis in certain cases are the unifying themes of modern economic analysis as it is applied to competition policy.

Economic analysis can play an important role in three different fields: improving existing rules, analysing individual cases and ex-post analysis of the effectiveness of the intervention. This chapter provides an overview of how and when economic analysis can be applied in those areas, based on some current examples. It discusses the limits and the benefits of a more effects-based approach.

2 ECONOMIC ANALYSIS IN EU COMPETITION POLICY

Economic analysis was marginal to EU competition policy until the late 1980s. Since then, the importance of economic analysis has increased significantly. The main feature of this extended reliance on economics is a reassessment of decision making in the light of economic principles – with respect to both better rules and an effects-based, case-specific analysis in some cases.

* The author is a member of the faculty of the European School of Management and Technology (ESMT), and Managing Director of ESMT Competition Analysis. From 2003 to 2006 he was a member of the team of the Chief Economist at the Directorate General for Competition (DG COMP), European Commission. Part of this chapter is based on a joint presentation with Lars-Hendrik Röller. The views expressed are those of the author alone.

The success of this reform strongly depends on the institutional environment in which it is embedded. It requires improved economic know-how and capabilities on the part of both the enforcer and the affected parties. In fact, one observes a steep increase in resources put into this reform. The current Competition Commissioner, Neelie Kroes, recently announced that the team of the Chief Economist, which is at the forefront of establishing economic analysis in the Directorate General for Competition, will double in size. Damien Neven, Chief Economist of DG COMP, argued in a recent article that the ratio of economists to lawyers at DG COMP, which was around 1 to 7 in the early 1990s, increased to 1 to 2 by 2007.[1] Furthermore national competition authorities, even those that have so far been rather reluctant to switch to economic analysis, have recently built up additional capacities.[2]

The increase in capacity by the competition authorities follows an even steeper increase in the commercial market for economic analysis. Starting from close to zero in the early 1990s, the turnover of economic consultancies has increased to around €30 million in 2004 according to some estimates.[3] Assuming that the market has grown in a manner comparable to previous years, one could consider a turnover of more than €60 million a plausible estimate of the size of this market in Europe.[4] Overall, recent estimates suggest that roughly 15 per cent of the fees for law advice are spent on economic analysis, with economists being more involved in phase-two cases or cases involving novel or complex analysis.

Introducing economic analysis into antitrust enforcement also requires a long-term commitment by policy makers to make it a success. Mario

---

[1]   D Neven, 'Competition Economics in Europe', in *Global Competition Review – The 2007 Handbook of Competition Economics* (2007) 4, and D Neven, 'Competition Economics and Antitrust in Europe' (2006) 21 *Econ Pol'y* 741.

[2]   For instance, the German competition authority recently appointed a chief economist.

[3]   *See* Neven, *supra* note 1, at 4, assuming an exchange rate of around 1.45€/£. Interestingly, the increase in economic consulting was closely linked to the introduction of the Commission Notice on the definition of relevant market for the purposes of Community competition law in 1997. In the same manner, the recent reform, ie the 'refined economic approach', is often linked to the introduction of an efficiency defence in the Merger Guidelines of 2004. However, this interpretation falls short of a proper, modern understanding of the role of economics in competition cases, in which economic analysis becomes an integral part of the case assessment.

[4]   According to Neven, the turnover doubled over the three years from 2001 to 2004. Accordingly, one could assume that the market size doubled again over the years 2004 to 2007. Whether this growth path is sustainable or simply due to the current merger trends in the US and Europe remains to be seen.

Monti, Competition Commissioner until 2004, stated: 'A major trend of this mandate has been to ensure that competition policy is fully compatible with economic learning'. By the same token, Commissioner Kroes more recently put forward: 'We are overhauling all our rules in order to firmly ground them in rigorous economic analysis and to improve speed, transparency and predictability of their application'. Important recent initiatives like the new R&D&I State Aid Guidelines,[5] which constitute the first Commission document to establish the refined economic approach in the field of state aid control, or the recently published Non-Horizontal Merger Guidelines,[6] indicate ongoing support for this reform by the current cabinet.

2.1 Elements of Robust Empirical Analysis

While in principle economic analysis is based on both economic theory and its empirical verification, one can identify four basic rules for a robust economic analysis. Firstly, it has to be based on cumulative knowledge, the economical canon, more than on marginal knowledge. Tailor-made economic theories of harm seem to be questionable and more prone to strategic manipulation than approaches that have been applied previously at various instances.[7] Secondly, the theory of harm, which is the legal concept, has to be confronted with economic theory early in the administrative process. In fact, one of the most important features of modern usage of economics in antitrust proceedings is its application from the very beginning of a case, thereby assuring convergence of legal and economic concepts up front. Thirdly, a robust empirical analysis has to be based on facts. The assumptions of the theoretical framework have to be checked, verifiable hypotheses have to be tested and expected effects need to be quantified. Fourthly, a robust empirical analysis should rely on various methods and should provide measures of the robustness of the estimates delivered.

---

[5] Community Framework for State Aid for Research and Development and Innovation, 13 December 2006, [2006] OJ C 323, p 1.

[6] Guidelines on the assessment of non-horizontal mergers under the Council Regulation on the control of concentrations between undertakings; http://ec.europa.eu/comm/competition/mergers/legislation/nonhorizontalguidelines.pdf (accessed 31 January 2008).

[7] There is some trade-off, though, in relying on standard models versus applying the most recent economic thinking. While the former may reduce the danger of strategic manipulation or intellectual domination, the latter ensures the application of the most recent economic thinking in antitrust policy. By updating economic guidelines on reasonable terms, this conflict can be resolved.

2.2   Change in the Commission's Handling of Economic Analysis

Interestingly one can observe a change in how the EC Commission has handled the subject of economic analysis over the last few years. In the 1999 decision on the *Volvo/Scania* merger, econometric analysis still seemed to be a rather novel feature for the Commission and the Commission did not see itself in a position to judge what was a robust interpretation of the studies put forward by various economists: 'Given the novelty of the approach and the level of disagreement, the Commission will not base its assessment on the results of the study'.[8]

In the same manner, the 2001 decision on the *GE/Honeywell* merger was rather half-hearted with respect to economic analysis. In this case, the Commission first put forward an economic model, the so-called Choi model, to support its case. But then, in its final decision, the Commission abandoned this model due to some criticism by the parties and their external economists – an approach that was commented on by the EC court rather cynically. In its 2005 decision, the Court of First Instance argues:

> The only economic evidence substantiating the Commission's argument concerning the future demise of Rolls-Royce and P&W was Professor Choi's economic model, commissioned by Rolls-Royce through the consultancy Frontier Economics ('the Choi model'), which has, however, been abandoned by the Commission. Furthermore, the Commission has not refuted the analyses submitted by rival experts who reached the opposite conclusion.[9]

A new self-confidence in applying and verifying economic modelling can be found in later EC decisions. In the 2005 *Oracle/Peoplesoft* decision, the Commission felt in a position to reason about mathematical models and to defend their application despite the fact that mathematical models are inevitably based on simple assumptions:

> For models to be mathematically tractable it is necessary to make simplifying assumptions and in this process it is important to ensure that the essential mechanisms that are left in the model adequately reflect the reality.
>
> But the debate over which simplifications to accept in the model should not obscure the fact that any prospective analysis of the effect of a merger will inherently be based on assumptions. A prediction of the effect of a merger made within the framework of a model is based on a high degree of transparency regarding the logical consistency of the prediction as well as its underlying assumptions. A prospective analysis made outside the framework of an

---

[8]   Commission Decision, 14 March 2000, Case No COMP/M.1672 – *Volvo/Scania*, para 75.

[9]   Case T-210/01 – *General Electric v Commission* [2005] ECR II-5575, para 109.

economic model based on qualitative assessment is equally, though in a less transparent and implicit way, based on a number of assumptions and may therefore equally be subject to the same kinds of criticisms.[10]

The simulation model applied in this case was, however, rejected due to the fact that the underlying assumptions did not coincide with the facts of the case.

The changed approach of the Commission might have peaked with the recent *Ryanair/Aer Lingus* prohibition decision.[11] In this decision, the Commission carefully reassessed the econometric study put forward by the parties and carried out its own empirical analysis. A 93-page appendix explains in detail the empirical method applied and the various robustness checks carried out. More importantly, the econometric analysis found its way from footnotes and appendices into the main body of the decision.[12]

2.3 Areas of Economic Analysis

The use of economic principles and analysis can vary substantially over the different possible areas of their application. In principle, three areas – depending on the relevant time horizon – can be identified where economic analysis can strengthen the enforcement of competition policy.[13]

Firstly, there is the application to individual cases. This type of investigation has a relatively short-term nature and concerns both the identification of *theories of harm* as well as their empirical testing. As mentioned previously, the stronger application of economic analysis has made the discussion of *theories of harm* necessary at an early stage. Resulting from the economic analysis is an increased focus on the resulting market equilibrium, which might be less well represented in a partial analysis. An appropriate weight in the analysis has also been achieved by the consideration of possible counter-strategies by competitors or buyers and potential efficiencies. Furthermore, due to the application of effects-based analysis, the counterfactual approach has become more important. This policy revision is especially visible in the field of state aid, where more recent Commission documents like the recently adopted R&D&I State Aid

---

[10] Commission Decision, 26 October 2005, Case No COMP/M.3216 – *Oracle/Peoplesoft*, paras 193 *et seq.*

[11] Commission Decision, 27 June 2007, Case No COMP/M.4439 – *Ryanair/Aer Lingus*.

[12] *Id*, paras 450–90 and Annex IV.

[13] *See* L-H Röller, 'Economic Analysis and Competition Policy Enforcement in Europe' in P van Bergeijk and E Kloosterhuis (eds), *Modelling European Mergers* (2005).

Guidelines directly refer to a counterfactual analysis as a central point for an analysis of whether a state aid measure will have an incentive effect or not.[14]

Secondly, economic analysis also plays a decisive role in the formulation of new guidelines or group exemptions. Compared to case-specific work – which, by definition, is more context-oriented – guidelines should be based on robust principles which endure in the long term. The definition of adequately robust economic rules demonstrates the challenge. Ideally, guidelines are based on an appropriate mix of form-based rules, in areas where economic effects over a wide range are not case-specific and effects-based rules, in areas where it is necessary to differentiate between cases on a contextual basis. The design of the new R&D&I Guidelines in the area of state aid control is an example of such an attempt.[15] Based on the balancing test as developed in the State Aid Action Plan, economic analysis has led to a careful adjustment of existing form-based rules and has introduced, among other things, an effects-based analysis for specific individual cases. The current discussion of the guidelines in the areas of Article 82 and the recently adopted Guidelines on non-horizontal mergers are additional examples of the relevance of economic analysis in the formulation of new guidelines or group exemptions.

Thirdly, economic analysis plays an important role in the evaluation and control of competition policy. When evaluating competition policy, one can examine the defectiveness of a decision made by the competition authorities in the sense of type 1 and type 2 errors. The study done by the Commission on remedies in merger cases[16] is a successful example of such an approach. The internal study evaluates the design and implementation of remedies in 40 merger cases during the period between 1996 and 2000. In total 96 remedies were examined, of which the majority addressed competition concerns by commitments to transfer a market position (divestiture). In 57 per cent of the investigated merger remedies, the competition objective was fully achieved and in 24 per cent of the cases it was achieved partially. Seven per cent of the merger remedies appeared to be ineffective. The main reason why some merger remedies were ineffective was

---

[14]   However, the acceptance of counterfactual analysis is also rising in other areas. *See*, for instance, the *O2* decision in the realm of Article 81; Case T-328/03 – *O2 (Germany) v Commission* [2006] ECR II-1231, paras 71–3.

[15]   *See* Community Framework for State Aid for Research and Development and Innovation, *supra* note 5.

[16]   European Commission, DG Competition, 'Merger Remedies Study, Staff Paper' (December 2005), http://ec.europa.eu/comm/competition/mergers/others/remedies_study.pdf (accessed 31 January 2008).

the incorrect definition of divestiture remedies, with regard to both their type and their extent. Other reasons for the ineffectiveness of some implemented merger remedies were the selection of inappropriate buyers and the incorrect or incomplete allocation of investment values to the divested businesses.

Ex-post analysis of, for example, merger decisions[17] or state aid decisions[18] is another example of the role that economic analysis can play in the evaluation and control of competition policy. Conceptually, however, there are ultimately two problems that can arise when executing such studies. The first is the identification of a plausible counterfactual (see above). The second is the endogeneity of the decision made by the competition authority. The latter denotes the possibility that the decision of the competition authority and the market outcome are not independent of each other. In this case, the evaluation will be incorrect. If, for example, only competitive firms are subsidized by a state agency, then in the ex-post evaluation that compares the performance of subsidized and non-subsidized firms one will find a positive effect of state aid. Because of these problems the number of potential applications of such studies is limited and additional efforts are required. The control of competition policy can be achieved especially by market observations and – closely related – by priority criteria. Market observations, for example as currently taking place through the sector enquiries in the energy and finance markets, enable an extensive collection of relevant factors and thereby provide the basis for a robust economic understanding of the respective sector. In return, this makes it possible to identify important competition problems and solve them – as far as is possible with the instruments available in competition policy. This way, the recent enquiry in the energy sector has identified material competition

---

[17] *See eg* PricewaterhouseCoopers, 'Ex Post Evaluation of Mergers. Study for Office of Fair Trading, Department of Trade and Industry and the Competition Commission' (2005), http://www.competition-commission.org.uk/our_role/evaluation/ex_post_evaluation_of_mergers.pdf (accessed 31 January 2008); and Lear (Laboratorio di economia, antitrust, regolamentazione), 'Ex-Post Review of Merger Control Decisions. Report for the European Commission' (2006), http://ec.europa.eu/comm/competition/mergers/studies_reports/lear.pdf (accessed 31 January 2008).

[18] *See eg* London Economics (2004), 'Ex-post Evaluation of the Impact of Rescue and Restructuring Aid on the International Competitiveness of the Sector(s) Affected by Such Aid, Final Report to the European Commission – Enterprise Directorate-General' (2004), http://ec.europa.eu/enterprise/library/lib-competition/doc/impact_rescue_restructuring_state_aid.pdf (accessed 31 January 2008); and NERA Economic Consulting, 'Case Studies of Public Subsidies, Study for the Office of Fair Trading' (2006), http://www.oft.gov.uk/shared_oft/reports/comp_policy/oft828.pdf (accessed 31 January 2008).

problems in the gas and electricity markets.[19] Especially the prolonged high degrees of market concentration, the damaging effect to competition of vertical exclusion strategies, the limited implementation of market integration and the problems with transparency and price setting were identified as significant restraints to effective competition. A balanced approach between regulatory and competition-policy interventions will be the consequence of these investigations. An economically meaningful demarcation of regulatory and competition-policy instruments thereby represents yet another area for economic analysis.[20]

2.4   Recent Examples of Economic Analysis

Reform takes time. On 1 May 2004 the new EC Merger Regulation came into effect and parallel to this, the corresponding Guidelines for horizontal mergers were adopted. The new substantive test put the hindering of effective competition in the centre of the analysis, and the concept of dominance – although still important – became a more secondary aspect. A first analysis of the merger decisions that have been handed down since then shows a slightly hesitant turning away from the dominance criterion and towards the concept of equilibrium analysis.[21] Of the 23 analysed decisions, 13 cases address concerns with respect to unilateral dominance and five relate to collective dominance. In three cases, the evaluation is built on an equilibrium analysis, whereas the dominance criterion plays only a secondary role.[22] The *Bertelsmann/Springer/JV*

---

[19]   The final report can be found at http://ec.europa.eu/comm/competition/sectors/energy/inquiry/index.html (accessed 31 January 2008).

[20]   The most elaborate framework with respect to phasing out regulatory instruments and introducing competition-policy instruments is applied to the telecommunications sector. For a recent study evaluating the impact of regulation in this sector, *see* HW Friederiszick, M Grajek and L-H Röller, *Analyzing the Relationship between Regulation and Investment in the Telecom Sector. ESMT Competition Analysis* (2007).

[21]   *See* L-H Röller and M de la Mano, 'The Impact of the New Substantive Test in European Merger Control' (2006) 2 Eur Comp J 1, 9–28. The paper analyses mergers notified between 1 May 2004 and 12 October 2005 over which the Commission expressed doubts about their effect on competition (ie all cases that were prohibited or were cleared subject to conditions). Altogether 23 cases were analysed, of which 18 were cleared in phase 1 and five in phase 2. In this period, no mergers were prohibited.

[22]   Commission Decision, 25 August 2005, Case No COMP/M.3687 – *Johnson& Johnson/Guidant*; Commission Decision, 13 July 2005, Case No COMP/M.3653 – *Siemens/VA Tech*; and Commission Decision, 4 July 2005, Case No COMP/M.3770 – *Lufthansa/Swiss*.

case[23] does not exhibit a direct reference to the dominance criterion either, but still refers to the clear market leadership of the newly founded joint enterprise. The *Total/Gaz de France* case analyses vertical problems for competition (third-party access to infrastructure) in the French gas market, but also without an explicit reference to the dominance criterion. This – initially only verbal – distance from the dominance criterion appears until now still limited but significant.[24]

Compared to the execution of past proceedings the reform process has also brought a stronger deployment of empirical methods. As part of the investigations around the *Volvo/Scania* (1999) merger,[25] for example, an econometric study was performed, even though in the end it was not included in the decision. In a similar way, the complainant in the *GE/Honeywell* merger case[26] put forward a theoretical work during the proceedings to which no reference was made in the later decision.[27]

In the last couple of years, one can however observe a change in attitude, although still a cautious one. This can be inferred from the fact that in various cases economic – in particular, empirical – techniques for analysis have been applied in a more marked way.[28] In the clearance decision of the merger between two Swedish electricity companies, *Sydkraft/Graninge*

---

[23]　Commission Decision, 3 May 2005, Case No. COMP/M.3178 – *Bertelsmann/Springer/JV*.

[24]　Due to the gradual character of the reform process, the clear identification of a 'gap case' is difficult. Röller and de la Mano, *supra* note 21, consider the *E.ON/MOL* case (Commission Decision, 21 December 2005, Case COMP/M.3696) a potential 'gap case'. However, the decision on this case also contains parts that refer to the dominance criterion. The *T-Mobile Austria/Tele.ring* case (Commission Decision, 26 April 2006, Case No COMP/M.3916) seems so far to best fit the profile of a gap case.

[25]　Commission Decision, 15 March 2000, Case No COMP/M.1672 – *Volvo/Scania*.

[26]　Commission Decision, 3 July 2001, Case No COMP/M.2220 – *General Electric/Honeywell*.

[27]　*See* discussion at 2.2 above.

[28]　It is not easy to show the application of economic theory, as there is not one specific theoretical model that is always applicable (*see* the *GE/Honeywell* merger discussed in section 2.2 above). For an attempt to determine the impact of the reformed merger analysis on EC decisions, *see* Röller and de la Mano, *supra* note 21. A closer connection to economic theory is easy to recognize in individual cases in the field of state aid control, in particular with respect to the application of the 'market failure' concept. *See eg* Commission Letter, 8 March 2006, Case No N 284/2005 – *Ireland: Regional Broadband Programme: Metropolitan Area Networks (MANs), phases II and III*, paras 58–63, or Commission Decision, 9 November 2005, Case C 25/2004 – *DVB-T Berlin Brandenburg*, [2006] OJ L 200, p 14, paras 95–119 (concerning state aid in Germany for the introduction of digital terrestrial television).

(2003),[29] there was, for example, a reference to the results of a merger simulation that was carried out based on a model of the Danish network operator Eltra. If the Commission, despite the relatively small increase in market share, had identified potential problems of dominance in the relevant electricity markets, then the simulation results would have done away with concerns about significant price effects as a result of the merger.[30]

In the merger case *Lagardère/Natexis/VUP* (2004), the Commission hired an expert to estimate a demand model, which was later used in the decision.[31] The model analyses the unilateral price effects of the merger and finds significant price effects of on average 4.48 per cent in the retail market for general literature (pocket format and large books).[32] The study furthermore predicts a considerable decline in consumer surplus of around 6 per cent as a consequence of the merger. This decline in consumer surplus corresponds to a not insubstantial part of the total turnover in the reviewed markets (namely 1.5 per cent).

In the merger case *GE/Instrumentarium* (2003),[33] a merger in the market for medical appliances, tender data were statistically analysed. Europe-wide information about tenders by the four main suppliers of patient monitors was gathered over a time span of five years – encompassing over a thousand tenders – with the objective of analysing the degree of competition between both merger parties. In this manner, for example, the frequency with which the two merger parties met each other during the tender periods – and especially the frequency with which one of the partners offered the second-best bid and the other partner actually won the tender – was used to make inferences about the degree of competition. It was also analysed whether as a result of the participation of the merger partner in a tender, the other partner could obtain only a relatively low price or needed to grant higher discounts.

---

[29]   Commission Decision, 30 October 2003, Case No COMP/M.3268 – *Sydkraft/Graninge*.

[30]   Also in the Commission Decision, 2 October 2003, Case No COMP/M.3191 – *Philip Morris/Papastratos*, a merger in the Greek cigarette market, there was a reference to the results of a merger simulation. The results of the study that was presented by the parties appear to have at most confirmed the results of the investigation by the Commission itself.

[31]   Commission Decision, 7 January 2004, Case No COMP/M.2978 – *Lagardère/Natexis/VUP*, paras 700–706.

[32]   With a probability of 95 per cent the price increase was estimated to be between 3.74 and 5.54 per cent. *See id*, para 702.

[33]   Commission Decision, 2 September 2003, Case No COMP/M.3083 – *GE/Instrumentarium*. A description of the empirical work is offered by G Loriot, F-X Rouxel and B Durand, 'GE/Instrumentarium: A Practical Example of the Use of Quantitative Analyses in Merger Control' (2004) *Comp Pol'y Newsletter* No 1, 58.

In the takeover case of Peoplesoft by Oracle (2004),[34] a merger in the market for software applications for businesses, tender data were also put forward. In particular, the analysis investigated whether the three main suppliers, Oracle, Peoplesoft and SAP, together presented a close oligopoly or whether other suppliers could exert significant competitive pressure as well. Based on three different data sets, the role played by individual firms in tenders was analysed (in a similar manner to the analysis in *GE/Instrumentarium*). In all three databases, no significant difference could be determined between the competitive conduct of Oracle towards SAP or Peoplesoft and its conduct towards other suppliers.[35] This result conflicts with the theory that the three parties present a tight oligopoly. Also the impact of the number of bidders in a single tender was analysed econometrically. However, in contrast to previous studies, no significant relation between the number of bidders in the final round and given discounts could be determined, given that the order size was controlled for in the analysis. In other words, the econometric results provided no additional evidence of a significant reduction in competition as a result of the merger. The broader market definition inferred from the previously mentioned results also led to the dismissal of the proposed simulation model, as this model was based on the assumption of a tight oligopoly in the relevant market.[36]

In the takeover of the Canadian chemical firm Acetex by the North American investment bank Blackstone (2005),[37] the results of an econometric analysis were relevant for market definition. The Commission initially expressed concerns regarding competition, as Blackstone also controlled another company that was active in the same market as Acetex. Besides correlation analyses, the parties also conducted an econometric study that analysed the regional effects of unexpected company shutdowns[38] on prices and trade flows in neighbouring markets. After the addition of more data and adaptation of the model, the Commission concluded that unexpected company shutdowns in Western Europe led to significant price increases not only in this region, but also in North America. This is evidence for the fact that North American producers react to a lower supply in Europe with increased imports, and therefore one can assume a broader

---

[34] Commission Decision, 26 October 2005, Case No COMP/M.3216 – *Oracle/Peoplesoft*.

[35] *Id*, para 143.

[36] *Id*, para 196.

[37] Commission Decision, 13 July 2005, Case No COMP/M.3625 – *Blackstone/Acetex*.

[38] Company shutdowns present natural experiments where this occurrence is both unexpected and without the influence of other market participants.

geographical market. A direct analysis of trade flows complemented the empirical investigation.[39]

The Commission also conducted an extensive investigation of empirical evidence when Sony and BMG wanted to create a music recording joint venture.[40] In the analysis of this tight oligopoly – the joint venture would reduce the number of 'majors' (Universal Music, Sony Music, EMI, Warner Music and BMG) from five to four, and these four again would control about 80 per cent of the relevant market – particular attention was paid to the potential development or enforcement of a collectively dominant position. In particular, the element of parallel pricing (as an indicator of existing coordination) and the aspect of transparency (as a necessary condition for future coordination according to the *Airtours* criteria) were evaluated by means of an extensive price analysis. For this purpose, price information regarding the 100 bestselling CDs of all time was collected and an analysis carried out on average prices. No significant support was found for the identification of past price agreements and the lack of transparency found as a result of the practice of giving rebates made future collective dominance seem unlikely. In spite of this data-intensive analysis, the decision was reversed by the Court of First Instance.[41] With this first dismissal of a clearing decision for a merger case, it becomes clear that the standard regarding empirical evidence in clearance decisions is just as high as when it comes to decisions that deny clearance. In 2007, the Commission reassessed the merger and concluded after 'the most thorough analyses of complex information ever undertaken by the Commission in a merger procedure' that the merger did not raise competition concerns.[42]

In the recent prohibition decision on *Ryanair/Aer Lingus* (2007), the Commission investigated the effect of entry by Ryanair on the routes on which Aer Lingus is active. Based on a data set detailing route intensity and covering monthly data over the period 2002 to 2006, the Commission found that the presence of Ryanair had a statistically and economically significant

---

[39]   B Durand and V Rabassa, 'The Role of Quantitative Analysis to Delineate Antitrust Markets: An Example. Blackstone/Acetex' (2005) *Comp Pol'y Newsletter* No 3, 118.

[40]   Commission Decision, 19 July 2004, Case No COMP/M.3333 – *Sony/BMG*, paras 67–119; P Eberl, 'Following an In-depth Investigation the Commission Approved the Creation of the Sony/BMG Music Recording Joint Venture on 19 July 2004' (2004) *Comp Pol'y Newsletter* No 3, 7.

[41]   Case T-464/04 – *Impala v Commission* [2006] ECR II-2289.

[42]   *See* Press Release IP/07/1437, 3 October 2007, http://www.ebu.ch/CMSimages/en/BRUDOC_INFO_EN_387%20_tcm6–55287.pdf (accessed 31 January 2008).

effect on the prices charged by Aer Lingus, ranging from 5 to 8 per cent lower prices depending on the particular specifications.[43]

Also, with respect to the efficiency analysis, a more careful treatment can be observed in some recent decisions. However, so far no case has been approved that was mainly based on efficiencies. After some careful discussion of the efficiencies in the above-mentioned *Ryanair/Aer Lingus* decision, the Commission concluded that the efficiencies were neither verifiable nor merger-specific. The passing on of benefits to consumers was considered rather unlikely.[44] In *Inco/Falconbridge* (2006),[45] again merger specificity was rejected due to the earlier proposal of a joint venture which would have resulted in comparable efficiencies. Here again the passing on to customers was questioned. In *Korsnäs/AD Cartonboard* (2006),[46] efficiencies seemed to be accepted, but the competitive assessment itself already indicated a clearance decision. In paragraph 64 of the decision, the Commission concludes: 'These efficiencies are thus likely to enhance the ability and incentive of the merged entity to act pro-competitively for the benefit of consumers, and therefore strengthen the conclusion that the proposed transaction will not significantly impede effective competition as a result of non coordinated effects'.

Besides merger control, economic analysis is also becoming important in the other fields of competition policy enforcement. In the Article 82 case regarding AstraZeneca[47] the method of natural experiments was applied for the market definition. In this case, the Commission accused AstraZeneca of abusing the patent and registration system for drugs with the objective of preventing market entry by competing generic drug manufacturers. In defining the market, the question was asked to what degree the affected product group of the so-called proton pump inhibitors (PPIs) was restricted by a previous generation product group, the so-called H2 blockers. With respect to the German market, among others, it was concluded that the entry of H2 generics showed a clear effect on the price and turnover of existing H2 products, but no effect was observed on the neighbouring market of PPIs. Also with regard to marketing efforts, a clear

---

[43]   Commission Decision, 27 June 2007, Case No COMP/M.4439 – *Ryanair/Aer Lingus*, paras 484 *et seq.*

[44]   *Id*, para 1151.

[45]   Commission Decision, 4 July 2006, Case No COMP/M.4000 – *INCO/ Falconbridge*, paras 529–50.

[46]   Commission Decision, 12 May 2006, Case No COMP/M.4057 – *Korsnäs/ Assidomän Cartonboard*, paras 57–64.

[47]   Commission Decision, 15 June 2005, Case COMP/A.37.507/F3 – *AstraZeneca*. Appeal was made against the Commission decision – also regarding the market definition, [2005] OJ C 271, p 24.

reaction to the introduction of the generics could be seen for existing H2 producers, but not for PPI producers. As a result of this, a narrower market definition was chosen that did not include H2 blockers.[48] An econometric study conducted by one of the parties was dismissed on the basis of conceptual shortcomings, however.[49]

Empirical methods have furthermore found their way into competition law enforcement regarding cartels. In the cartel case concerning copper plumbing tubes[50] – fines were imposed in the amount of €222.3 million – the parties presented several econometric studies with the intention of showing that the cartel had no significant effect on market prices.[51] Based on a so-called dummy-variable model it was demonstrated that only in niche markets – if at all – could price effects be observed. The Commission analysed the raw data, presented estimation procedures in a detailed manner and concluded that the results of the study did not contradict the conclusion of strong price effects over several time intervals and countries.[52] On the contrary, the Commission concluded that significant price effects as reported by whistleblowers were supported by the model.[53]

However the most dramatic turnaround may be observed in the field of state aid control. Whereas traditionally most aid measures are scrutinized under a 'one size fits all' approach based on formal criteria as described above,[54] a more systematic assessment of the positive and negative effects of the aid is implemented in some recent Commission decisions and guidelines, in particular for aid measures involving large amounts of aid.[55]

---

[48]   *Id*, paras 423 *et seq.*
[49]   *Id*, paras 462–72.
[50]   Commission Decision, 3 September 2004, Case COMP/E-1/38.069 – *Copper Plumbing Tubes*. Appeal was made against the decision, [2005] OJ C 82/39.
[51]   *Id*, paras 612 and 625.
[52]   *Id*, paras 655–66.
[53]   *Id*, para 664.
[54]   *See* at 2.3 above.
[55]   *See* Community Framework for State Aid for Research and Development and Innovation, *supra* note 5, section 1.3.1.; State Aid Action Plan – Less and better targeted state aid: a roadmap for state aid reform 2005–2009 (consulation document), 7 May 2005, COM(2005) 107 final, paras 11 and 20; Communication from the Commission – Consultation Document on State Aid for Innovation, 21 September 2005, COM(2005) 436 final. In several cases, a more explicit balancing has been applied. These include: Commission Decision, 20 December 2006, Case No C 36/2005 – *United Kingdom: Investbx*, [2008] OJ L 45, p 1; Commission Letter, 8 March 2006, Case No N 284/2005 – *Ireland: Regional Broadband Programme: Metropolitan Area Networks (MANs), phases II and III*; Commission Decision, 19 July 2006, Case No C 35/2005 – *The Netherlands: Broadband development Appingedam*, [2007] OJ L 86, p 1; Commission Decision, 5 June 2007, Case No C

As a conceptual framework for evaluating state aid measures, the Commission puts forward the use of a general balancing test. In essence, this test asks whether (1) the state aid addresses a market failure or other objectives of common interest; (2) the state aid is well targeted (ie is the aid an appropriate instrument, does it provide an incentive effect and is it kept to the required minimum?); and (3) the distortions of competition are sufficiently limited so that the overall balance is positive. Fundamentally, the test balances the positive and negative effects of state aid in the same way, as it was already the underlying principle under the old regime. The balancing test is now explicitly spelled out, though, measuring the 'benefits' of a state aid measure under steps 1 and 2 and the 'cost' or negative effects of an aid measure under step 3, including the balancing.

The balancing test provides a consistent framework for both reforming existing per se rules and an effects-based analysis for cases involving large amounts of aid. It therefore allows the introduction of a new architecture allowing a light assessment of standard cases and a more detailed assessment for some specific cases. Under the new architecture, one will find block exemptions and guidelines (eventually further distinguishing between standard and detailed assessment) in parallel,[56] allowing a better targeting of the assessment efforts on those measures that are likely to be the most distortive and reducing red-tape and administrative burden by block-exempting more measures than before.[57]

The detailed assessment, as spelled out in the R&D&I Framework, has been applied recently in various cases – most notably in several R&D state aid measures granted by the French Industrial Innovation Agency to industry consortia led by large firms. For instance, in the *NeoVal* case, the Commission approved aid of €26.5 million to the firms Siemens and Lohr for developing a new generation of metro trains featuring innovative

11/2005 – *Bavaria: Aid for an ethylene pipeline*, [2007] OJ L 143, p 1; Commission Letter, 21 February 2006, Case No N 674/2006 – *France: Soutien de l'Agence de l'innovation industrielle en faveur du projet NeoVal*.

56   The old architecture allowed either block exemptions or guidelines, but not both at the same time. The only exception to it was the block exemption for R&D aid for SMEs, which coexisted with the R&D Guidelines. *See* Commission Regulation No 364/2004 of 25 February 2004 amending Regulation (EC) No 70/2001 as regards the extension of its scope to include aid for research and development, [2004] OJ L 63, p 22.

57   *See* H-W Friederiszick, L-H Röller and V Verouden, 'European State Aid Control. An Economic Framework' in P Buccirossi (ed), *Handbook of Antitrust Economics* (MIT Press 2008) for a broader introduction to the new architecture.

functions.[58] In its detailed assessment of the aid amount granted to Siemens, the Commission identified well-defined market failures justifying the aid. It also applied standard investment decision techniques to assessing the incentive effect. As significant distortions of competition seemed to be unlikely (here the relevant antitrust markets were defined and the likely anticompetitive effects assessed), the aid was approved. While some other comparable measures were approved along those lines,[59] the Commission opened a formal investigation procedure regarding a €96 million aid package that France planned to grant Peugeot-Citroën and other partners for the development of a hybrid diesel car under this aid scheme.[60] Interestingly, the concerns raised by the Commission, that is, that no well-defined market failure exists and that the incentive effect may not be given in this case, seemed to have influenced the decision by the French state to abandon the underlying aid scheme and re-focus the budget towards SMEs.[61]

3   CONCLUSION

In recent years, economic analysis has become central to the assessment of competition cases throughout all fields of competition policy – ranging from merger control to Articles 82 and 81 to state aid cases. Acknowledging that reform needs time, that is, resources have to be built up, guidelines to be rewritten, standard practices to be developed –

---

[58]   *See* Commission Letter, 21 February 2006, Case No N 674/2006 – *France: Soutien de l'Agence de l'innovation industrielle en faveur du projet NeoVal*; *see* also Press Release, IP/07/227, http://europa.eu/rapid/pressReleasesAction.do?reference=IP/07/227 (accessed 31 January 2008).

[59]   Commission Letter, 12 September 2007, Case No N 185/2007 – *France: Soutien de l'Agence de l'innovation industrielle en faveur du programme (NANOSMART)*; Commission Letter, 12 September 2007, Case No N 89/2007 – *France: Projet d'aide de l'Agence de l'innovation industrielle au PMII HOMES*; Commission Letter, 10 December 2007, Case No N 887/2006 – *France: Projet Bernin 2010*; Commission Letter, 10 May 2007, Case No N 854/2006 – *France: Soutien de l'Agence de l'innovation industrielle en faveur du programme mobilisateur pour l'innovation industrielle TVMSL*. *See* also Press Releases IP/07/137, IP/07/1058 and IP/07/642.

[60]   Case No N 530/2007; *see* Press Release IP/07/1679, http://europa.eu/rapid/pressReleasesAction.do?reference=IP/07/1679&format=HTML&aged=0&language=DE&guiLanguage=en (accessed 31 January 2007).

[61]   F Delaye, 'Big Companies Lose Out as France Merges its Two Main Innovation Agencies' (2007), http://bulletin.sciencebusiness.net/ebulletins/showissue.php 3?page=/548/2648/9371 (accessed 31 January 2008).

the implementation has to be considered a success up to this point: as the various cases reviewed in this chapter show, economic analysis has helped to take not only better justified, but also significantly better decisions.

2. Competition law and the institutional embeddedness of economics

David J Gerber*

1 INTRODUCTION

Transnational debates about the role of economics in competition law have paid relatively little systematic attention to the embeddedness of economics in institutions. They typically proceed as if embeddedness were not an issue. The assumption appears to be that economics looks, acts and functions the same wherever it is applied. This assumption is often the basis for claims supporting increased use of economics in legal systems around the world. The claim is that economics represents a standardized and internationally applicable language and thus that its increased use in competition law will lead to or at least support global harmonization of antitrust law. In particular, European discussions of a 'more economic approach' to competition law often refer to the use of economics in US antitrust law, and they frequently assume that if economics works in a particular way in the United States and has particular consequences there, it will function the same way in Europe and have similar consequences.

Lack of attention to the embeddedness of economics in institutions can be attributed to two sets of closely related factors. One is a lack of sufficient incentives to explore these issues. Economists themselves generally have little reason to study the institutional application of economics. It is not their issue. Their role and function is to talk about the substance of economics itself and to apply its methods.[1] Legal scholars may be dissuaded from approaching these issues because they do not fit neatly into any exist-

* Distinguished Professor of Law, Chicago-Kent College of Law, Chicago, Illinois.
[1] The field known as 'new institutional economics' might be expected to be a locus for this kind of analysis, and there is valuable work in this field that can be used in the type of analysis I engage in here. In this body of scholarship, institutions are important, because they influence economic outcomes. In general, however, institutional economists do not focus on how economics itself is embedded in

ing category of legal scholarship and, as a result, few intellectual tools have been developed for analysing them. Scholars in the specific field of law and economics might be expected to have some interest in this area, but they have been primarily concerned with importing economics into law at a substantive-law level, and this enterprise provides few incentives to discuss the institutional-embeddedness issues. Finally, practising attorneys may have experience in specific procedural contexts, but seldom have incentives to engage in systematic study of the phenomenon. For each of these groups, the seeming 'messiness' of procedural issues further reduces incentives to study the issues. Institutional embeddedness involves procedural and institutional complexities and irregularities, and it does not easily lend itself to the development of either generalizations regarding methods or predictions about outcomes.

A second set of factors involves institutional and professional interests that may provide disincentives for systematic study of the issues. For example, scholars and lawyers from the United States generally seek to export the US antitrust model. Given that this model is based on a specific role for economics, paying attention to differences between the systems that might interfere with success in exporting the US model might be perceived as counterproductive.

Yet to ignore this institutional factor invites serious distortions in analysing the relationship between economics and competition law.[2] Institutions condition the use of economics. Their practices and procedures influence not only the norms that are applied, including the appropriate role of economics, but also the factual material that is produced for use by economists and the myriad decisions that are made in reaching outcomes.

My main claim in this chapter is that we need to analyse institutional embeddedness if we wish to evaluate and analyse the role of economics in legal institutions, in general, and in antitrust law, in particular. The underlying issues in virtually all legal analysis are 'what decisions will be made?' and 'what kinds of factors influence those decisions?' Given the extraordinary increases in the value of economics in some areas of the law, it is critical to identify and assess the modalities through which economics influences decisions, and here the institutional-embeddedness issue is of central importance.

---

institutions. For discussion of recent developments in the field, *eg* JN Drobak and JVC Nye (eds), *The Frontiers of the New Institutional Economics* (1997).

[2]   I use the term 'competition law' here to refer to general legal regimes that impose sanctions on conduct because such conduct restrains competition. The term 'antitrust' is often also applied to this type of legal regime, particularly in reference to the competition law of the United States.

The need for this type of analysis is particularly striking where claims are made that extend beyond the borders of a single legal system. Any claim or assumption that experience with economics in one system is relevant to decisions in another system is suspect if it does not take institutional embeddedness into account. In these contexts, economics is applied by different institutions and subject to different institutional and procedural influences. The respective institutional contexts will each shape decisions in their own ways, and these will often lead to very different roles for economics and economists and thus potentially very different outcomes.

To illustrate these issues, I here examine them in an arena in which they are of particular importance. Europe is moving toward greater use of economics in competition law, and in this context there are frequent references to US antitrust experience with economics. There are claims, for example, that increased use of economics in European competition law will lead to greater convergence in competition law between the US and Europe and thus more uniform rules to guide transatlantic business. Such claims are of little value and may even be harmful unless they are based on appropriate analysis of institutional-embeddedness factors.

This chapter examines the issue of institutional embeddedness and some of the ways in which it is important.[3] I apply the analysis to the European discussion of a 'more economic approach', examining some of the procedural and institutional differences that deserve to be considered where the role of economics in US antitrust law is viewed as relevant to the use of a 'more economic approach' in Europe. Failure to appreciate the institutional and organizational *embeddedness* of economics in US antitrust law and to recognize differences between US and European decisional contexts can distort assessments of US experience and may reduce the potential value of references to it. It may lead to inappropriate and unfounded expectations and thus to ill-advised decisions. Sharper awareness and clearer analysis of these differences may, however, increase the potential value of references to US experience and lead to a clearer vision in Europe of some of the implications of increasing the role of economics in competition law.

I have four main objectives. One is to examine the embeddedness of economics in US antitrust law. Revealing the factors that condition the use of economics in institutions makes clear the value of taking them into account in analysing the role of economics in competition law. A second is to compare the factors that influence how economics operates in US antitrust

---

[3] Although in this chapter I limit the discussion to the competition-law context, I believe that the analytical principles can also be applied with value to other areas of law in which economics is used.

law and the way it operates and could operate in Europe. A third aim is to identify some of the implications of this type of analysis for decisions that are now being made in Europe and those that will have to be made in the future. The fourth is to offer a method of analysing the embeddedness issue that can be of value not only in the context of individual legal systems, but in any situation in which references or claims are made about the role of economics that transcend the boundaries of a single system.

2   ECONOMICS AS SCIENCE: THE UNIVERSALITY POSTURE

A starting point for thinking about the institutional embeddedness of economics is its universalist posture. Universality is at the core of the scientific enterprise, and thus as a social science, economics seeks universally valid principles. The language of economics is, therefore, necessarily abstract, and its methods are intended to be applicable everywhere.[4] In general, economists assume that economics is the same here, there and everywhere, regardless of cultural or other contexts.[5] The 'internationalization' of economics over the last half century is largely based on this postulate, as is much of the extraordinary development of economics as a science.[6]

This does not mean, of course, that economists are unaware of such contexts, but rather that they view their analytical tools as independent of context. Most economists recognize that cultural and institutional factors may influence not only legal and political decisions involving economic issues, but also economic processes themselves. Nevertheless, these issues are not generally considered part of the discourse of economics itself. They are relegated to a separate realm referred to as the practical application of economics. In this realm, economics can be, and often is, applied by non-economists.[7]

This universalist perspective is fostered by the orthodoxy of a particular set of goals and methods within the economics profession. Among the most important of these are the assumptions that economic actors

---

[4] For general discussions of economics methodology, *eg* M Blaug, *The Methodology of Economics: Or How Economists Explain* (2nd edn, 1992) and LA Boland, *The Methodology of Economic Model Building* (1999).

[5] For discussion, *see* MW Reder, *Economics: The Culture of a Controversial Science* (1999).

[6] This development is described and analysed by AW Coats, *The Post-1945 Internationalization of Economics* (1997).

[7] For analysis of the use of economics in government, *see eg* AW Coats, *Economists in Government: An International Comparative Study* (1981).

generally act 'rationally', at least in most spheres of activity,[8] that efficiency assessments are at the core of economic analysis and that mathematics must play the central role in the development of economic theory. These core values and postulates have developed as a result of a specific set of concerns and objectives, and the culture of the economics profession now replicates and reinforces them.[9]

From the standpoint of economic analysis, there is great value in this universalist posture. It fosters analytical precision, permits the broad applicability of analytical work, and, above all, releases the power of abstraction in the formulation of economic principles. These are primary considerations within the economics community, and they have proven their value in developing both theory and policy. In addition, they provide status to practitioners of the science, which in turn contributes to both the social and market value of the roles that economists play.

3   INSTITUTIONAL EMBEDDEDNESS: SOME USES OF ECONOMICS IN COMPETITION LAW

This universalist posture tends, however, also to conceal and to be confused with a different set of issues that involves the use of economics in institutions. Institutions *use* economics for specific purposes. Here the universality posture is misplaced and may be misleading. The scientific claims, universal methods and abstract language – the factors whose very universality makes the scientific enterprise of economists valuable – now become embedded within institutional contexts in which they cannot operate as they operate within the scientific community of economists.

In these contexts, the methods of economics become tools to be applied according to the rules and procedures of the institutions and organizations that use them. Where economics is used in institutions, the categories, methods and language of economics share decisional space with other factors. Specific institutional and procedural contexts shape the ways in which economics is used and the outcomes reached by those using it. It cannot operate at its accustomed level of discursive universality, but must now contest with other specifically institutional factors in influencing legal decisions and outcomes.

---

[8]   This rationality assumption has been subject to increasing limitations among some groups of economists, especially in recent years. In the context of the use of economics in competition law, it remains little challenged. For discussion of the most recent movements of this kind within the economics profession, *see* D Coyle, *The Soulful Science: What Economists Do and Why it Matters* (2007).

[9]   For discussion of that cultural function, *see eg* Reder, *supra* note 5.

When used in the specific context of competition law, economics plays two main roles, each of which is shaped by specific institutional and procedural factors.[10] One is normative. In it, economics supplies the content of legal norms. It provides the normative standards that are applied to conduct in order to assess whether the conduct is deemed to violate law. In doing this, it shapes the questions to be asked in competition law, supplying the concepts and categories that are used in the process of assessing the lawfulness of conduct. Concepts and categories drawn from economic science – such as, for example, 'efficiency' – become operative standards of the legal system. This requires some mechanism for relating the economics concepts and language to those of the legal system. In effect, it requires that economics be grafted onto the authoritative legal-political basis for decisions in the competition-law system.

The other role is that of fact interpretation. Here the role of economics is to specify methods to be used in answering factual questions – questions about what has happened or what the consequences of particular conduct are likely to be. Given that antitrust law is designed to prevent particular kinds of harm to the competition process, the issue is often 'Did particular kinds of conduct "cause" particular results?' This may involve issues such as the assessment of the market power of the enterprises involved, the characteristics of the markets in which they operate and other purely factual issues. Economic science can provide abstract models and testable hypotheses for use in making these factual determinations, and it can supply methods (eg econometrics) for analysing them.

4 TRANSNATIONAL COMPETITION LAW ISSUES AND ECONOMIC EMBEDDEDNESS

With this distinction in mind, we can see that any cross-system reference involving the role of economics requires careful analysis of the embeddedness issues. Each competition system conditions these two roles of economics in specific ways. With regard to the normative role, for example, it will use different institutional means to relate the substantive principles of economics to legal norm-setting processes of the competition-law system. Depending on the legal system, this may require specific authority located in a statute or it may be within the authority of courts to establish and define the relationship. On this issue, there are major differences between

---

[10]   I develop this distinction more fully in DJ Gerber, 'The Future of Article 82: Dissecting the Conflict' in C-D Ehlermann (ed), *European Competition Law Annual 2007: A Reformed Approach to Article 82 EC* (forthcoming).

the US antitrust system and European systems: US courts typically have far greater authority to shape this relationship than do analogous European courts.[11]

The second or fact-interpretation function is also performed in system-specific ways. Specific institutional arrangements in the competition-law system will, for example, provide the means for acquiring data, specify the kinds of data that can be acquired, identify the agents that are permitted to acquire the data, designate the potential sources of data, assign spheres of control of the data and so on.

Of the many elements of US litigation that are relevant to the embeddedness of economics, I have chosen three for closer examination here. One involves the amount of data that is available for evaluation by participants in the fact-interpretation process. This includes the procedures for access to information. A main value of economics in competition law is its capacity to evaluate data, and the amount of data available and access to data are central to making use of its potential value. A second involves control over data. Who can get, use and control data, under what circumstances and subject to what kinds of constraints? The third relates to the interpretation of data. Economics 'interprets' data, and thus the institutional mechanisms for performing that function are keys to the outcomes that are reached.

These three components of the US system condition the use of economics in fundamental ways. They determine how much data is available and thus the degree of empirical testing of abstract propositions that is possible. They determine how the presentation of data is organized and controlled, thereby determining the roles of economists and the relationship between those roles and the roles of lawyers and judges. And, finally, they determine the factors that will influence the process of interpreting the data, the process on which much of the value of economics rests.

One criterion for selecting these three factors is the centrality of their roles in both the operation of the system generally and in relation to the embeddedness of economics. Another is my experience that they are often overlooked or misunderstood by outside observers. I look first at the amount of information available for economic analysis, then at control over information and, finally, at the interpretation of the data that is available.

---

[11] For comparative analysis of these types of differences, *see* DJ Gerber, 'Competition Law' in P Cane and M Tushnet (eds), *Oxford Handbook of Legal Studies* (2004) 510, and DJ Gerber, 'Comparative Antitrust Law' in M Reimann and R Zimmermann (eds), *Oxford Handbook of Comparative Law* (2007) 1193.

5 USING US ANTITRUST EXPERIENCE IN THE EUROPEAN CONTEXT

We can now apply this analysis to the specific example of the use by Europeans of US antitrust experience. As noted, the European Commission's efforts to use a 'more economic approach' have been much influenced by US experience, and thus it is valuable to analyse the intellectual basis for references to that experience and the kinds of issues that need to be explored in making such references effective.

In the late 1990s, the European Commission began to change fundamental components of its competition law. Since then, European competition law has moved toward what is generally described as a 'more economic approach'.[12] The term is used loosely to refer to increased use of economics in competition law and includes increased reliance on economic science to inform the norms of competition law. Economics increasingly is given the role not only of improving the interpretation of data in competition-law cases, but also of supplying its norms and methods.[13] With the introduction in 2004 of the requirement that European Union competition law be applied by Member States in virtually all competition cases, this movement toward increased reliance on economics has expanded in scope and become relevant to the application of competition law throughout Europe. Many questions remain as to how economics will actually be used, especially by Member State competition authorities and courts, and thus the role of economics is likely to remain a topic of central concern for many years.

US experience has played an important role in this development. The role of economics in competition law that is espoused by the European Commission is essentially the same as the role that economics now plays in US antitrust law. This conception of the role of economics is the basis for the substantive law changes that the European Commission has introduced into the assessment of vertical and horizontal agreements as well as mergers and that it is currently proposing for use in the context of unilateral conduct (Article 82 of the EC Treaty).[14] In this process of change, US

---

[12] For discussion of the more economic approach, *eg* LH Roeller, 'Economic Analysis and Competition Policy Enforcement in Europe' in PAG Bergeijk and E Klosterhuis (eds), *Modeling European Mergers: Theory, Competition Policy and Case Studies* (2005) 11.

[13] For analysis of some of the controversies concerning the use of economics in European competition law, with particular reference to distinguishing among the various uses of economics in applying Article 82, *see* Gerber, *supra* note 10.

[14] The Commission's recent thinking about the future of Article 82 can be found in 'CDG Competition Discussion Paper of application of Article 82 of the

experience has frequently been used to support and justify the move toward increased use of economics, often under the rubric: If the US does it, and it seems to be associated with positive economic developments there, perhaps we should do it as well. In that sense and others, US antitrust law experience has been a major reference point in Europe's 'more economic approach' movement.

These references in Europe to US experience seldom pay significant attention, however, to embeddedness issues, in particular, differences in the institutional and procedural contexts that condition the operation of economics in these two decision-making contexts. References to US experience typically proceed as if either there were no significant differences between the two decisional contexts or such differences were irrelevant to assessing the use of a 'more economic approach' in Europe. As we shall see, however, there are major differences in the institutional and procedural contexts of the use of economics between the US and Europe, and these need to be taken into account in relating one to the other.

5.1   The Role of the Federal Courts

In order to pursue this analysis, we need to limit its scope and compare similar institutions performing analogous roles. Several institutions are instrumental in the US antitrust system, but by far the most important are the federal courts, and thus this article focuses on the roles played by those courts. It examines how economics is embedded in their decisional processes and assesses the importance of that embeddedness for the use of US antitrust experience in Europe.[15]

I have chosen this example because of its importance, but also because foreign observers often misunderstand it. Litigation in the federal courts is the central institutional context for the creation and application of US antitrust law and thus for the use of economics in the US antitrust system. For most purposes, it is here that antitrust law is made. Decisions of the federal courts are the authoritative pronouncements that officially guide decision making in antitrust law. They are particularly important in this area of law, because other forms of authority and guidance play limited

---

Treaty to exclusionary practices', December 2005, http://ec.europa.eu/comm/competition/antitrust/art82/discpaper 2005.pdf (accessed 31 January 2008).

[15]   For discussion of the role of litigation in the US antitrust system from a comparative perspective that relates US experience to the situation in Europe, *see* DJ Gerber, 'Private Antitrust Enforcement in the U.S. and Europe: A Comparative Perspective' in TMJ Moellers and A Heinemann (eds), *The Enforcement of Competition Law in Europe* (2008) 431.

roles. Legislation plays virtually no role in the area. The basic antitrust statute was enacted in 1890, and the last major legislative change occurred almost a century ago.[16] Moreover, administrative decision making is also far less influential in the US system than it is in most other competition-law systems.

Because federal courts play a role in the development and operation of the US antitrust system that is more central than that played by courts in most competition-law systems, foreign observers often underestimate the centrality of that role. In most systems, courts either play no direct role or merely review administrative decisions for procedural or constitutional flaws. Courts there may engage in varying degrees of review of administrative action, but typically their role is relatively limited. In the US, however, the federal courts do far more. They are the centres of the system – the principal arbiters of what the law is and the primary factors in developing the law. Court decisions and case-law interactions among courts are the reference point for both public enforcers and private lawyers in making competition-law decisions. In most other competition-law systems, the administrative authority responsible for competition law plays a far more central role in the system than it does in the United States.

The federal courts are central to both public and private enforcement of the antitrust laws. In the US system, two agencies of the federal government are authorized to enforce the competition laws. One is the Antitrust Division of the United States Justice Department, which is part of the executive branch of government. It has often been considered the more influential of the two agencies. Yet the Department of Justice generally cannot enforce the antitrust laws directly! When it wishes to take action, it must generally do so by commencing litigation in the regular jurisdiction federal courts. It must win its lawsuit there in order to effectuate its enforcement decisions and achieve its enforcement goals. Moreover, when the Justice Department goes to court, it is generally subject to the normal procedural rules of the federal courts. The Justice Department may choose to bring a civil suit or a criminal suit, depending on the claims involved, and the corresponding procedural rules are applied to the litigation. With limited exceptions, there is no separate procedure specifically designed for antitrust litigation. I emphasize these points because foreign observers are often 'shocked' by the fact that the US Justice Department must actually go to the regular courts in order to take enforcement action and by the further fact that when it does go to court, it is typically subject to the

---

[16] Some might also consider the 1950 expansion of the scope of application of the merger control provisions to be a major legislative change.

ordinary procedural rules of those courts. The other enforcement agency is the Federal Trade Commission. It operates as an independent agency, and it may issue orders directly. Nevertheless, its actions are subject to both procedural and substantive review by the federal courts, which impose the same substantive antitrust rules to decisions by the FTC as they apply to all other antitrust litigation.

The centrality of the federal courts in the US system is further enhanced by the importance of private antitrust litigation. This form of litigation takes place in the same federal courts that control public enforcement. Private antitrust litigation is common, providing most of the decided cases in the area, and it is often viewed as at least as important as public enforcement in implementing the antitrust laws, if not more important.

5.2   Some Key Procedural Features of Antitrust Litigation in US Federal Courts

As background, it is important to note several basic features of litigation in the US that are relevant to the issues treated here.[17] The common-law model of litigation that evolved in England and that operates in modified form in the US relies on a set of roles for judges in first-instance (ie trial) litigation that is quite different from the roles usually played by judges in continental Europe. In it, the judge is primarily a referee or umpire whose role is to enforce the rules of procedure and ensure fair proceedings within those rules. She has no obligation to know all the substantive law that might be applicable in a case before her, and she does not develop the case herself. The system relies on the attorneys for each side to develop their own cases and to present fully developed legal and factual arguments to the respective decision makers (judge or, as the case may be, jury), who must choose among the elements presented. The judge's primary role during first-instance litigation is to monitor this interplay between the attorneys.

A second key feature of this litigation model is the basic principle that competition or conflict between the attorneys is likely to produce the best outcome. In order to achieve this result, the procedural mechanism provides extensive power and responsibility to the lawyers for each side. The image is that the attorneys are empowered to make their best cases; the procedure identifies the conflicts between the two sides; and a neutral and impartial jury or judge makes the factual determinations based on the

---

[17]   For an analytical framework for comparing procedural systems that treats many of these issues, *see* DJ Gerber, 'Comparing Procedural Systems: Toward an Analytical Framework' in JAR Nafziger and SC Symeonides (eds), *Law and Justice in a Multistate World: Essays in Honor of Arthur T. Von Mehren* (2002) 665.

material and arguments presented.[18] The procedure does not centre on the judge's knowledge of the law or assign to the judge responsibility for developing either legal or factual arguments.

US federal procedure has added another important component to this model that plays a key role in the issues here – the centrality of factual density to the litigation process.[19] At one level, this factual density is captured by the common claim among US lawyers and judges that 'facts win cases' – that is, that the central issues in litigation are generally factual issues and that whoever has the most and best evidence is likely to win. It also reflects, however, a concept of procedural justice that often goes unnoticed. This basic conception is that maximum access to factual data produces the best and fairest results.

Both ideas reflect an underlying view of the litigation process in which the substantive law appears as flexible and somewhat indeterminate and in which, therefore, factual detail and the sensitivity of the procedure to the specifics of the case are key means of legitimating the process. This means that the foremost objective of lawyers is often to present a convincing factual presentation and to master the factual contours of the case. The importance of this function is further enhanced by the heavy reliance on factual comparisons in a case-based system. Similarities and dissimilarities between the facts of a case being decided and the facts of prior authoritative cases (precedents) are central to legal decision making. Effective comparison of factual scenarios is a key to successful litigation strategies.

Given the importance of this factual analysis, access to data is seen as key to producing the best outcomes for the parties and legitimating the system itself. This, in turn, supports the proposition that the procedural mechanism should provide extensive rights for the lawyers to acquire information. In no area of US law is this more important than antitrust law, because, as noted above, virtually all antitrust law is made by the courts.

Three additional factors are important for assessing the role of courts in antitrust cases and understanding the embeddedness of economics in US antitrust law. First, the US antitrust system assumes that private litigation is of primary importance in securing compliance with antitrust law. In fact,

---

[18]   In US civil litigation, a defendant is generally guaranteed a right to jury trial by the US Constitution. If a jury is present, it resolves all issues of fact, leaving the legal issues to be dealt with by the judge. If no jury is present, the judge resolves issues of fact as well as law. Basically, the same evidentiary and procedural rules are followed in both cases.

[19]   For discussion of procedural-justice issues in US and European litigation, *see* DJ Gerber, 'Extraterritorial Discovery and the Conflict of Procedural Systems: Germany and the United States' (1986) 34 *Am J Comp L* 745.

most antitrust litigation in the US is private litigation, and many of the most important cases are private cases. Private litigation is thus at the centre of the system. Second, several procedural provisions are intended specifically to encourage private litigation. For example, successful private plaintiffs are awarded compensation in an amount equal to three times the actual damage sustained (so-called treble damages). This provision is specifically intended to encourage private litigation. Third, antitrust litigation can take several forms – private, administrative and criminal, and, as noted, the procedural rules vary according to the form of the litigation. Private litigation follows the basic rule of civil procedure, while Department of Justice litigation may follow civil litigation rules or criminal procedure rules, depending on the type of conduct involved, and Federal Trade Commission litigation generally follows administrative procedural rules.

5.3   The Comparative Reference Point: Analogous European Institutions

In relating this role of economics in US antitrust litigation to the European context, a key issue is finding an appropriate reference institution – what exactly is to be compared? As noted, European competition law relies far more heavily on administrative decision making in applying and enforcing its norms than does US antitrust law. This, by itself, represents a major dissimilarity between the two systems and raises fundamental questions about the use of US experience in the European context, but comparative issues of that magnitude are beyond the scope of this chapter. Instead, the chapter compares courts with courts. This permits an analysis of specific issues of competition-law decision making in the judicial context itself and avoids the fundamental differences between court procedures and administrative procedures.[20] This will enable us to identify differences in the ways in which analogous European institutions condition the use of economics.

It also compares European national courts with US courts, thereby leaving aside the special institutional roles of the two European Union courts. Moreover, the comparison focuses on the first-instance competition law courts in which litigation typically takes place. This is necessary in order to ensure that the comparison relates institutions performing analogous functions. While it is true that national courts have so far played a relatively minor role in the European competition-law context, our concern here is with identifying aspects of the institutional embeddedness of economics, and from this perspective the current amount of private litigation in Europe

---

[20]   These comparisons are also relevant in many respects to many administrative proceedings, not only in Europe, but also in many other systems that have been influenced by European models.

is not at issue. Nevertheless, there is also significant practical importance in the comparison, because private litigation in competition law has been increasing in Europe, and because the European Commission is currently advocating a major increase in reliance on such litigation in Europe.[21] The issue is thus of particular importance for the future development of European competition law.[22]

Comparing the decision-making contexts of US courts with those of European courts at this level of generality requires identifying features that are common to continental European procedural systems. There are, of course, significant differences among procedural systems in courts on the European continent, especially between those with predominantly Germanic influence (eg Austria and Sweden) and those with predominantly French influence (Italy and Spain are examples). Nevertheless, we can identify patterns that generally appear in continental procedural systems, and we will here focus on those widely shared features. This chapter does not refer to the common-law-based procedural systems of the United Kingdom and Ireland, because their deviations from the continental pattern are too extensive to be tractable in the space available.

Finally, even in a specific national court system there are sometimes significant procedural differences among the types of courts that may be involved in antitrust litigation. For example, there may be differences in procedure between general-jurisdiction courts and administrative courts. This chapter does not address such differences directly, but many of the features of procedure used in this analysis are often applicable to other courts, because they rest on many of the same principles of procedural justice. In any event, the purpose here is to identify differences rather than to engage in detailed description of specific courts.

5.4 Continental Civil Procedure: Some Basic Principles

The starting point for any such comparison is to recognize that courts in continental Europe generally operate according to a principle of centralization of procedural authority and responsibility that contrasts sharply with the principle of dispersion of procedural responsibility that we have

---

21 European Commission, Green Paper – Damages actions for breach of the EC antitrust rules, 19 December 2005, COM(2005) 672 final = http://eur-lex.europa.eu/LexUriServ/LexUriServ.do?uri=COM:2005:0672:FIN:EN:PDF (accessed 31 January 2008).

22 Although the Commission's modernization plans call for increased reliance on private enforcement, many in Europe do not share this objective. For discussion, *see* W Wils, 'Should Private Antitrust Enforcement be Encouraged in Europe?' (2003) 26 *World Comp* 473.

identified in US procedure. The basic image is that the court represents 'the state' and that it is the responsibility of the state's employees – that is, the judges – to control the proceedings.[23] This means that typically a judge will have the full responsibility for developing the litigation and controlling the procedure. She will, for example, decide whether there is enough evidence for litigation to commence and then develop a file (or 'dossier') that represents the official record of the proceeding. She determines herself issues such as what data is to be presented to the court, which witnesses, if any, may be heard by the court and which questions, if any, may be posed to witnesses.[24] She thus determines the scope and shape of the factual material. The file is all important. It contains, in essence, the litigation data, such as, for example, the judge's determinations on points of fact and law and her notes on witnesses and the like. In this procedural context, the role of lawyers tends to be far more limited than in the United States. For example, they typically do not call their own witnesses, cross-examine witnesses, prepare witnesses, hire their own experts, control what witnesses say and so on.

This model rests on a specific conception of judicial professionalism.[25] While US federal judges are often appointed to the bench after many years of experience in practice (or, occasionally, in law teaching) the continental judge is typically a lifetime career civil servant who is trained specifically for the judicial role immediately after university training and who generally remains a judge throughout her career. The judge *is required to know* the substantive law applicable in the cases she handles and to apply it fairly to the disputes before her. Her professionalism and her knowledge of the substantive law are central legitimating features of the system.

Key elements of the US system are simply not present in these systems or play marginal roles. I mention only two. First, whereas the central concept of US procedure is that justice is best served by a procedure in which competition and conflict between the parties to the litigation are encouraged and the parties are given maximum opportunity to develop and present their own cases, the central idea of continental procedural systems is that the professional judge's knowledge and control of the proceedings is the primary source of procedural justice.[26] Second, the idea fundamental

---

[23]   For analysis, *see* M Damaska, *The Faces of Justice and State Authority* (1986).

[24]   In these courts, witnesses normally provide their material in 'raw form' – ie as a single, connected narrative rather than in response to questions from lawyers or from judges. In some systems, especially those of the French procedural tradition, 'live' witness testimony plays a minor role in most litigation.

[25]   For discussion, *see* Gerber, *supra* note 19, at 767–9.

[26]   For useful analysis of the issues, *see* JH Langbein, 'The German Advantage in Civil Procedure' (1985) 52 *U Chi L Rev* 823. Some of the factual references in the article are no longer accurate, but the analysis remains valuable.

to US procedure that access to factual material is the key to effective justice has at best minimal resonance in continental systems.

6 DATA ACCESS AND THE QUANTITY OF INFORMATION

The amount of data available for analysis by economists is a key factor affecting the role and operation of economics in a competition-law system. Where economists have large amounts of data and a high degree of access to data that they wish to obtain, their roles and value are significantly enhanced. The importance of these data-access issues has tended to increase in both the US and Europe over the last two decades, as per-se rules have been discarded or tempered in order to allow courts to look more carefully at specific factual circumstances in assessing harm to competition.

6.1 US Procedure: The Abundance of Data

A central aspect of procedure in US federal courts is the extensive capacity it provides to litigants to acquire data. The so-called 'discovery' process is of immense importance to the entire embeddedness issue.[27] This mechanism provides litigants with broad rights to request and, in practice, virtually to compel the presentation (so-called production) of information from other parties and sometimes even from others who are not parties to the litigation. These rules require a litigant, on request by another litigant, to make available to her all information requested by her that can reasonably be expected to lead to evidence that is 'admissible' (ie that can be presented in court). This includes allowing requesting attorneys to examine large numbers of documents and depose (ie formally interrogate) those who may have relevant information.

The form and extensiveness of these rights to demand information require emphasis, because they represent a process that is distinctive for US procedure. A key to understanding the importance of this feature is recognizing the standard used in assessing the 'relevance' of information sought. This standard is often misunderstood by foreign observers.[28] It is far broader than relevance standards in most litigation systems in

---

[27] For discussion of US discovery practices from a comparative perspective, *see* DJ Gerber, 'International Discovery after *Aerospatiale*: The Quest for an Analytical Framework' (1988) 82 *Am J Int'l L* 521.
[28] For further discussion, *see* Gerber, *supra* note 19, at 761–7.

that it encompasses information that may simply be expected to lead to admissible evidence. It is not limited, as in most systems, to data that is directly probative of claims in the litigation. This often enables litigants to acquire very large amounts of information, some of which may be sought for strategic business reasons unrelated to the litigation.

The discovery mechanism can, and often does, yield massive amounts of information that then become part of the litigation process. Many rooms filled with physical documents (or their digital representations) are not uncommon in large litigation. Teams of many lawyers and legal assistants may spend years investigating, sorting and evaluating documents. While there are some judicial controls on the extent of discovery, as noted below, the main constraints are often those of cost. Note also that throughout this process the lawyers for the parties are often in contact, coordinating aspects of the discovery process, negotiating over the extent of discovery and often arguing about matters such as the propriety of particular requests for information. This interaction typically proceeds with little or no judicial supervision.

Several additional features of this 'discovery' process are important for purposes of comparison. First, the process occurs before the first-instance procedure (ie the trial) begins. This means that it is carried out by the attorneys in developing their own respective presentations of the data and before there has been any evaluation by a judicial official of the legal claims to which the data relates. Second, the discovery process is typically not closely supervised by a judge. Judicial supervision is normally only available with respect to specific issues involving the scope of a request, and it must typically be requested by one of the parties. Again, the contrast to continental European litigation systems is stark.[29]

This aspect of US civil procedure has profound implications for the use of economics in the context of antitrust litigation. First, and above all, it means that there is an open and relatively unencumbered field of operation for economic analysis. There is an abundance of data to be examined and explored. Moreover, economists and lawyers are basically in charge of the process of gathering the data. They can ask for and usually obtain data that they think might be relevant to the cases that they are constructing. As we shall see, European procedural systems do not provide this freedom of operation for economists and their methods.

---

[29] A practice called 'managerial judging' is found in the federal courts, and it does involve some supervision of the discovery process. It does not, however, fundamentally change the basic situation created by discovery. First, it is not used in all cases, usually only in larger cases. Second, it involves nowhere near the kind of control of the procedure that is found in continental procedure.

Second, it provides extensive opportunities for testing theories. The claims of economists can be based on a far broader data set than can be created under continental procedures. In essence, where lawyers and economists seek to evaluate an economic claim, they have procedural tools available that aid them in identifying data that might be relevant to supporting that claim and additional tools for actually acquiring it. Economists can then use this data to test the claim and, presumably, to achieve more reliable and effective analysis of the data. The extensiveness of the data available to economists can thus significantly enhance the weight and probative value of the work of economists and generally support their role.

The availability of data and the capacity to acquire such extensive data also generate *incentives* for testing economic claims. Where the capacity to acquire such data exists, the lawyer/economist team for each party has an incentive to acquire and analyse it. Moreover, each litigation team has strong incentives to gather and analyse during the discovery process all data that might later be considered relevant at the trial stage of the proceedings, because it must seek to avoid encountering claims made at the trial by the other party that relate to factual data that it has not evaluated. Once the trial has commenced, it is generally too late to seek such data.

6.2   Europe: Bring your Own

Data access in continental civil procedure is far more limited than in US federal courts, and US-style discovery has no close analogues in continental procedure. The state is not considered responsible for providing a mechanism by which litigants can coerce the presentation of data from other litigants or from third parties. Moreover, the court itself usually has limited authority to demand such information. A judge can typically do so only under highly restricted conditions such as, for example, where a party provides evidence that such data is likely to be directly relevant to a specific claim (ie directly probative of an essential element of the claim). In general, therefore, the lawyers for the parties have little or no access to data from other parties or from third persons. In addition, the only data typically available to the judge is that which can be found in the public record, data that the parties themselves voluntarily bring to the case, and some limited and specific forms of data that the judge is authorized to require a party to submit to the court (eg a document to which a witness has referred in the proceedings). Moreover, even in situations where a judge has authority to require the presentation of data, she has little incentive to do so, because she may not have the resources in time or personnel support necessary to process or analyse it. In addition, the costs must typically be borne directly by her employer, the state. This represents a significant impediment to the gathering of extensive data and again contrasts with the situation in the US, where the incentives are aligned to encourage the development of such data.

So-called piggy-backing procedures are available under the competition laws of some continental countries. Here private litigation follows administrative enforcement and can make use of at least some of the factual material presented in the administrative procedure. These procedures do increase the availability of data, but even here the data access is relatively limited compared with US procedures.

The litigation thus proceeds with access to far less data than is available in the United States litigation system, and, as a consequence, there is less data available for economic analysis. This has three main consequences for the use of economics. First, it means that the value of economics is reduced because there is less opportunity to use it. There is limited material to which economic analysis can be applied. Second, the material that is available tends to be 'thin', potentially reducing the value of certain forms of economic analysis. For example, there may not be sufficient data to adequately support particular kinds of econometric analysis. Third, it means that economic theories cannot be tested to the same degree as they can be tested in the US. One important use of economics is to provide theory-based hypotheses and models that can inform the analysis of factual data. Where the data is insufficient to test these models, their value is limited.[30] In general, much of the value of economics in antitrust litigation is its utility in analysing complex factual situations. In the European context, the limited amount of data reduces that value.

7   DATA CONTROL

A second key issue relating to the institutional embeddedness of economics involves control over data. The procedural system conditions the role of economics by determining the extent to which lawyers and economists can control components of the data set. This includes issues such as whether the data can be used by economists without restrictions, whether there are obligations to make acquired data available to opponents prior to litigation and how data can be presented to those who make decisions regarding the 'facts' of the case.

---

[30]   For further discussion of economic modeling issues, *see* Boland, *supra* note 4.

7.1 US Antitrust: Control by Lawyers

In the US federal courts, data is controlled to a very significant extent by the lawyers for the parties. Lawyers for each side not only acquire their own data, but also have basic control over the presentation of data to judges or, as the case may be, juries. The discovery process is in their hands, subject, as mentioned above, to controls to prevent abuse. They decide, for example, which witnesses will be heard in court, and they ask the questions to which the witnesses must respond and beyond which their answers may not go. The questions of the lawyers thus structure the data presented to those who decide factual issues. In addition, the lawyers may prepare their own witnesses, and they often discuss in detail with their witnesses what the latter will say, what questions will be presented and so on. The lawyers also cross-examine the witnesses of their litigation opponents. In short, the presentation of data by the lawyers structures the discussion and analysis of the data that is then subsequently presented to the official decision makers (ie judge or jury). This treatment of witnesses also applies to expert witnesses, who are hired by each side and who form part of the respective litigation 'teams'.

This data control by the lawyers has at least three significant consequences for the use of economics in antitrust. First, it allows economists (working with lawyers) to develop economic analysis according to their own needs and objectives, subject only to reasonableness requirements and the cost constraints imposed by their clients. They can use the discovery process to seek information relevant to economic theories that are being considered, and subject the resulting data to econometric or other forms of economic analysis – all generally without interference from the court.

Second, and related, it means that economists can direct their data-analysis efforts specifically to the legal arguments of their respective teams. They are not expected to be neutral arbiters, as are the judge and the expert witness in continental procedure, but to give the interpretation that best favours their clients' position. Their incentives are, therefore, to explore new theories and to 'push' the theoretical and factual basis for their claims as far as possible.

Third, the process creates opportunities for contesting economic claims and arguments. As the economists work during the proceedings, their claims are often used by the lawyers in negotiations with opposing lawyers. For example, if one line of investigation seems particularly strong, it may strengthen the negotiating position of the lawyer in settlement negotiations. In this process, however, each side often has opportunities and incentives to challenge the other side's economic and factual analysis. Ideally, this process reveals the strengths and weakness of the economic analysis and leads to more accurate and valuable factual analysis.

7.2   Europe: Control by the Judge

In continental European courts, the control of data has rather different characteristics. As noted above, continental civil procedure generally features the judge as the director of the entire litigation process, controlling the development of the case and, in particular, the acquisition and presentation of data. Unlike the situation in the US, the lawyers do not shape and define the presentation of data to the decision maker. The judge builds a file that contains the data and/or descriptions of it by the judge. She also determines and generally controls the process of data collection. Lawyers may not present the factual case as they wish and subject to their own control, as is the case in the US. There is also no broad cross-examination mechanism (and sometimes no cross-examination at all) that allows lawyers (and economists) to challenge the presentations made by the other party (and her economists). Finally, experts are designated and called by the court in most cases, and they are responsible only to the court. They are not presented by each of the parties as is the case in the US.

Timing factors in the relationship between legal assessment and factual presentation also differ dramatically from the situation in the US. In Europe, the judge typically begins to assess both factual and legal claims at the commencement of the process, long before there is full argumentation in court or detailed presentation of factual material. Substantive law is applied not at the end of a procedure that has been structured by lawyers and economists, as in the US, but throughout the development of the litigation. This means that the collection and organization of data is subject throughout the procedure to the judge's control. It is thus filtered through her eyes and her methods and shaped by her knowledge of principles and prior cases. In that context, she may often make factual determinations without providing opportunities for the parties to present fully developed analysis of the data.

These factors create a far more limited and constrained process for the application of economic methods to data than is found in US antitrust litigation. Whereas in the US system economists can analyse data subject only to the controls by the lawyers (and their clients) for whom they are working, they cannot operate this way in continental civil procedure. The judge is responsible for development of the factual material, not the lawyers and economists. There is thus far less freedom for economists to develop factual analysis and employ the tools of economic science.

As a result, there is also little opportunity to contest varying forms of economic analysis. Whereas in the US system economists for each side can analyse and contest the claims of opposing economists both during the discovery phase of litigation and during the process of presenting the data to the judge, this type of contest is seldom, if ever, possible in continental courts. This lack of procedural opportunities for confrontations between opposing views may significantly reduce the value of economic analysis. Moreover, these diminished opportunities for contesting opposing views reduce incentives for thorough economic analysis that can push the interpretive limits of the available data.

The continental model of centralized procedural authority thus significantly constrains the operations of economists, and it may, as a consequence, reduce the value of economic science. Accordingly, reduced data access combines with reduced opportunities for the development of economic analysis in ways that may diminish the quality of the factual material presented.

8   THE ROLE OF DATA INTERPRETATION

The procedures of legal institutions and the decision-making methods within them transform raw data into legally relevant 'facts'. This process of transformation is usually referred to as the 'interpretation' of data. It involves assessing the relevance of data, sorting and categorizing data and generally relating specific elements of data together to form 'factual' narratives that form the basis for decision making. Economics can be of enormous importance in deepening, broadening and enriching this interpretive process – that is, in the 'transformation' of 'data' into legally approved and procedurally accepted 'facts'. Indeed, its primary value may be that it can generate a more insightful and sophisticated interpretation of data.

8.1   US Antitrust: Relatively Free Rein for Economists

In the US system, the judge plays only a limited role in this interpretive process. It is not her responsibility to acquire and assemble the data and piece together the construction of a credible narrative. These functions are the primary responsibility of the lawyers. They organize, sort and give meaning to the data. They then present their interpretations to the judge or jury for choices among the pre-formulated narrative items. Regardless of whether there is a judge or a jury, the decision maker is faced with choices presented by the lawyers, and her role is to choose among the elements of interpretation that have been provided by the parties. This difference between US and continental procedures is fundamental and often not adequately understood by outside observers.

One major consequence of this characteristic of US litigation is that economists in US antitrust litigation tend to be relatively unfettered in performing their interpretive functions by the constraints that often influence the process of factual interpretation in other systems. The economists and lawyers for each side are permitted to perform their interpretive functions with minimal need to conform to pre-established institutional influences and constraint. They are free to pursue particular interpretations that are structured neither by the concepts of the legal system nor by existing legal precedents.

8.2   Europe: The Impact of the Judge's Roles and Incentives

In continental court procedures, the factors that influence data interpretation differ in important ways from those typical in US antitrust litigation. In particular, the judge interprets economic data subject to constraints and influences that play little or no role in the interpretation of data in US federal courts. I mention here only some of those differences.

First, it is important to remember that data interpretation in continental European litigation procedure is done only by judges. This, by itself, distinguishes it from US procedure, where a jury may perform that function. Where there is a jury in the US, it alone is responsible for interpreting facts.[31] Moreover, even where there is no jury, procedures are used that tend to place the judge in the role of the jury. This means, for example, that determinations of law and determinations of fact are strictly separated rather than temporally interspersed as is typical in the continental model.

Second, and unlike the US judge, the continental European judge is obligated to know the substantive law that is potentially applicable to the cases she is assigned to handle and to apply the substantive law continually to the procedural development of the case. The entire procedural structure centres on the professional expertise of the judge in both substantive and procedural law, and, as noted above, many features of the entire legal system are intended to maximize the judge's knowledge of substantive law and underscore its importance.

This means that the judge starts with often highly developed and specialized knowledge about the abstract principles to be applied in cases and about prior interpretations of similar data. She necessarily interprets the new data through the concepts, categories and prior cases that comprise that field of substantive law. These concepts and categories necessarily shape and guide her interpretation of that data. Moreover, the judge's interpretation of data through these categories takes shape not only after

---

[31]   There are special and rare cases in which, on request of a party, the judge may take responsibility for overriding a jury's determination of the facts. This may occur, for example, where the judge is convinced that the jury could not reasonably reach the conclusion that it has reached.

the presentation of data by the parties, as in the US, but throughout the procedure, often before there has been opportunity for the parties' representatives to develop their own factual analysis. In some systems, party representatives have almost no role in interpreting data.

The consequences for the use of economics are striking. The role of economists in interpreting data is constrained to a very significant extent by the role of the judge in interpreting data. In sharp contrast to the US situation, where there are few procedural constraints on the opportunities for economists to develop their interpretations of the data, the economist in the continental context is far more constrained in performing her interpretive role. The judge's interpretations are driven by the categories and concepts of the substantive law and may be established and fixed early in the procedure – prior to any opportunity for economists to influence the interpretation. In contrast to the US practice of allowing the parties to use economics to develop interpretations of data and then seeing which ones can be substantiated under applicable legal norms, the continental practice works the other way round. The judge decides which provisions of the law, if any, need to be supported by economic analysis of the data. The cognitive impact of this difference can be profound.

9   CONCLUDING COMMENTS

This brief review illustrates the degree to which economics is embedded in the institutions and procedures of the competition-law system in which it is used. These institutions and procedures transform the abstract language and universalist posture of economics into a set of decisional influences that compete with other influences in generating specific decisions. The way economics functions in one institutional context may thus differ greatly from the way it operates in others, and it certainly operates very differently than it does within the economics community itself.

These institutional and procedural factors condition the use of economics in fundamental ways. They determine how much access economists have to data, what data is actually made available for economic analysis and in what quantities, what kinds of incentives there are for acquiring data, how the tools of economics can be employed, what incentives there are for their use and many other factors. In order to analyse the decisions that are likely to be made using economics in competition law, it is necessary to understand those factors. As we have seen, however, these influences are susceptible to systematic analysis.

Our application of this analysis to the relationship between US and EU competition laws demonstrates its potential value. Taking institutional embeddedness into account in relating US experience to decisions about the use of economics in competition law in Europe reveals dimensions of the issue that are critical for a full understanding of it. The factors that condition the role of economics in the US courts and those that operate in European courts often differ in fundamental ways. To the extent that the conditioning factors are similar, US experience can provide guidance for European decision makers, serve as a basis for predicting outcomes and, perhaps, support decisions there. To the extent that the conditioning factors are dissimilar, however, the potential value of referring to US experience with the use of economics may be diminished. At least it requires a more thorough and careful comparison of the differences.

Economics can play valuable roles in the development and application of competition law in Europe. It has in the past, and it will continue to do so in the future. It is indispensable for effective competition-law analysis. The institutional-embeddedness issues raised here do not detract from that value, but seek to enhance it by pointing to a more nuanced and presumably, therefore, more valuable view of how economics can be used, particularly in transnational contexts.

3. The goals of Japanese competition law

Shuya Hayashi[*]

1 COMPETITION LAW AND POLICY IN JAPAN

1.1 The Intrinsic Value of Competition

This chapter considers the goals of competition law, focusing on the various aspects of Japanese competition law. The general theme of the goal of competition law, one of the most challenging and controversial in the field, is addressed as well. Then the chapter explains the Japanese perspective on this topic, although a detailed discussion about what the goal of competition law generally should be, will be avoided.[1]

The goal of competition law is difficult to explain comprehensively. Of course, generally speaking, it is to promote free and fair competition. Promoting competition leads to improving economic efficiency and stimulating innovation and, as a result, maximizing consumer welfare. However, what is and what should be the concept of fair and free competition is highly controversial.[2] As Kenneth Arrow has pointed out,[3] many economists have focused on the consequences of resource allocation. Any

* Associate Professor of Law at Nagoya University Graduate School of Law, Nagoya (Japan).

[1] In principle, I will confine the footnotes on Japanese law to the materials written in English, mainly because of space constraints.

[2] Similarly, it is also controversial that the ultimate goal of competition policy should be to maximize consumer welfare. Not a few economists think that the goal of competition policy is to maximize net social welfare including consumer welfare. Even if many economists accept the consumer-welfare standard, they will have negative attitudes towards such additional goals of competition policy as economic freedom, protecting small and medium-sized firms, measures to achieve international competitiveness of domestic firms and international economic integration. But this chapter contends that competition policy should be a hybrid including these additional objectives.

[3] KJ Arrow, 'Arrow's Theorem' in J Eatwell, M Milgate and P Newman (eds), *The New Palgrave: A Dictionary of Economics Vol 1* (1987) p 1, 127: 'It has been

standards represented by Pareto-efficient resource allocation or net social surplus are forms of evaluation based on results that can be attained through the perfectly appropriate redistribution of resources. In fact, most economists prefer the 'net social welfare' standard and are reluctant to accept the 'consumer welfare' standard. They implicitly assume that because maximizing consumer welfare is a matter of wealth allocation, focusing only on it is not necessarily socially desirable.

However, when we lawyers think about the value of fair competition, we contemplate not only the consequence of economic performance involved in competition but also the competitive process, the richness of opportunities brought about by competition. Securing such 'competition as procedure' and the opportunities it affords is of crucial value for us in considering what fairness in competition means.[4] In the sense of procedural value of competition, it is revelatory for me that the prominent welfare economist Professor Kotaro Suzumura, who emphasized the intrinsic value of competition as procedure, pointed out as follows:[5]

> In evaluating the social performance of regulation versus competition, we should pay due attention not only to the welfaristic effects and/or the non-welfaristic effects on consequences, but also to the non-consequentialist effects thereof as exemplified by the procedural fairness of regulation versus market competition, the richness of opportunities thereby opened, and the liberty and rights of individuals and private enterprises under these social contrivances.

1.2 Consumer Surplus versus Social Surplus: A Hypothetical Example

Let us explain why this chapter from a lawyer's perspective esteems that the consumer-surplus standard is more acceptable than the net-social-surplus

---

taken for granted in virtually all economic policy discussions since the time of Adam Smith, if not before, that alternative policies should be judged on the basis of their consequences for individuals'.

[4] However RH Bork, *The Antitrust Paradox: A Policy at War with Itself* (1978) 58, criticized the understanding of competition as rivalry: '[T]his identification of competition with rivalry will not do for antitrust purposes. It makes rivalry an end in and of itself, no matter how many or how large the benefits flowing from the elimination of rivalry. And it is clear what those benefits are. Our society is founded upon the elimination of rivalry, since that is necessary to every integration or coordination of productive economic efforts and to the specialization of effort. No firm, no partnership, no corporation, no economic unit containing more than a single person could exist without the elimination of some kinds of rivalry between persons.'

[5] K Suzumura, 'Competition, Welfare, and Competition Policy', CPRC Discussion Paper Series CPDP-3-E, December 2003, http://www.jftc.go.jp/cprc/DP/CPDP-3-E.pdf (accessed 31 January 2008).

standard in the following hypothetical example. Let us compare two same-sized markets. Let us say that one is a pharmaceutical market and the other is a jewellery market.

Company A and company B are the only two pharmaceutical companies that manufacture an essential vaccine for curing or preventing a certain intractable disease such as AIDS. Let us assume that companies A and B have merged. As a result of this merger, some efficiencies, such as production or distribution-cost reduction and/or management rationalization accompanying the integration of management resources, will be expected. On the other hand, the market for the vaccine will become highly concentrated (duopoly to monopoly), as a result of which the price of the vaccine may tend to increase seriously (for example, 10 per cent or more from its current level). In this case even if the price of the vaccine increases significantly, patients of the disease cannot dispense with the purchase of the essential vaccine. Therefore, total production output of the vaccine circulating in the market as a whole may hardly decrease.

In contrast to this example, we also assume that the companies C and D have merged. Companies C and D are manufacturers of certain luxury items such as jewellery. In this case as well, we assume that some efficiencies, such as production or distribution-cost reduction and/or management rationalization are to be expected as the result of this merger. On the other hand, as the market for jewellery will become concentrated as a result, the price of the jewellery may increase seriously (for example, 10 per cent or more, as in the former vaccine case). However, consumers can do without luxury items such as jewellery, because they are not a necessity of life, in contrast to the former vaccine case. People don't need jewels in order to live. In this case, if the price of the jewellery increased significantly (for example, by 10 per cent), consumers could dispense with its purchase as an extravagance. Therefore total production output of the jewellery circulating in the market as a whole may significantly decrease.

Ceteris paribus, there may be little possibility that the former merger case of pharmaceutical companies is considered to be illegal if an increase of net social surplus is to be expected that exceeds the reduction of consumer surplus accompanying the price increase of the vaccine.

By contrast, in the latter merger case of jewellery companies, a significant number of consumers may cease to purchase jewels from the merging companies at the monopoly price charged by the merged companies, although those consumers were willing to purchase them at the competitive price. Thus the total wealth disappearing from the overall market as a result of these consumers' activity (their ceasing to purchase) may be more significant than in the vaccine case. Therefore there may be a greater possibility that the latter merger case of jewel companies will be considered illegal from the viewpoint of the net-social-surplus standard, because the decrease of net social surplus due to the price increase of the jewellery will be greater than in the vaccine case, all other things being equal. However, I have serious doubts that people, at least lawyers, will widely accept that result.[6]

1.3   The Objectives of the Japanese Antimonopoly Act

Whilst the philosophical arguments are many and varied, my idea about the general goal of competition policy is relatively straightforward, and is shared by many others. Competition policy is there to help nations achieve economic prosperity and increase the welfare of society by forcing companies to run themselves efficiently and ensuring a level playing field. Competition forces economic operators to adjust to changes and it forces them to innovate. Competition leads to lower prices, to higher quality and to more variety of product choice for the consumer as a whole. It leads to greater dynamism in industry, to inspiration of entrepreneurship and to the expansion of employment.[7]

Turning to the purpose of the Japanese competition law specifically (hereinafter referred to as the Antimonopoly Act),[8] Section 1 of the Antimonopoly Act provides that the purpose of the Act is 'to promote free and fair competition, to stimulate the creative initiative of entrepreneurs, to encourage business activities of enterprises, to heighten the level of employment and people's real income and thereby to promote the democratic and wholesome development of the national economy as well as to assure the interests of consumers in general'. As a means to these ends, the Antimonopoly Act eliminates any unreasonable constraint to business

---

[6]   In order to take account of efficiency claims in assessment of mergers, Part IV 2(7) of the Japanese Guidelines to Application of the Antimonopoly Act Concerning Review of Business Combination (revised on 28 March 2007, hereinafter referred to as 'Japanese Merger Guidelines'), explicitly require that improvements in efficiency should contribute to 'users' welfare'.

[7]   Former EC Commissioner Mario Monti remarked on the goal of competition policy as follows: 'Actually, the goal of competition policy, in all its aspects, is to protect consumer welfare by maintaining a high degree of competition in the common market. Competition should lead to lower prices, a wider choice of goods, and technological innovation, all in the interest of the consumer'. *See* M Monti, 'The Future for Competition Policy in the European Union', speech of 9 July 2001, http://europa.eu/rapid/pressReleasesAction.do?reference=SPEECH/01/340&format=HTML&aged=0&language=EN&guiLanguage=en (accessed 31 January 2008).

[8]   The Act Concerning the Prohibition of Private Monopoly and Maintenance of Fair Trade (Act No 54 of 1947).

activities creating, maintaining or reinforcing market power, such as restraint on price, by prohibiting private monopolization, unreasonable restraint of trade, unfair trade practices and anticompetitive mergers.

As seen above, Section 1 of the Antimonopoly Act has a multilayered structure. The first part, 'to promote free and fair competition', is widely understood as being the 'direct objective' of the Antimonopoly Act. The next part, 'to stimulate the creative initiative of entrepreneurs, to encourage business activities of enterprises, to heighten the level of employment and people's real income' is only to indicate the value or importance of the competition policy enforced under the Antimonopoly Act. The last part, 'thereby to assure the interests of consumers in general, and also to promote the democratic and wholesome development of the national economy', is generally considered to list the ultimate objectives accomplished by the Antimonopoly Act.

It must further be noted that the objectives of the Antimonopoly Act are of a hybrid nature, consisting of economic and non-economic elements, and divided into direct objectives and ultimate objectives. Therefore in Japan 'efficiency' is not the only goal of the Antimonopoly Act. Actually, in almost all cases except for merger cases, the concept of efficiency does not function as the explicit benchmark of enforcement of the Antimonopoly Act.[9] It goes without saying that as a result of promoting 'free and fair competition' as specified in Section 1 of the Antimonopoly Act, efficiency will be accomplished 'reflexively'. Of course, economic inefficiency is of great concern in Japan too.[10] However, in Japan other goals, such as dispersion of economic

---

[9]   In merger cases, efficiency evaluation is the important factor in the competition-law analysis of the merger. If improvement of efficiency due to the merger is expected, the merger will be cleared. In its assessment, the Japan Fair Trade Commission (JFTC) will consider both the possible anticompetitive effects arising from the merger and the procompetitive effects stemming from efficiencies identified and substantiated by the parties. For the JFTC to take account of efficiency claims in its assessment of the merger, the efficiencies have to benefit consumers, be merger-specific and be verifiable; *see* the Japanese Merger Guidelines, *supra* note 6, Part 4 2(7). According to the Japanese Merger Guidelines, efficiency is judged from the following three viewpoints: (i) efficiency should be improved as an effect specific to the merger (*merger-specific* efficiency); (ii) improvement of efficiency should be materialized; and (iii) improvement of efficiency should increase the welfare of consumers.

[10]   Of course, improvement of efficiency is an effect to be achieved through competition. In addition, companies' most appropriate competitive behaviour is that to increase their efficiency. In merger cases, almost all merging companies insist that the purpose of their mergers is to achieve and improve efficiency. Therefore, when examining a merger, the manner of assessing the efficiency caused by a merger and the manner of using the assessed efficiency for the judgment on the illegality of the

power, freedom and opportunity to compete on the merits, satisfaction of consumers and protection of the competitive process, must also be considered as important factors. Needless to say, because the Antimonopoly Act is the law for eliminating obstacles to free and fair competition, the protection of small and medium-sized companies cannot be a direct objective of our competition policy. As a result of free and fair competition in the markets, the strong companies may become stronger and smaller and weaker firms may be driven out of the markets, as this is quite a natural result of the competitive process.

Hence any provisions[11] in competition laws protecting the weak and small firms usually work in such a way as to regulate free and fair competition. As *protectionist* regulation brings about socially inefficient resource allocation, the Antimonopoly Act does not protect competitors but competition itself, and most other nations' competition laws support the same philosophy.

1.4   The Need for Variety in Competition Policy

Of course competition policy is one of the various means of achieving economic growth and the goal of competition law should be considered through the long-term historical experiences in each country. In this sense, there may be wide gaps in defining the goal of competition law between highly developed countries and developing countries.[12] Competition policy itself is influenced by a country's own cultural background.

For example, there has been some concern among developing or transition economies that the enactment of competition law and its vigorous enforcement may be an obstacle to the development of the national

---

merger are very important. Consideration of efficiency is sometimes treated in the form of an 'efficiency defence'. According to a common theory among Japanese antitrust scholars, however, it is not strictly a 'defence', because bare comparison between a merger's effect of restraining competition and efficiency is not accepted (that is, efficiency is not accepted as a justification for the effect of restraining competition). Japanese Merger Guidelines, Part IV 2(7). (When improvement of efficiency is deemed likely to stimulate competition, these positive impacts are considered.) There is, however, an alternative to the above common theory: when a merger leads to market power, but economies of scale would reduce costs and therefore tend to lower the price, the efficiency defence should only be accepted if it is found on balance that there is no possibility of raising the price.

[11]   They often take the form of exemptions from the competition law, such as the exemption for cooperatives of small or medium-sized enterprises or of consumers.

[12]   *Compare*, for instance, the regulation of the 'administrative monopoly' by the new Chinese Antimonopoly Law.

economy. The reason is that domestic firms may be replaced by competitive foreign firms in the national markets. The active enforcement of competition law may discourage entrepreneurship and innovation on the part of the national firms. In sum, not a few people in developing countries may consider that competition law and its enforcement are likely to impede economic development. There is probably wide agreement that the one desirable competition law does not exist. Competition laws vary between countries, and their enforcement is even more varied. Furthermore, the judicial system and the institutional structure for enforcement procedures depends on historical elements of each country. Still, even if competition policy partly consists of industrial policy, it is also important to understand that enforcement activities against violations of competition law should not be commingled with industrial policy.

Competition policy[13] should promote fair and free competition by providing a level playing field. It should seek to achieve fair and free competition not by directly affecting the players in the market, but instead should ensure that the market is controlled by fair rules.[14] This is what is meant by the saying that competition law does not protect competitors, but competition itself. Industrial policy, on the other hand, promotes, regulates or suppresses particular sectors of the industry by providing subsidies, encouraging consolidation of firms and sometimes facilitating cooperative relationships among competing enterprises. It focuses on the players in the market and tries to directly affect them in order to implement national competitiveness strategy and promote and protect certain industry groups. In this sense, the philosophy underlying the two policies seems to be very different.

In the rapid globalization of the world's economy, competition policy is required to be harmonized with free-trade policy around the world, which is based on GATT/WTO rules. Under these circumstances we should also bear in mind that competition policy is sometimes inconsistent with

---

[13]   For a definition of 'competition policy', for example, take that of M Motta, *Competition Policy* (2004) 30: 'the set of policies and laws which ensure that competition in the marketplace is not restricted in such a way as to reduce economic welfare'.

[14]   It is revelatory for me that Milton Friedman pointed out the non-discriminatory value of the market mechanism as follows: 'No one who buys bread knows whether the wheat from which it is made was grown by a communist or a republican, by a constitutionalist or a fascist, or, for that matter, by a negro or a white. This illustrates how an impersonal market separates economic activities from political views and protects men from being discriminated against in their economic activities for reasons that are irrelevant to their productivity – whether these reasons are associated with their views or their color.' *See* M Friedman, *Capitalism and Freedom* (1962) 21.

industrial policy, which often focuses solely on the interests of domestic industry.

2   FOR A COMMON MARKET: ANOTHER GOAL OF COMPETITION LAW

2.1   The Growing Importance of Competition Law and Policy in Japan

In Japan competition policy is indeed becoming an important policy instrument both at the domestic and at the international level. For multilayered consideration of the goal of competition policy, we must recognize the growing importance of competition policy in contemporary Japan. The Japan of today seeks to achieve fair and free competition not by directly affecting the players in the market, but instead by ensuring a level playing field for market players. Industrial policy of the past in Japan tried to directly protect the market players in order to achieve national growth. But this type of protectionism was a holdover from the past. In what follows, I will first roughly sketch the genesis of the philosophy of the Japanese competition policy in the ongoing structural reform of the domestic economy. One aspect that should be noted is the rapid globalization of the economy. Under these circumstances, competition policy must be harmonized with the worldwide free-trade policy based on GATT/WTO rules.

At the domestic level, competition policy penetrates the entire Japanese economy. First of all, the most recent amendment to the Antimonopoly Act of 20 April 2005 revised the surcharge system (including an increase in the surcharge rate), introduced a leniency programme, introduced compulsory measures for criminal investigations and revised the hearing procedures. The amendments came into effect on 4 January 2006 and significantly strengthened the powers of the JFTC to enforce the Antimonopoly Act and to eliminate and deter anticompetitive activities, in particular hard-core cartels. This legislation represents Japan's strong will to promote competition policy in order to establish a free, fair and global competitive environment for the 21st century based on market mechanisms and the principle of self-determination.[15]

Then I will turn to my second focus and consider how Japan has gradually promoted the privatization of individual government-affiliated entities.

---

[15]   Chairman of the JFTC, Kazuhiko Takeshima, frequently says that 'there is no economic growth without competition'. He asserts that in order to maintain the economic competitiveness of Japan, competition throughout the economy is needed.

The relevant ministries and agencies in charge of the privatization will be required to ensure that the competitive process in the relevant market is not distorted. Thus competition policy is becoming important in almost all spheres of the Japanese economy.

The most prominent example of privatization is the liberalization of the telecommunications market and the introduction of fierce competition to that. Since the privatization of Nippon Telegraph and Telephone Public Corporation and the liberalization of the telecommunications market in 1985, a number of telecommunications carriers have entered the market, and due to the advancement of technological innovations, the emergence of diverse services such as mobile communications and Internet access, the promotion of deregulatory measures and other factors, the competition among the telecommunications carriers has progressed, prompting the significant development of the telecommunications market. It was a notable milestone in Japanese history to bring competition into this strictly regulated industry.

In 2003, with the advancement of competition policy, the Telecommunications Business Law, which entered into force on 1 April 2004, was substantially revised to realize drastic institutional reforms, including the abolition in principle of regulations on market entry, tariffs and agreements. The system experienced a major shift from ex-ante to ex-post regulations. Under the policy system with ex-post regulations at its core, rapid technological innovations facilitated a shift to IP and broadband communications, and in the fast-changing telecommunications business field, it is now becoming necessary to grasp market trends precisely in order to ensure fair competition and reflect them in policy-making.[16]

2.2 Importance of Competition Policy for Economic Integration

At the international level, there is widespread movement towards international cooperation on competition policy among a number of countries and

---

[16] Therefore, taking into account the framework for market analysis in the EU Member States and the Antimonopoly Act and other factors, the Ministry of Internal Affairs and Communications (MIC) of Japan initiated a Competition Review from Fiscal Year 2003 as part of its measures for promoting fair competition in telecommunications business. Article 1 of the Telecommunications Business Law refers to the concept of 'fair competition' set out as follows: 'The purpose of this Law, considering the public nature of telecommunications business, is, by ensuring the proper and reasonable operations of such business as well as promoting fair competition thereof, to secure the consistent provision of telecommunications service, to protect the users' benefit, and thereby to ensure both the sound development of telecommunications and the convenience of people, and to promote the public welfare.'

regions in order to adjust and ultimately integrate substantive competition law and procedure of competition law enforcement systems. For example, in the European Union competition policy has special value for the purpose of creating the integration of internal markets within the EU. Currently, an active competition policy is needed in order to discourage business practices that have the effect of restraining free and fair trade for a common market. In this sense, the functioning of competition policy is also crucial for regional integration systems in East Asia. It could provide some solutions at the global level. Almost the only solution to the problem of a lack of competition law or competition-law enforcement is the dissemination of competition law and policy. The JFTC has been making efforts to disseminate competition law and policy to such countries in various ways. One such effort is technical assistance on competition policy.[17]

There is an increasing awareness that trade and competition are closely linked. Although government-imposed trade barriers, including tariff and non-tariff barriers, have been substantially reduced thanks to successive global trade rounds, private barriers have remained unabated. In the context of US-Japan economic relations, many on the US side believed in the past that competition-restrictive business practices and distribution systems had been hindering the access of US products to Japanese markets.

The importance of competition-law enforcement cooperation has intensified with an increase in transnational mergers. One notable case is the merger of Boeing/McDonnell Douglas[18] in 1997. Japan, a major purchaser of their passenger aircraft, was one of the countries that could have been affected most seriously by the merger. However, under the provision of the Antimonopoly Act in those days, the JFTC could do nothing about the proposed merger because the JFTC was empowered to examine only those mergers that involved at least one Japanese company. This inability on the part of the JFTC was rectified by the amendment of the Antimonopoly Act in June 1998.

---

[17]   Technical assistance activities are very important for the development of competition law and policy. Along with the increase in the number of developing economies that have introduced or are preparing to introduce competition laws, the need for technical assistance has also expanded. The JFTC has been implementing a variety of technical assistance programmes during the past decade. The purpose of technical assistance is to build capacity, especially in developing economies, by making better use of the accumulated knowledge and expertise on competition policy.

[18]   Commission Decision of 30 July 1997, Case No IV/M.877 – *Boeing/McDonnell Douglas* [1997] OJ L 336/16; for the US FTC decision, *see Boeing/McDonnell Douglas*, FTC File No. 971-0051, 5 Trade Reg Rpt (CCH) ¶ 24,295 (1997).

Regarding the need for greater adjustment of competition laws and legal systems, I wish to point out two factors briefly. One is the fact that, for merging companies, the burden of getting clearance from a number of competition authorities has sometimes become enormous. The second factor is the view that the difference in the strictness of competition law enforcement in different regions brings about uneven competitive conditions for individual companies. In other words, companies in a jurisdiction with lenient competition-law enforcement are in a more advantageous position than those in a jurisdiction with strict enforcement. Therefore international cooperation and coordination on competition law and its enforcement in the cause of a common market is and should be another goal of Japanese competition law, because Japan undoubtedly enjoys the benefit of liberalization of international trade and will do so in the future.

2.3   Worldwide Cooperation on Competition Policy

There has been increasing awareness that competition policy and trade policy are closely related and affect one another. Based on this awareness the International Competition Network (ICN) has set up some working groups on specific competition issues.[19] Discussions at the ICN have contributed greatly to promoting understanding of competition policy among developing nations as well as to strengthening the belief that trade policy should be in line with competition principles. As potential problems of this kind of policy cooperation, the following concerns were pointed out. One was the fear that trying to reach an agreement in the ICN, WTO or any other international body on the principles of competition policy may end up attaining the lowest common denominator, because many member countries have little or no competition policy experience. Another reason for reluctance is that 'negotiating' an agreement on competition policy in this kind of international body may spoil the traditionally amicable relationship between competition authorities. For example, the atmosphere prevailing in the WTO is far from camaraderie.

I find such reservations understandable. But the arguments in favour of the ICN or any international body as the venue for trade-competition discussions are even more compelling. In this sense, the ICN is virtually the only active organization in the competition-policy field with almost

---

[19]   Based on this awareness, the ICN has set up a number of working groups. These working groups discuss various issues, including cartels, competition policy implementation, mergers and unilateral conduct.

universal participation.[20] In order to promote the international convergence of competition laws and policies among countries, two challenges to be overcome in the future are as follows. One is the need for convergence of substantive rules on competition. This, of course, is not easily agreed to on a multilateral or global basis. However, agreeing to rules on a multilateral basis in ICN, as was possible in the EU member countries, could be a solution. The second need is for rules on evidence. Since competition issues are fact-intensive issues, there need to be appropriate rules for verifying evidence. Each one of these requirements is an enormous challenge for the international community. No one expects that these needs will be met in the near future, but considering the benefits of the ICN's capacity to handle competition-related issues, it is a long-term objective worthy of pursuit.

This is why I strongly support the continuing discussion on competition law and policies among countries in such international fora as the ICN in order to achieve the goals of Japanese competition law and policy as a common rule of market economy. At least such discussions would contribute to the establishment of common principles of competition policy.

3   THE GOAL OF COMPETITION LAW FROM A HISTORICAL PERSPECTIVE

3.1   A Brief History of Competition Law and Policy in Japan

In this section I would like to explore the goals of competition law in the context of the economic history of Japan.[21] It is helpful to emphasize that the establishment of competition policy after World War II was not only a means of achieving economic efficiency, but also of *economic democratization* in Japan, by preventing excessive concentration of economic power and preserving an atomistic market structure. Many people believed that economic democratization laid a solid foundation for political freedom and the establishment of democracy. The goal of the original Antimonopoly Act, enacted in 1947, was mainly focused on achieving economic democratization through the maintenance of the atomistic market structure of Japanese industries, not on the economic consequentialism of welfare. The Japanese government and the public had previously thought that excessive

---

[20]   However, the ICN is not equipped with a functioning international dispute-settlement mechanism.

[21]   For a detailed discussion of the history of Japanese competition law, *see* H Iyori and A Uesugi, *The Antimonopoly Laws and Policies of Japan* (1994) 1–66. For a recent discussion, *see* TA Freyer, *Antitrust and Global Capitalism* (2006) 160–243.

concentration of economic power in *zaibatsu* groups was needed and a cartel-promoting policy was essential for the development of the national economy, especially for a wartime economy. As a result of such policies, *zaibatsu* colluded with Japanese military forces for the purpose of profit maximization and growing economic and political power in Japanese society, promoting the Pacific War. Finally, Japan fell into ruin. At the time, the establishment of the Antimonopoly Act had a symbolic meaning, reflecting past experience. That is why the Antimonopoly Act is known as the economic constitution of Japan.[22] In considering the goal of competition law comprehensively, we cannot forget the original intent of the Antimonopoly Act [23] as the basis of the liberty and rights of individuals and private enterprises in a democratic society.[24] In order to identify the goal of Japanese competition law historically, the section will roughly sketch the vicissitudes of the 60 years' life of the Antimonopoly Act in Japan.[25] Today, after many twists and turns, competition policy has taken root in Japanese economic society and the enforcement of antimonopoly law is becoming more effective.

3.2 The Period Preceding the Antimonopoly Act

Historically, before the end of World War II, there were no laws regulating cartels, trust and market concentration in Japan. The Japanese government was tolerant of such activities. Indeed, it encouraged businesses or trade associations to establish cartels by providing laws or administrative guidance. A small number of families gained control over a lot of companies in various industries under a holding company owned by each family. Such groups of companies were called '*zaibatsu*', among which Mitsui, Mitsubishi, Sumitomo and Yasuda are famous examples. During the World War II period, the top four *zaibatsu* groups controlled, either directly or indirectly, over 500 companies, which together occupied a very significant

---

[22] In this regard, it is revelatory that the US Supreme Court, in *United States v Topco Associates, Inc* 405 US 596, 610 (1972), held as follows: 'Antitrust laws in general, and the Sherman Act in particular, are the Magna Carta of free enterprise. They are as important to the preservation of economic freedom and our free-enterprise system as the Bill of Rights is to the protection of our fundamental personal freedoms.'

[23] For a detailed discussion of the original intent of the Antimonopoly Act, *see eg* H First, 'Antitrust in Japan: The Original Intent' (2000) 9 *Pac Rim L & Pol'y J* 1.

[24] For a European discussion, *see* DJ Gerber, *Law and Competition in Twentieth Century Europe: Protecting Prometheus* (1998) 232–65.

[25] However, this chapter cannot undertake a detailed discussion of the history of Japanese competition law and policy, mainly because of space constraints.

position in the economy; they accounted for a quarter of the total capital of all industrial sectors, almost half the capital of financial businesses, and almost one third of the capital in heavy industries.[26]

The modernization of almost all elements of Japanese society started at the time of the *Meiji* restoration, which took place in the second half of the 19th century. Japan's economic system since the *Meiji* era has changed dramatically from feudalism to capitalism, or market economy. It is true that in the early *Meiji* era the Japanese government established a number of state enterprises, but they were mainly for quickly introducing modern advanced technology from abroad with less accumulated private capital. Once this objective was attained, those state enterprises were privatized, and the development of the Japanese economy was left mainly to the initiatives of the private sector. It was only during the rather limited period from the Great Depression in the early 1930s until the end of World War II that the Japanese government regained extensive control over the economy, mainly through trade associations, in order to mobilize all the country's national resources for military purposes. The symbol of this extensive governmental control is the Important Industries Control Act, which was enacted in 1931. Many compulsory cartels and cartel associations were formed in many important industries such as steel, coal, paper, cement etc by the Act. The government in this era believed that rationalization of industries through cartels was the way to cope with greater recession, and that the regulation of excessive competition under strong government control was crucial to get through the wartime economy.

3.3 The Birth of Japanese Competition Law: The Antimonopoly Act of 1947 and a Successive Decline for Japanese Competition Policy

After World War II, and under the occupation by the allied powers, drastic democratization measures were introduced into all spheres of Japanese society. In the economic field, the democratization measures consisted of the following three main pillars: (i) democratization of industry, (ii) farmland reform; and (iii) labour legislation reform. The democratization of industry was to be attained by (i) dissolution of the *zaibatsu* and other enterprise combinations, (ii) abolition of various measures for promoting private monopolization and (iii) establishment of a system of free competition. As for the

---

[26] The three largest *zaibatsu* groups, Mitsui, Mitsubishi and Sumitomo, controlled, either directly or indirectly, 488 companies, which together constituted a very significant part of the economy. *See* Holding Company Liquidation Commission, *Nihon Zaibatsu to Sono Kaitai* (Japan's *zaibatsu* and their dissolution), Volume 95, 113, and 122; and Data Volume 426, 428 and 468 (1950).

zaibatsu dissolution,[27] 18 giant companies were ordered to restructure their organizations under the Law on Exclusive Measures for the Excessive Concentration of Economic Power (Deconcentration Law). Their stocks in other companies and some of their factories were disposed of by order of the allied forces, and they divided themselves into smaller companies.

For the purpose of firmly establishing a freely competitive economic system, the Antimonopoly Act was enacted in July 1947, and the JFTC was established as an independent regulatory commission. The Antimonopoly Act was strongly influenced by the American antitrust laws, namely the Sherman Act, Clayton Act and Federal Trade Commission Act. The Antimonopoly Act prohibits various types of anticompetitive business conduct, such as monopolization, price and other types of cartels, bid-rigging, resale price maintenance and other types of unfair trade practices. Furthermore, the original Antimonopoly Act included much stricter pro-hibitions and regulations than the US antitrust laws they were modelled on, such as (i) the general prohibition of stockholding by any company not authorized by the JFTC, in addition to the general requirement that all mergers be authorized by the JFTC, (ii) general authorization of interna-tional contracts by the JFTC, (iii) the per-se prohibition of certain con-certed practices and (iv) remedial measures against undue and substantial disparity of economic power. Later all of these measures were recognized as overregulation and consequently deleted or relaxed. Prevalent attitudes towards the original Antimonopoly Act in economic circles were as follows: first, the Antimonopoly Act was thrust upon Japan by the allied forces as a means of preventing economic recovery from its war-devastated condi-tion; second, the Antimonopoly Act was an 'outrageous' law because of its extreme 'prohibition principle'; and third, the Antimonopoly Act's notification requirements were heavy regulatory burdens for businesses.

Too strict and idealistic, the first version of the Antimonopoly Act was amended soon. On the one hand, this may have been suitable for the Japanese economy at the time, in order to avoid 'false positives'. On the other hand, however, it initiated the fatal process that has gradually taken the bite out of the Antimonopoly Act. In conclusion, the goal of the Antimonopoly Act in this era was mainly focused on achieving the 'atomistic' market structure of Japanese industries, not on the economic 'consequentialism' of welfare.

As indicated above, the philosophy of Japanese competition policy is to minimize government intervention in the economy, prohibit cartels and

---

[27] For a detailed analysis of the process of the *zaibatsu* dissolution, *see* EM Hadley, *Antitrust in Japan* (1970).

other collusive conducts of enterprises, control monopolies when they lead to an excessive concentration of market power and thereby promote competition. However, many people in the industrial and political communities of the 1950s understood competition policy as being an obstacle to economic development in Japan. Consequently, the original Antimonopoly Act experienced successive amendments in 1949, 1953 and 1958 to cut back strict enforcement.[28] Against that background, there was great tension between industrial policy[29] and competition policy, since the former is designed to protect a particular industry and, as a means to that end, may step in to allow cartelization and concentration of market power, while the latter generally takes a negative attitude toward such intervention.

If industrial policy and competition policy are considered as economic policy as a whole, we should not be overly critical of the decline of competition policy exemplified by the Antimonopoly Act, because such rapid economic growth as Japan experienced may result from the protectionist industrial policy embodied in the Antimonopoly Act. On the other hand, if we believe the goal of competition law is to maximize 'consumer welfare', the transfer of wealth from consumer to producer by way of anticompetitive price increases or oligopolistic behaviour should be condemned strongly. The JFTC could not resist the introduction of industrial policy measures such as exemption of cartels and anticompetitive administrative guidance to weaken the Antimonopoly Act, and naturally the enforcement activities by the JFTC remained stagnant until about the mid-1960s. The JFTC's only real efforts in this period were public-relations activities to secure confidence in and support for its activities and competition policy.

3.4   Incipient Restoration of the Antimonopoly Act in the 1960s and Public Support for Competition Policy

The 1960s were a period when rising consumer prices, which were an undesirable by-product of rapid economic growth, became a major economic political issue. Various measures for fighting the inflation were proposed and debated. In September 1960, the government announced countermeasures to curb inflation, in the form of a cabinet policy statement, which

---

[28]   The details of the three amendments are omitted because of space constraints. For a detailed explanation *see* Iyori and Uesugi, *supra* note 21, at 30–40 and Freyer, *supra* note 21, at 183–96.

[29]   For comprehensive discussion of Japanese trade and industry policy, including in part competition policy, *see* M Sumiya (ed), *A History of Japanese Trade and Industry Policy* (2000).

included a request to the JFTC to enforce the Antimonopoly Act more strictly. This was the first cabinet-level statement calling for stricter enforcement of the Antimonopoly Act. The Price Problem Conference, organized by the government, also proposed that Antimonopoly Act enforcement be strengthened. In response to such proposals, the JFTC started to engage in industry-by-industry analysis of competitive conditions of oligopolistic industries. In the latter half of the 1960s, the JFTC issued many decisions condemning price-fixing cartels and resale price maintenance.

In the 1960s, Japan started to take measures to open itself fully to foreign trade and investment, as the country joined GATT, IMF and OECD. The government of Japan was concerned that, unless an appropriate industrial policy were designed, the Japanese market and industries would be taken over by highly competitive foreign imports and powerful foreign capital. Driven by such concern, it took measures to, among other things, encourage the expansion of corporations through mergers and consolidation. As a result, a number of mergers involving big companies were proposed in the late 1960s. The most important case was the merger of Yawata Iron & Steel Co. and Fuji Iron & Steel Co., which produced the merged company of New Nippon Steel (1969).[30] This case was most controversial, and the JFTC approved it on certain conditions after lengthy discussions and quasi-judicial hearing procedures.[31] Through these cases and the controversy they generated the business circles realized that they could not evade merger regulation under the Antimonopoly Act any more.

In 1973, the first oil crisis shook the Japanese economy, quadrupling the import price of crude oil, which resulted in a sharp increase of almost all prices in Japan. Businesses by and large tried to absorb this cost increase by forming illegal cartels. That year the JFTC issued 67 orders against cartels, which was a record number for cartel regulation by the JFTC. In February 1974, the JFTC filed a criminal accusation with the Public Prosecutors' Office, accusing 12 petroleum-refining companies and 15 of their directors of price-fixing. This case, in effect, was the first criminal accusation against a cartel. This instance showed the public the JFTC's tougher stance against cartels. At the same time, it also showed that the Antimonopoly Act at that time was not sufficiently strict to effectively tackle price cartels and oligopolistic business activities.

---

[30] *Re Merger of Yawata Steel Company et al.*, JFTC Decision of 30 October 1969, 16 Shinketsushu (JFTC Decision Reporters) 46.
[31] On the other hand, a planned merger of three major paper companies (Oji, Honshu and Jujo) was given up after they received an informal negative reaction from the JFTC.

This cartel had been organized on the recommendation of the government (i.e. the Ministry of International Trade and Industry, or MITI[32]), but this was held to be illegal by the JFTC. This cartel, known as the petroleum cartel, was engaged in by the petroleum industry for the purpose of limiting the production of petroleum products by collusion. The MITI had recommended and made use of this cartel as a part of its petroleum policy limiting the amount of production and stabilizing prices. The MITI dealt with the oil crisis in this way. Then the oil cartel became part of governmental, in particular MITI's, policy.

However this policy failed. As seen above, the petroleum cartel was investigated by the JFTC. As a result of this investigation the JFTC issued an order to break up the cartel and recommended that the Public Prosecutor General seek a criminal indictment. The Public Prosecutor General challenged the cartel before the court.[33] In the end, the cartel was held illegal and the defendants guilty in the Supreme Court. In the trial, the defendants claimed that their conduct of joint price-fixing was based on the administrative guidance of the MITI, not on private initiative. However, the Supreme Court rejected this argument.[34] Thereby, a great source of tension and conflict between industrial policy and competition policy disappeared. Competition policy, which is intended to reduce active government intervention in the economy as much as possible and keep it at the level of maintenance for the free and fair market mechanism by prohibiting collusive conduct such as cartels or bid-rigging, and controlling abusive conducts by dominant firms, became the dominant philosophy in Japan. In contrast, industrial policy, which is meant to intervene in a specific sector of industry in the form of compulsory or discretionary governmental control of industries with the tools of price control, production quotas, state subsidiary and so on, declined.

The role of competition law and policy as a safeguard of free and fair markets has even been reinforced in the years to come.

3.5   First Strengthening: The Antimonopoly Act Amendment of 1977

In the years that followed several studies were carried out on administered price problems. Based on those proposals, divestiture orders against

---

[32]   The MITI has been reorganized as the METI (The Ministry of Economy, Trade and Industry) since 2001.

[33]   Decision of the Tokyo High Court of 26 September 1975, 983 Hanrei Jiho (Court Cases Reporter) 22.

[34]   Decision of the Supreme Court (2nd *Petit* Session) of 24 February 1984, 38 Keishu (Criminal Cases Reporter) No 4: 1287.

monopolistic companies and certain disclosure requirements for parallel price increases came about. Also, as a result of studies on the stockholdings of major business groups and general trading companies, proposals for setting ceilings on giant companies were made and financial institutions tightened restrictions on stockholding. In view of the insufficiency of sanctions against cartels, proposals for the introduction of a surcharge (or administrative fine) system and an increase in criminal penalties arose. In September 1974, the JFTC proposed amendments to the Antimonopoly Act, effectively incorporating all those proposals.

As expected, this proposal encountered strong opposition not only from business circles but also from the government authorities in charge of industrial policy, although consumer organizations and academics were in favour of the amendments. After many twists and turns, a bill amending the Antimonopoly Act finally passed the Diet in May 1977. This amendment empowered the JFTC (i) to order cartel participants to pay surcharges, (ii) to order divestiture of a part of a business if a monopolistic situation was found to exist, (iii) to order firms to file reports should a parallel price increase have occurred in highly oligopolistic industries, (iv) to impose restrictions on aggregate total stockholding by giant companies and so on. The newly introduced surcharge system turned out to be the most effective provision among those amended in 1977 and was quite well accepted, even though it was a rather unfamiliar system in Japan. Moreover, after the 1977 amendment, enforcement of the Antimonopoly Act was generally tightened.

3.6 Fierce Trade Conflict and the Renaissance of Competition Policy

After Japan had successfully surmounted the second oil shock, trade conflicts with other countries became even more serious. Around the mid-1980s, allegations of possible anticompetitive practice by Japanese firms and trade associations were raised by the US Trade Representative (USTR) in the framework of Japanese-US trade negotiations. During the Market-Oriented Sector Specific (MOSS) talks between Japan and the United States, which began in 1985, and also during the Structural Impediments Initiative (SII) talks, which began in 1989, issues related to the competition problems were taken up.[35] In concluding the SII talks, Japan announced its intention (i) to increase the number of JFTC investigators, (ii) to use formal remedial power, particularly in such fields as price-fixing cartels and

---

[35] On the SII, *for instance*, M Matsushita, 'The Structural Impediments Initiative: An Example of Bilateral Trade Negotiation' (1991) 12 *Mich J Int'l L* 436.

bid-rigging, (iii) to increase the publicizing of Antimonopoly Act enforcement by disclosing the identities of the persons involved and (iv) to increase the surcharge rate. All of these measures have been put into effect. In addition, such a declaration of the JFTC's intentions convinced many in Japanese business circles that it was time to adopt an Antimonopoly Act compliance programme for their companies.

In December 1992, the Antimonopoly Act was amended so as to increase the maximum criminal penalties on a legal person in the case of double punishment (on parties who are both natural and legal persons). The maximum fine for certain Antimonopoly Act violations has been increased to 100 million yen, which means an increase by 20 times. In June 1996, the Antimonopoly Act was amended to upgrade the status of the secretariat of the JFTC. Before the amendment, the Commission's secretariat was equivalent to a bureau in a government ministry. The total number of bureaus in all the ministries amounts to more than 120. After the amendment, the JFTC's former secretariat was transformed into a general secretariat with two bureaus under it. In June 1995, the Diet passed, on a proposal made by the JFTC, an omnibus bill to amend 20 laws by abolishing provisions in those laws that exempt certain cartels from application of the Antimonopoly Act. Also in June 1997, the Diet passed, again on the proposal of the JFTC, a bill to change the regulation of holding companies. Previously, holding companies had been totally prohibited. The amendment aims to limit prohibition only to those holding companies that are expected to bring about an excessive concentration of controlling power over businesses. Finally, in 1998, the Diet passed a bill changing the notification systems and jurisdictional coverage of mergers and acquisitions. Until 1998, all mergers, large and small, were required to be notified to the JFTC. Mergers among foreign companies were outside the jurisdiction, even though they might have an effect on the Japanese market. With this amendment of the Antimonopoly Act of 1998, the scope of notifiable mergers became limited to mergers of a significant size. In addition, certain categories of foreign merger fell under the jurisdiction of the Antimonopoly Act.

3.7 Concluding Summary after the 1977 Amendment and the Review of the 2005 Amendment of the Antimonopoly Act

From the 1970s to the 1990s, competition law and policy took root in the economic soil of Japan. The JFTC also made efforts in the area of public relations to raise confidence in and support for its activities and competition policy. The Antimonopoly Act was amended to reinforce its effective enforcement on several occasions in this era. The SII was the favourable wind blowing in this situation.

To effectively enforce competition law, it is quite important to gain public support for competition law and policy, and to that end, to conduct public-relations activities. The successive amendments to the Antimonopoly Act to achieve effective regulation were the result of public support for competition law and policy. Indeed, the government (including MITI) and even the public have gradually come to recognize competition policy as being important. More specifically, the economic policy makers in Japan came to understand that competition policy is an essential element of an open market economy, and markets need to be protected against the creation of dominant positions and cartels and abuses of market power. That is also why we believe in the importance of a strong competition authority. That is why we must apply the competition rules in a rigorous and transparent way. A solid institutional arrangement for antitrust enforcement is essential for promoting competition policy. Such a system is based on an independent antitrust agency that enforces the rules under the control of the judiciary.

It is in this sense that the above-mentioned Amended Antimonopoly Act of 2005,[36] which revised the surcharge system (including an increase in the surcharge rate),[37] introduced a leniency programme, introduced compulsory measures for criminal investigations and revised hearing procedures,

---

[36]   The amendment to the Antimonopoly Act was enacted on 20 April 2005 and came into effect on 4 January 2006. For an outline of the amendment, *see* OECD, *Annual Report on Competition Policy in Japan* (January–December 2004).

[37]   The rate of surcharge paid by an enterprise engaged in unreasonable restraint of trade was increased as follows:

Manufacturers etc	Large enterprises: 6% → 10%
	Small and medium-sized enterprises (SMEs): 3% → 4%
Wholesalers	Large enterprises: 1% → 2%
	SMEs: 1% (no change)
Retailers	Large enterprises: 2% → 3%
	SMEs: 1% → 1.2%

The 2005 amendment introduced a leniency programme and will grant immunity from or a reduction in surcharge payments to enterprises that have committed price-fixing and that meet statutory conditions. According to this programme, the first applicant will be granted total immunity provided that the application is made before the investigation is initiated. Second and third applicants will enjoy a reduction of 50 and 30 per cent respectively. Any applicant who makes an application after the initiation of the investigation will receive a reduction of 30 per cent. The number of undertakings that may be granted leniency may in no case be higher than three.

is very important in promoting competition policy in the new Japanese antitrust era.

4   THE LONG JOURNEY TO THE GOALS OF JAPANESE COMPETITION LAW

As seen above, competition policy is now permeating all sectors of the Japanese economy. The Antimonopoly Act Amendment of 2005 significantly strengthened the power of the JFTC to enforce the Antimonopoly Act and to eliminate and deter anticompetitive activities, in particular hard-core cartels. Given a long history of collusive conduct and offenders who repeatedly engaged in hard-core violations, the 2005 Amendment sought to deter these sorts of nakedly anticompetitive practice by increasing the surcharge applied to hard-core cartels from 6 per cent to 10 per cent and applying a still higher rate to repeat offenders. This is the noteworthy reinforcement of enforcement against cartels and bid-rigging. Thus, with respect to these two practices, the actions taken by the Japanese government in the 2005 Amendment are consistent with the recommendations of the OECD and with the actions of governments around the world.

However, some people are beginning to think that the Antimonopoly Act should be further revised to intensify its enforcement power and deterrent effect in view of the fact that actions violating the Act are still being committed one after the other. A supplementary provision of the 2005 Amendment provides that, while taking into account the actual state of enforcement of the new law and changes in socioeconomic circumstances, the government must examine the surcharge system, the procedures for cease-and-desist orders and the hearing procedures and take the necessary measures based on the result of this examination within two years after entry into force of the 2005 Amendment (Article 13 of the Supplementary Provisions).

In accordance with the Supplementary Provisions of the 2005 Amendment, 'the Antimonopoly Act Study Group' (hereinafter referred to as 'the Study Group') was held for the first time in July 2005 as a private discussion body of the Chief Cabinet Secretary,[38] and has since been held over 30 times, including input from academics. The Study Group has decided to publicize 'Points at Issue',[39] entailing a summary of the issues

---

[38]   The Study Group is organized by the Office of the Antimonopoly Act of the Minister's Secretariat of the Cabinet Office, Japanese Government.

[39]   The Office of the Antimonopoly Act, Basic Study of the Minister's Secretariat of the Cabinet Office of 21 July 2006; http://www8.cao.go.jp/chosei/

discussed at those meetings, to solicit public comment. The main points proposed by the Study Group for further improvement of the current Antimonopoly Act are as follows:

(i)   to ensure sufficient deterrents to acts in violation of the Act;
(ii) to set up a system under which effective law enforcement is provided;
(iii) to guarantee the due process of law upon administrative measures; and
(iv) to compare the Antimonopoly Act with other domestic and foreign legal systems.

Although many interesting issues are raised by the 'Points at Issue', it seems remarkable that the Antimonopoly Act should gain more deterrent effect according to the discussion of the Study Group. Needless to say, the measures imposed against cartels and bid-rigging must have a sufficiently deterrent effect and must be implemented so as to achieve their intended purpose, as the Study Group has recognized. Based on our unfortunate history with collusive conduct, especially with respect to cartels and bid-rigging involving Japanese companies, I strongly question whether the current level of surcharges under the Antimonopoly Act is sufficient by itself effectively to deter hard-core cartel behaviour in Japanese markets. In order to deter companies from engaging in what would otherwise be very profitable cartel conduct, pecuniary penalties should be at levels that will take away more than merely the unlawful profits. Because cartels usually operate in secret, the probability of detection and prosecution of a part-icular cartel is quite low. Therefore if companies are to be deterred from engaging in such collusive conduct when they know that there is little chance of their being caught, pecuniary penalties should be significantly higher than the actual unlawful profits.

In any case, the Japanese Antimonopoly Act should have more deterrent effect if we are to follow the trend of the times against cartels as follows:[40] Cartels are unambiguously bad. They cause harm amounting to many billions of dollars each year. They interfere with competitive markets and with international trade. They affect both developed and developing countries, and their effect in the latter may be especially pernicious. Their participants operate in secret, knowing that their conduct is unlawful. Their detection and prosecution should be a top priority of governments everywhere.

---

dokkin/kaisaijokyo/publiccomment/publiccomment_en.pdf (accessed 31 January 2008).
[40]   OECD, *Hard Core Cartels: Third Report on the Implementation of the 1998 Council Recommendations* (2005) 7.

5 CONCLUSION

The public has increasingly come to understand that in the globalized world effective competition policies are the trustee of our economic prosperity. Developing countries and countries in transition are restructuring their economies in an effort to create free and fair competitive conditions and to integrate them fully into the world's economy. In order to claim their share of the benefits of globalization, more developing countries are adopting economic reform packages to liberalize entire sectors, privatize state-owned enterprises and introduce competition laws and policies. They naturally look to established competition authorities – including that of Japan – for support and technical assistance. The reason is that Japan has a long history of struggling to establish a competitive environment through the instrument of an effective competition policy. In the trend of economic globalization, competition law and policy should rank as a common rule of the market economy of the world. This is one of the goals of competition law, including the Japanese Antimonopoly Act.

The goal of antimonopoly law and policy is the creation of enforcement mechanisms that should seek to strongly deter clearly anticompetitive conduct, while at the same time ensuring that there is no chilling effect on conduct that enhances efficiency or is otherwise beneficial to consumer welfare. There is a clear and wide international consensus that hard-core cartel conduct such as bid-rigging harms consumer welfare and has no economic efficiency benefits. In order to deter effectively such unlawful behaviour, cartels should be given the highest enforcement priority and subjected to severe sanctions. On the other hand, other types of business practices, and in particular a certain type of unilateral conduct, often will have procompetitive justifications that would make antimonopoly enforcement inappropriate and possibly harmful to both consumers and the economy. Because the competitive implications of certain types of corporate strategies such as unilateral conduct can often be evaluated only after careful, case-by-case analysis, a deliberate review must be undertaken to ensure that procompetitive, efficiency-enhancing conduct is not inhibited under the threat of possible antimonopoly sanctions. We must avoid the kind of regulation that results in the fallacy of false positives. In the light of these considerations, economic analysis in the area of competition law will be crucially important in achieving sophisticated case reviews.

Acting on the recognition that consumers and companies alike are increasingly citizens of a globalized economy, international integration of markets leads to sustained competitive outcomes, thus making the globalization process both economically more efficient and socially more acceptable. If we are to enjoy the prosperities brought about by globalization, competition policy has an important role to play now and in the future. This is the goal of competition law in Japan in which I believe.

4. Efficiency of competition law in economies of transition

Luboš Tichý*

1 INTRODUCTION

Advancing an economic argument, or alternatively an economic or economizing concept of commercial competition, primarily means understanding the categories of competition law from the perspective of their economic content. This involves a two-fold procedure:

(a) interpreting all terms, that is, the words in the text, from the perspective of their economic content, and
(b) incorporating terms with economic significance into the regulatory text.

This chapter attempts to analyse the law on regulation of competition in the Czech Republic from this perspective, covering succinctly the entire course of its development; to compare and contrast the current state of the law with that in Europe and in two new member states, Poland and Hungary; to point out certain broader contexts for the understanding of commercial competition in the Czech Republic; and to evaluate the existing law in terms of its significance for the market economy.

2 DESCRIPTION OF BASIC TERMS

2.1 Economic Analysis of Competition Law and Efficiency

The economic aspect[1] or concept of competition and its regulation of course includes the issue of economic efficiency.[2] Economic efficiency no

* Prof. Dr., Head of the Department of European Law, Faculty of Law, Charles University Prague.
1 U Schwalbe and D Zimmer, *Kartellrecht und Ökonomie* (1990) 10.
2 H Eidenmüller, *Effizienz als Rechtsprinzip* (1998) 4 *et seq.*

doubt serves as an assessment criterion for legislators, but also for case law, and constitutes one of the requirements of economic analysis of law. Last but not least it involves the issue of whether economic efficiency represents an attractive political aim for the regulation of competition within the whole system of law.[3]

My ideas ensue from the fact that this concept is based on an economic analysis of law. Its basic programmatic principles may be summarized as follows:

- People react to legal norms and legal decisions as *homines oeco-nomici*, that is, rationally, and they make decisions so as to achieve maximum profit gain.[4] Legal sanctions have an effect similar to prices, meaning that they make certain forms of behaviour more expensive than others. Predictions on the consequences brought about by legal norms and court decisions should be carried out in realistic terms based on this economic model of behaviour.[5]
- Those consequences are economically efficient that increase the general welfare, and those consequences are inefficient that limit or reduce the general welfare. The assessments and decisions of courts and other bodies and the consequences thereof, as well as consequences brought about by legal norms, should be based on the economy of welfare.
- It is the task of all the institutions of a legal system, not only the legislature, but also the courts and other bodies, to make such decisions as lead to desirable consequences in the above sense, that is, decisions that will improve the general welfare, or at least not decrease it.[6]

Further, it is necessary to distinguish between the positive economic model of behaviour on the one hand and the normative economic task of promoting efficiency on the other.

Economic theories, for instance, those advanced by Pareto,[7] Coase[8] and Posner,[9] constitute the basis for the economic concept applied in case law and written into legislation, including competition law and therefore competition regulation as well.

---

[3] *Id*, at 58.
[4] Schwalbe and Zimmer, *supra* note 1, 15 *et seq*.
[5] S Bishop and M Walker, *The Economics of EC Competition Law: Concept Application and Measurement* (2002) 10 *et seq*.
[6] E Hoppmann, *Wirtschaftsordnung und Wettbewerb* (1988) 75 *et seq*.
[7] V Pareto, *Manual of Political Economy* (1906, 1971).
[8] RH Coase, 'The Nature of the Firm' (1937) 4 *Economica* 386.
[9] RA Posner, *Economic Analysis of Law* (1972).

The so-called more economic approach,[10] currently being advanced in competition policy, implies the use of economic methods in applying cartel law, as for instance in the instruments of market definitions, merger-simulation models, in the modernization of Article 82 of the EC Treaty and especially in connection with private enforcement of claims, including damage claims.

2.2   The Ordoliberal School

It must be acknowledged that the concept of the more economic approach is not new, as we will show based on an example from the Czech Republic, and as can also be seen in the theories of Kantzenbach[11] or Hoppmann,[12] for example. In other words, implementation of what is considered an American concept in European cartel law means, to some extent, dusting off the ideas of the Ordoliberal School.

These doctrines grew from the idea that economic instruments are more effective than a purely legal, formalistic approach. Without doubt, these theories contribute to an improvement of a purely specialist quality of court decisions. Even now the discussion involves not the question of whether to use such methods, but to what extent and in what scope to economize cartel law.

Thus, for example in determining relevant markets, an empirical quantitative analysis is used, as well as an analysis of price correlates, analysis of elasticity of prices or a hypothetical test of a monopolist (HM test), which methods minimize the risk of a too narrow definition of a market. Simulation methods are used in reviewing mergers as a prognosis of the effects of a potential merger of enterprises.

2.3   Modernization of Competition Law

The modernization of Article 81 EC consists of modifications or a reform of per-se rules and their progressive replacement by economic facts and prognoses.[13]

The methods of calculating damage are very important mainly in the case of private enforcement of claims. They include, for instance, a before-

---

[10]   D Hildebrandt, 'Der "more economic approach" in der Wettbewerbspolitik' (2005) *WuW* 513.

[11]   E Kantzenbach and J Kruse, *Kollektive Marktbeherrschung* (1989).

[12]   Hoppmann, *supra* note 6.

[13]   *See* Communication from the Commission – Notice: Guidelines on the Application of Article 81(3) of the Treaty, [2004] OJ C 101, p 97, para 13.

and-after method, the concept of comparison, a concept based on a hypothetical calculation of costs, an approach that is based on market simulation etc.[14]

We can also state a certain penetration into European law of the rule of reason, which is an element that has its origin in American cartel law; however, we can also find it in the Czech Act of 1991.[15] This idea was born in interpretation of the Sherman Act of 1890 in the United States and is based mainly on the decisions *US v Trans Missouri Freight Association*[16] and *Standard Oil Co. of New Jersey v US.*[17] In the ECJ's decisions this approach has been shown, for example, in the verdict in *Maschinenbau Ulm*[18] and in the case law following this decision, as in, for example, *Lancôme,*[19] *Pronuptia,*[20] *Erauw,*[21] *Metro,*[22] *Dansk Rørindustri*[23] and others.

3 ANALYSIS OF COMPETITION LAW IN THE CZECH REPUBLIC, HUNGARY AND POLAND

3.1 Development and Current Status of Cartel Law in the Czech Republic

In assessing the regulation in the Czech Republic, we can state the following: in terms of the *definition of a cartel*, there has been basically no significant improvement over the history of the country's competition policy. The *exemptions* from the cartel prohibition are significant. The Act of 1991[24] and also the Act of 2001[25] contained, until 2004, exemptions from the prohibition of cartels based on industrial or other intellectual property if they do not restrict the assignee in a manner exceeding the extent of the legal regulation of these rights.

[14] Schwalbe and Zimmer, *supra* note 1, at 98.
[15] Section 3 of the Law on Economic Competition No 63/1991 Coll.
[16] 166 US 290 (1897).
[17] 211 US 1 (1911); followed by the judgment in *Chicago Board of Trade v US*, 246 US 231 (1918).
[18] Case 56/65, *Société Technique Minière v Maschinenbau Ulm GmbH*, [1966] ECR 235.
[19] Case 99/79, *Lancôme v Etos* [1980] ECR 2511, para 24.
[20] Case 161/84, *Pronuptia de Paris GmbH v Schillgalis* [1986] ECR 353.
[21] Case 27/87, *Erauw-Jacquery v La Hesbignonne*, [1988] ECR 1919.
[22] Case C-376/92, *Metro SB-Grossmärkte v Cartier* [1994] ECR I-15.
[23] Joined Cases, *C-189/02 P, C-202/02 P to C-205/02 P, C-208/02 P and C-213/02 P Dansk Rørindustri and others v Commission* [2005] ECR I-5425.
[24] Section 3 of the Law on Economic Competition No 63/1991 Coll.
[25] Act No 143/2001 Coll, on Protection of Economic Competition.

The Act of 1991 also exempted a whole range of types of agreements pursuant to Section 3(3), for example agreements using uniform contract terms or those enhancing rationalization of economic activity,[26] mainly by its specialization, unless such agreements lead to a substantial restriction of competition in the market; provision of trade discount if it represents a real compensation for the performance and does not lead to discrimination or, as the case may be, where the share of the market is below 5 per cent of the market of the entire separate Czech Republic or below 30 per cent of the local market. The Act of 2001 includes a statutory exemption for horizontal agreements if the joint share of the participants in the relevant market is below 5 per cent, and for a vertical agreement if the share of the participants does not exceed 10 per cent.[27]

A facultative exemption was formerly granted by the Act of 1991, provided that the agreement did not contain a cartel obligation and did not conflict with any statutory prohibition or the good morals of competition and unless its restrictions intolerably interrupted the economic activity of the assignee of the right or licence, having thus a significant adverse impact on economic competition in the market.[28] For the facultative exemption, the current regulation is in line with the wording of Article 81(1) of the EC Treaty.[29]

Mergers   It was considered as a limitation to merger control and therefore a condition for allowing a merger if the share of the participating undertakings did not exceed 30 per cent of the total turnover in the relevant market (Section 8(3) of the 1991 Act). The current legislation does not contain this statutory exemption anymore.[30]

Abuse of Dominance   According to the 1991 Act (Section 9(2)) a dominant position is held by an undertaking that provides through its supplies in the relevant market for the period of one calendar year at least 30 per cent of the supplies of identical, comparable or mutually substitutable goods. In comparison, the current regulation (Section 10(2) of the 2001 Act) establishes a threshold of 40 per cent. At the same time, it defines market power by considering the quantity of supplies or purchases in the market of the goods in question attained by the competitor or competitors through joint dominance during the period that is examined under this Act, but also

---

[26]   Section 3(3), Act 1991.
[27]   Section 3(5), Act 2001.
[28]   Section 4, Act 1991.
[29]   Section 8, Act 2001.
[30]   Act 2001.

considering other indices, including, but not exclusively, the economic and financial power of the competitors, legal or other obstacles preventing other competitors from entering the market, the degree of vertical integration of the competitors, market structure and the market shares of the closest competitors. The current Act also has very similar rules for the calculation of turnover.[31]

Compared to the current regulation, the 1991 Act provided for class actions as the first act in history in what was then known as Czechoslovakia. It provided for the possibility of legal action to obtain cease-and-desist orders, removal of the defective state and compensation for damages and provided reasonable compensation for persons whose rights had been breached by an illegal restriction of competition. Once proceedings had commenced through this action, legal actions by persons in the same case were not allowed. In this case, victims were allowed to join the pending dispute as additional participants. Rulings awarded with respect to these claims were also binding for other eligible persons.[32]

3.2   Description of the Current Situation in Hungary

Like the Czech Republic, competition legislation in Hungary was also implemented through two acts that have been amended several times. The first regulation was implemented under the Act of 1990,[33] which, compared to corresponding legislation in the Czech Republic and Poland, has rather a lengthy text (67 articles). In 1996, this Act was replaced by the act that has been in force since 1997[34] and has been amended several times. Its length is considerable, as it originally had 98 articles and even currently, after a number of amendments, contains 97 articles.

Cartels   There is a general prohibition allowing a few exemptions, namely the de-minimis exemption, exemption under the rule of reason and finally the legal exemptions.[35]

De-minimis Exemption   In principle, agreements whose parties' share in the relevant market does not reach 10 per cent are exempt from the ban.

---

[31]   Section 14, Act 2001.
[32]   Section 17, Act 1991.
[33]   Act No LXXXVI/1990 on the Prohibition of Unfair Behaviour on the Market of 5 December 1990.
[34]   Act No LVII/1996 on the Prohibition of Unfair Trading Practices and Unfair Competition and Restrictions on the Market of 10 July 1996; amended by Act No XXXVIII/2000 of 23 December 2000.
[35]   Section 11, Act 1996.

However, in the case of vertical agreements that have a restrictive effect and that bring about no benefits, cartels whose parties' market share does not reach 10 per cent may be prohibited, too. This is the case in particular where ties are extensive. Nevertheless, the 'cumulative ties' criterion (cumulative ties that bind a far greater number of undertakings, thus increasing the firm's market share substantially) constitutes an exception to this exemption.[36] This exemption rule is no longer provided for expressly, but it is still applied in practice. Another rule stipulates that even some vertical cartels exceeding a 10 per cent market share may be exempt from the prohibition.[37]

Additional exemptions are provided for by other laws besides the Cartel Act. The legal framework is very complex. Exceptions apply to several types of mainly free professions, including attorneys, pharmacists, doctors, sales representatives and notaries. These provisions then distinguish, in several hierarchies, between various types of markets that are subject to legal exemptions.[38]

These exemptions are governed by a relatively exhaustive list and definitions of admissible restrictions. A relatively extensive catalogue of banned restrictions in cartel agreements permitted by group exemptions is in place. For instance, sales agreements are not exempt if the cartel parties are manufacturers of goods subject to the cartel etc. On the other hand, there are lists of admissible restrictions, for example, for cartels between suppliers and a purchaser who may sell back to the supplier only etc.[39]

Abuse of Dominance   The concept of the relevant market is defined in relatively great detail, mainly in terms of substance and space. This applies to the substitutability of goods as well, although the law does not require that all the stipulated conditions be met and satisfied in full.[40] Dominance is considered on the basis of a large number of complex criteria; in addition to the market share, potential competition is also taken into account. In principle, all relevant aspects of the case must be considered. Beyond the detailed regulation of market dominance, the Hungarian provision on unilateral conduct[41] is formulated according to Article 82 EC.

Mergers   The method used shows a relatively high degree of complexity and includes a number of economic criteria (turnover between parties;

---

[36]   Section 13, Act 1996.
[37]   Section 11(2), Act 1996.
[38]   Sections 16 and 17, Act 1996.
[39]   Section 15, Act 1996.
[40]   Section 21, Act 1996.
[41]   Section 22, Act 1996.

special provisions on enterprises located abroad).[42] Even here the Hungarian provisions employ a number of relatively complex criteria, including the market-dominance test. The limit of a 25 to 30 per cent share in the relevant market usually triggers considerations of a possible abuse of market dominance, and thus the inadmissibility of the merger.[43] The Hungarian law and the merger-clearance practice employ a fairly complex system of criteria when considering the admissibility of mergers.

3.3 The Situation in Poland

The first antitrust law in Poland was enacted in 1987,[44] only to be replaced in 1990[45] by a new law that was substantially amended three times. Another new law was enacted in 2000.[46]

The 1990 Act was characteristic, in particular in the way it regulated cartels, as it expressly contained the rule of reason in Article 6, which means only a general, fundamental prohibition of monopoly practices, unless it is necessary to retain them because they do not restrict competition in a material way, with the cartelist bearing the burden of proof.[47]

Definitions The Polish legislation is characterized by the Act itself and the definitions specified in Article 4 thereof; the definition of dominant undertaking and dominant position must be mentioned in particular,[48] since these allow the use of economic criteria.

Cartels Articles 5 and 6 prohibit cartels pursuant to Article 81(1) of the EC Treaty, save for (Article 6) horizontal agreements between undertakings whose market share does not exceed 5 per cent and vertical agreements between undertakings whose market share does not exceed 10 per cent.[49] What is important is the wording of the authorization of the government (Article 7), which may exempt cartels from the restrictions imposed on the condition that they are equal to those stipulated in Article 81(3) EC.[50]

---

[42]   Section 24, Act 1996.
[43]   Section 23, Act 1996.
[44]   Act of 28 January 1987 on Combating Monopoly Practices in the National Economy (Coll 3/18).
[45]   Act of 13 April 1990 on Combating Monopoly Practices (Coll 60/704).
[46]   Act of 15 December 2000 on Protection of Competition and Consumers (Coll 122/1319).
[47]   Article 6, Act 1990.
[48]   Article 4, Act 2000.
[49]   Articles 5 and 6, Act 2000.
[50]   Article 7, Act 2000.

Abuse of Dominance   Article 8 of the Act lists examples of abuse in part differently from Article 82 of the Treaty.

Mergers   The provisions on the control of mergers (Article 12 *et seq.*) differ from the EU provisions, but only at first sight.[51]

3.4   Comparison

First of all, it is necessary to emphasize one characteristic feature of all three legal systems and of the European regulation as well. Each of these concepts differs from the others at the level of detail of the legal regulation and, as the case may be, the subordinate rules. Clearly, the Hungarian regulation is the most detailed, the Czech regulation is significantly less detailed, and the Polish regulation is rather brief and, regarding the substantive-law conditions of the regulation, thus basically identical to the provisions of EC law.

It is also important to keep in mind that this situation has existed in all three jurisdictions. However, the Czech and particularly the Polish legislation were previously very concise. They allowed rather broad scope for deliberations by the competition authority or a court, as the case may be, though in the latter case to a much lesser extent.

The Republic of Poland has the most extensive case law, the vastness of which makes it comparable to the European practice. The other two jurisdictions have far fewer cases by comparison and thus not as plentiful a judicature. This applies to the Czech Republic in particular.

Economic concepts are most clearly represented in the Hungarian legislation. The Czech and Polish provisions, in their brevity (particularly the Polish), regulate by law just a few more aspects than does the European regulation. However, in the case of the European regulation, it is necessary to stress the importance of secondary legislation and particularly the judicature, which is decisive for the development of an economic approach.[52]

A significant aspect of cartel law is private enforcement. It was previously regulated only in the Czechoslovakian Act of 1991, though in the Czech Republic this option is no longer included in the Cartel Act of 2001, like the Polish and Hungarian laws, which have never contained such a provision. In all three countries, it is necessary to proceed under general law principles and procedural regulations of the Civil Code, the Commercial Code and the Code on Civil Procedure in particular.

---

[51]   Article 12, Act 2000.

[52]   *See eg* decisions of the Czech Office for the Protection of Competition, S 18/01 *Eurotel Ltd*, S19/01 *Radio Mobil* and S 105/99 *ČEZ*.

4 THE CONTEXT OF THE ECONOMIC APPROACH TO COMPETITION LAW REGULATION

In assessing the influence of competition, its regulation and, as the case may be, the economic approach to these phenomena, the following aspects must be taken into account with respect to economies in transition.

None of these states previously featured an economic market. In 1933, a legal framework for the regulation of competition was set up in Czechoslovakia. Although very modern at the time of its enactment, it aged with time to the point of impracticability. Nevertheless, its marks on the first Czech law regulating competition must be noted, which is attributable to the creators of the first law. The other two countries being compared here have no tradition of competition regulation, with no real competition and no real legal framework in place.

At the beginning of the transition process, the state was almost a monopoly owner. At that time, the EU witnessed speedy development, particularly due to the actions of the Commission, which vigorously advocated the introduction of modern national regulatory systems. However, the situation in the field of 'network sectors' in particular was quite unclear. In these countries, this sector was controlled mainly by the state or by the public sector. Even state aid was at first governed by no rules, with EU regulations through the European Treaties becoming valid relatively late – five years after the above legal provisions had been enacted.

5 EVALUATION OF THE IMPORTANCE OF COMPETITION AND ITS REGULATION FOR MARKET ECONOMIES

Continuing evaluation of the significance of competition and its regulation for market economies must be based on further aspects, including:

- creation of competition and a competitive environment;
- risk of cartelization and monopolization;
- risks involving the state and public sector, including their influence on competition through aid;
- legal uncertainty due to a general framework and lack of experience.

6 CONCLUSION

It must be concluded that the attempts of all the countries examined here to create fundamental preconditions for modern regulation and, in particular, their attempts to create a competitive environment as part of a market economy have been successful.

5. The treatment of efficiencies in South African merger consideration

Geoff Parr*

The South African Competition Act has explicit public-interest objectives, including the promotion of employment, which sometimes conflict with other objectives such as efficiency and competitive prices. This chapter discusses the treatment of efficiencies in the Act, and the interaction of efficiency considerations with the public-interest consideration of employment. The chapter also discusses the definitive decision by the Competition Tribunal on efficiencies, the *Trident/Dorbyl* merger. In that decision, the Tribunal held that job savings cannot be counted as efficiencies in an efficiency defence of an anti-competitive merger, because the promotion of employment is in the public interest.

1 INTRODUCTION

This chapter will consider some of the issues about efficiencies as they apply to South Africa, particularly in respect of merger consideration. The South African Competition Act, Act No 89 of 1998, is a well-drafted piece of legislation that has been successfully applied since 1999 by the three competition agencies established in terms of the Act. These institutions are the Competition Commission, which investigates mergers and complaints, decides on 'intermediate' mergers and refers all 'large' mergers and selected complaints to the Competition Tribunal. The Tribunal is a world-class adjudicative body that hears large mergers and complaints referred to it by the Commission. It also hears appeals on intermediate mergers ruled on by the Commission. In turn, the decisions of the Tribunal are subject to appeal to the Competition Appeal Court, which is constituted as and when needed.

The South African (SA) competition authorities have made steady progress and, following the recommendation of an OECD peer review in

---

* Economist, Deneys Reitz Attorneys, South Africa.

2003, the Competition Commission has increasingly focussed on enforcement activity. Significant developments in the last few years have been the investigations into car prices, the development of a leniency programme and the holding of a banking enquiry, which is still in progress and which appears to be following the EC enquiry in some respects. Merger review probably still constitutes the bread and butter of the activities of the competition authorities, however. The international standing of the SA competition authorities was boosted in May 2007 when they successfully hosted the annual conference of the International Competition Network in Cape Town.

This chapter will discuss the treatment of efficiencies in the SA Competition Act and by the SA Competition Tribunal, and concentrates on the consideration of efficiencies in merger review.

2   THE TREATMENT OF EFFICIENCIES IN THE SOUTH AFRICAN COMPETITION ACT

There should be no reason why economic rules, if correctly specified and applied, should not fit all jurisdictions. Indeed, one of the objectives of the International Competition Network is to bring about convergence where appropriate. Realistically, however, differences in opinion and ideology about the rules may prevent complete convergence from happening.

There are instances in which economic considerations are permitted to influence decisions of the SA competition authorities, but there are others in which there are rules that do not allow for any consideration of economic effects. For example, the prohibitions against fixing prices or trading conditions, and the prohibition against minimum resale price maintenance, are form-based or per-se rules. On the other hand, there is room for efficiency considerations in the treatment of other restrictive horizontal and vertical practices, as well as in the treatment of certain exclusionary acts of dominant firms.

There are certain named exclusionary acts that are prohibited outright for a dominant firm, such as excessive pricing, refusal to give a competitor access to an essential facility and prohibited price discrimination, but in each case there are substantial hurdles for a complainant to overcome. For example, to prove excessive pricing, a complainant or the Commission must convince the Tribunal that a particular price is in fact excessive, but the Act does not explicitly define what criteria are to be used in making that determination. In respect of an essential facility, the complainant must demonstrate not only that the facility is indeed 'essential', but also that it is 'economically feasible' for the respondent to give access to that facility – both grey areas. Finally, in respect of price discrimination, there are several possible defences that a respondent can rely on in order to show that its price discrimination is not 'prohibited' price discrimination.

Therefore, with regard to the exclusionary acts of a dominant firm, the SA Competition Act does not stipulate form-based rules, but rather allows for effects-based analysis of some kind. In summary, the only provisions of the Act that are truly form-based or per se are the prohibitions on hard-core cartels and the practice of minimum resale price maintenance. This means that the SA Competition Act provides for a wide scope for examining the economic effects of restrictive practices.

3   EFFICIENCIES IN MERGER REVIEW

In terms of the consideration of efficiencies in merger review, the SA Act was based on the Canadian law, with some differences. Efficiencies are not treated as one of the factors in considering a merger, but may be used in defence of an anti-competitive merger. There are also explicit public-interest considerations written into the SA Act that can conflict with the objective of efficiency.

Consideration of mergers is set out in section 12A of the Act:

(1) Whenever required to consider a merger, the Competition Commission or Competition Tribunal must initially determine whether or not the merger is likely to substantially prevent or lessen competition, by assessing the factors set out in subsection (2), and

  (a) if it appears that the merger is likely to substantially prevent or lessen competition, then determine

      (i) whether or not the merger is likely to result in any technological, efficiency or other pro-competitive gain which will be greater than, and offset, the effects of any prevention or lessening of competition, that may result or is likely to result from the merger, and would not likely be obtained if the merger is prevented; and

      (ii) whether the merger can or cannot be justified on substantial public interest grounds by assessing the factors set out in subsection (3); or

  (b) otherwise, determine whether the merger can or cannot be justified on substantial public interest grounds by assessing the factors set out in subsection (3).

(2) When determining whether or not a merger is likely to substantially prevent or lessen competition, the Competition Commission or Competition Tribunal must assess the strength of competition in the relevant market, and the probability that the firms in the market after the merger will behave competitively or co-operatively, taking into account any factor that is relevant to competition in that market, including

(a) the actual and potential level of import competition in the market;
(b) the ease of entry into the market, including tariff and regulatory barriers;
(c) the level and trends of concentration, and history of collusion, in the market;
(d) the degree of countervailing power in the market;
(e) the dynamic characteristics of the market, including growth, innovation, and product differentiation;
(f) the nature and extent of vertical integration in the market;
(g) whether the business or part of the business of a party to the merger or proposed merger has failed or is likely to fail; and
(h) whether the merger will result in the removal of an effective competitor.

(3) When determining whether a merger can or cannot be justified on public interest grounds, the Competition Commission or the Competition Tribunal must consider the effect that the merger will have on

(a) a particular industrial sector or region;
(b) employment;
(c) the ability of small businesses, or firms controlled or owned by historically disadvantaged persons, to become competitive; and
(d   the ability of national industries to compete in international markets.

The Competition Tribunal had to consider efficiency claims in a steel merger in 2001, and its decision contains the definitive approach to the treatment of efficiencies in terms of the SA Competition Act.

4   THE COMPETITION TRIBUNAL'S DECISION IN THE TRIDENT DORBYL MERGER

The important SA case on efficiencies is the 2001 decision by the Competition Tribunal in the merger between Trident Steel (Proprietary) Limited and Dorbyl Limited.[1] The merger concerned the relevant market

---

[1] Approval Decision of 30 January 2001, Case 89/LM/Oct00, http://www.comptrib.co.za/comptrib/comptribdocs/163/89LMOCT00.pdf (accessed 31 January 2008).

for cut flat steel products of varying quality, such as improved surface finish (ISF) or non-ISF steel. Non-ISF steel is often used in the inner panels and unexposed parts of motor vehicles, whereas ISF steel is a high-quality steel specific to the automotive industry, used for the outer body panels of cars. The proposed transaction did not alter the competitive situation in the non-ISF market, but in the ISF market, the merger combined the parties' market shares of roughly 35 per cent each into a 70 per cent share for the merged entity. Imports accounted for 30 per cent of the market, but the competing import was not completely substitutable and tariffs (32.5 per cent to 43.5 per cent), incentive schemes, transport costs and exchange rate fluctuations all undermined the foreign product. Accordingly, the Tribunal noted:[2] 'Substitution in one of these forms will not necessarily constrain Trident's market power or prevent Trident from raising prices on ISF flat steel products up to the import parity ceiling'.

The Tribunal further stated:[3] 'Accordingly, considering that Trident will be the only domestic steel processor of outer blanks for the automotive industry post-merger, as well as the unreliability of imports as a likely competitive force, we find that the merger will result in a substantial lessening of competition in the ISF market'.

Next, the Tribunal had to consider whether the merger was likely to result in any technological, efficiency or other pro-competitive gain that, in the words of Section 12A(1)(a)(i), 'will be greater than, and offset, the effects of any prevention or lessening of competition, that may result or is likely to result from the merger and that would not likely be obtained if the merger is prevented'.

The Tribunal proceeded to examine the aspects of efficiency claims: first, it stated that the onus of proving efficiencies rested on the parties. Second, it discussed whether efficiencies were verifiably 'cognizable' or speculative, real or pecuniary, dynamic or static efficiencies. Third, the Tribunal mentioned the complexities in the formulaic (Williamson[4]) approach to comparing efficiencies with deadweight losses, coming out in favour of 'a flexible approach that recognises and weighs the evidence of a formulaic result'.[5]

The Tribunal next considered whether the benefit of the efficiencies must be passed on to consumers (the 'consumer welfare standard') or not (the

---

[2]   *Id*, at para 26.
[3]   *Id*, at para 40.
[4]   O Williamson, 'Economies as an Antitrust Defense: The Welfare Tradeoffs' (1968) 58 Am Econ Rev 18.
[5]   *Trident/Dorbyl*, *supra* note 1, at para 67.

'total welfare standard'). The Tribunal noted the Canadian preference for the total welfare standard, as opposed to the 'passing on' requirement in the USA, whereby consumers must receive at least some of the benefit of efficiencies.

As mentioned above, the SA legislation on efficiency consideration in merger review was based on the Canadian Act, although the main differences are noted in the following passage (paras 78 to 80) in the *Trident/Dorbyl* decision:[6]

> (78) Our statute differs from its Canadian counterpart in some important respects. Firstly our concept of efficiency is used in section 16 [note: now section 12A] in combination with the words 'technological or other pro-competitive gain'. Adopting an eiusdem generis approach and trying to discern a common meaning between these three words, this would suggest that in this context, efficiencies that equate to 'technological gains' ie dynamic efficiencies or 'pro-competitive gains' ie those that constitute real economies, not mere pecuniary gains, are to be favoured.

> (79) Secondly in the 'purpose' clause, which we find in section 2(a) of the Act, efficiency is conceptually linked to notions of a dynamic nature: '*to promote the efficiency, adaptability and development of the economy*'. . .[7] This choice of language is, once again, suggestive of notions of dynamic and productive efficiencies.

> (80) Thirdly the use of employment as a public interest concern in section 16(3)(ii) [note: now section 12A(3)(b)] which must be taken into account in assessing the desirability of the merger suggests that employment reduction should not be recognized as an efficiency in terms of section 16 (1)(a)(i) [12A(1)(a)(i)]. The legislature can hardly be seen to be giving a defence in one section (16(1)(a)(i)) [12A(1)(a)(i)] and taking it away in another (section 16(3)(ii)) [12A(3)(b)].

The Competition Tribunal then concluded on efficiency considerations as follows:[8]

> (81) . . . We propose the following test – where efficiencies constitute 'real' efficiencies and there is evidence to verify them of a quantitative or qualitative nature, evidence that the efficiencies will benefit consumers, is less compelling. On the other hand, where efficiencies demonstrate less compelling economies, evidence of a pass through to consumers should be demonstrated and although no threshold for this is suggested, they need to be more than trivial, but neither is it necessary that they be wholly passed on. The test is thus one where real economies and benefit to consumers exist in an inverse relationship. The more compelling the former the less compelling need be the latter. When we talk of real economies

---

6   *Id*, at paras 78–80.

7   Emphasis added by the author.

8   *Id*, at 81 *et seq.*

we would, without proposing an exhaustive list, include dynamic efficiencies, production efficiencies ranging from plant economies of scope and scale to research and development efficiencies that might not be achieved short of merger. Pecuniary efficiencies would not constitute real economies nor would those that result in a mere redistribution of income from the customers, suppliers or employees to the merged entity. Without categorically rejecting them we would be more sceptical than the Canadian courts in accepting certain efficiencies such as administrative efficiencies since these can be established in most mergers. As our discussion of the textual features of our Act has shown, it could not have been the intention of the legislature that a merger that is anticompetitive could be immunized by a demonstration of savings on clips and clerks.

(82) Whilst this approach might be criticized for giving the competition authority too much discretion at the expense of business certainty, the alternative which is to interpret this section as a mathematical comparison of two areas on a Williamson diagram, permits an approach so clinical and rigid that it would reduce the proper exercise of a discretion to a matter of calculus.

It is apparent from paragraph 81 above that the Tribunal decided to adopt an 'inverse sliding scale'. Under a normal 'sliding scale', the more competition is restricted, the higher the efficiency claims must be. The SA Competition Tribunal's 'inverse' sliding scale means that the stronger the showing of real efficiencies, the less need there would be to show how consumers would benefit directly.

In the event, the Tribunal accepted several of the claimed efficiencies raised by the parties as being merger-specific and substantial, such as rationalization and re-organization of production facilities, reducing wastage, getting the steel supplier (Iscor – now Mittal) to put more of the parties' products on its standard list and so on. However, the Tribunal did not accept that volume discounts from Iscor were real efficiencies.

The efficiencies were stated by the Tribunal to be so overwhelming that they would dwarf the anti-competitive effects, and they took some comfort in the fact that the parties' pricing was constrained by the import parity price, which they accepted was about 20 per cent higher than the ruling domestic price.

Nowhere in its decision did the Tribunal actually anticipate a reduction in prices to consumers as being likely to occur as a consequence of the claimed efficiencies. The Tribunal adopted the stance that as long as there are large enough, verifiable efficiencies, it is likely that, in part, those gains will be passed on to consumers.

As an aside that perhaps illustrates the danger of accepting efficiency claims (no matter how overwhelming) in mergers to monopoly or near-monopoly, the exchange rate of the SA Rand significantly depreciated late in the very next year (2001), giving firms in the steel supply chain (including Iscor and the downstream steel de-coiling and cutting firms) a greatly increased pricing wedge up to the import parity level. As a result, steel product prices soared and there were complaints made about excessive pricing against Iscor in 2002 to the Competition Commission, complaints that were only decided by the Competition Tribunal in March 2007, but even that decision has been appealed by Mittal to the Competition Appeal Court.

Had the Tribunal anticipated the sharp change in the exchange rate, it might not have approved the *Trident/Dorbyl* merger. As the Tribunal stated:[9] in paragraph 91:

> Since this import parity price is not likely to be much higher than the current market price, the anticompetitive effects whilst real, are constrained. [Footnote: August Lapple, a major customer (the press shop for BMW), have suggested that this would be approximately 20%] Had this not been the case, we may have either found the trade-off had not been sufficiently established or we might have considered approving the merger, but subject to appropriate behavioural conditions.

5   SAVINGS IN EMPLOYMENT AS EFFICIENCIES

As noted above, the SA Competition Tribunal regards efficiency gains arising out of savings in employment as being inconsistent with the further objective of the Competition Act to promote employment, as found in section 12A(3)(b). This should be seen in context: the most serious macro-economic problem in South Africa is (and has been for many years) the very high rate of unemployment.

Accordingly, section 2(c) on the purpose of the Act reads:

> The purpose of this Act is to promote and maintain competition in the Republic in order . . .
>
> (c)   to promote employment and advance the social and economic welfare of South Africans

Is it true therefore that savings in employment can never constitute a valid efficiency defence for an anti-competitive merger? Section 12A(3)(b) (ex 16(3)(ii)) reads as follows:

> When determining whether a merger can or cannot be justified on public interest grounds, the Competition Commission or the Competition Tribunal must consider the effect that the merger will have on . . .
>
> (b)   employment . . .

---

[9]   *Id*, at para 91.

This does not appear to exclude the consideration of proposed mergers that contemplate job losses that, in creating efficiencies and reducing costs, will allow the merged entity to continue to operate, thereby saving the remaining jobs.

But that eventuality is catered for in the list of factors that must be taken into account in the prior consideration of whether the merger substantially prevents or lessens competition, in section 12A(2)(g): 'whether the business or part of the business of a party to the merger or proposed merger has failed or is likely to fail'. This is the failing-firm defence in the SA Competition Act. Therefore it seems that the Tribunal was correct in surmising that savings in employment cannot be raised as an efficiency defence of an anti-competitive merger.

The feature of the South African Competition Act that it does not recognize employment savings as part of an efficiency defence in merger consideration is unusual in that efficiencies are usually expected to be associated with job savings. Therefore the higher the efficiency claims associated with an anti-competitive merger, the higher the expected job savings will be. Indeed, if substantial efficiencies are claimed but there are no claims of associated job savings, then the merger filing might be regarded with some suspicion by the authorities.

Furthermore, the legislation predisposes the authorities to prohibit an anti-competitive merger that entails large efficiencies, including substantial job savings, because the job savings are a negative in terms of the public interest. Therefore the exclusion of job savings as part of an efficiency defence could be seen as a 'double whammy', because not only are these efficiencies excluded from the efficiency defence, but they count against the approval of a merger on public-interest grounds.

6   CONCLUSION

This chapter has summarized the treatment of efficiencies in the South African Competition Act, particularly in relation to merger review. The definitive decision by the Competition Tribunal that addressed efficiencies was the *Trident/Dorbyl* case, in which the Tribunal listed the types of efficiencies it would accept and those it wouldn't. The Tribunal also held that it could not accept job savings as part of an efficiency defence, because the effect of a merger on employment is listed in section 12A(3)(b) of the Act as a public-interest consideration. As a result, job savings are not only excluded but also subtracted from any other efficiencies claimed in the calculation of the magnitude of the efficiency defence.

PART II

The status of efficiency analysis in competition law

6. Should competition law promote efficiency? Some reflections of an economist on the normative foundations of competition law

Wolfgang Kerber*

1 INTRODUCTION

After the introduction of the 'more economic approach' in EU competition policy, the question of the importance of economic efficiency as a goal of competition law has become even more relevant. To what extent should competition law promote efficiency? What is the relation between competition and efficiency? This problem has always been relevant for exemptions from the prohibition of horizontal and vertical agreements according to Article 81(3) EC (with its balancing test). It also emerged in the discussion about efficiencies in merger control, leading to a major change in EU merger control in 2004. Recently this problem has also popped up with regard to the discussions about the application of the 'more economic approach' concerning Article 82 EC. Whereas economists vehemently emphasize the importance of efficiency considerations for competition policy, legal scholars are much more uneasy about this development.

This chapter (written by an economist) intends to contribute to a better understanding between economists and legal scholars about the goals of competition law. My main point is that the discussion on the normative foundations of competition law is not well developed: The main problem on the side of economics is that the theory of industrial organization, which

* Professor of Economics, Philipps University Marburg, Department of Business Administration and Economics. The author would like to thank Oliver Budzinski, Arndt Christiansen, Eleanor Fox and Daniel Zimmer for important discussions as well as the NYU Law School and the Hauser Global Law School Program for providing abundant support and a stimulating intellectual atmosphere during his stay as Global Professor of Law in the spring term of 2007.

dominates the 'more economic approach', does not focus its research on normative questions. Usually the normative issues are narrowed down to the question of total welfare standard versus consumer welfare standard. However, normative approaches in economics can offer a much broader set of arguments which might allow for a more differentiated discussion about the goals of competition law. In the legal discussion, the main problem is that the goals of competition law primarily emphasized by legal scholars, such as economic freedom or legal certainty, do not easily relate to modern economic approaches. Economists often do not understand the arguments of legal scholars, and legal scholars are appalled by the apparently exclusive reliance of economists on economic efficiency. These problems stem partly from misunderstandings between economists and lawyers, and partly from an underdeveloped normative discussion about the goals of competition law. Therefore, more interdisciplinary research is necessary to clarify the relevant normative issues and to develop more sophisticated concepts for the goals of competition policy.

In this chapter, I can only discuss some of the relevant issues and will briefly suggest some ideas for a broader perspective on the normative foundations of competition law. In section 2, I will try to clarify the normative key concepts that economists use with regard to competition policy – such as static and dynamic efficiency as well as the problem of redistribution through market power. Section 3 presents another normative perspective based upon constitutional economics, which may lead to a more differentiated normative approach to competition law. Its basic idea is that the preferences of citizens should be the relevant normative criterion for appropriate decisions about the objectives of competition policy. This will lead to a different perspective on the questions of how, to what extent and what kind of economic efficiency should be considered in the different realms of competition law. It might also allow for more consideration of normative issues currently emphasized primarily by legal scholars, such as the protection of rights of market participants or concepts like 'competition on the merits'.

2 CURRENT DISCUSSION ABOUT GOALS OF COMPETITION POLICY: SOME CLARIFICATIONS AND COMMENTS

2.1 Introduction

Current overviews of the goals of competition policy written from an economic perspective primarily emphasize allocative and productive efficiency, based upon welfare economics. Dynamic efficiency also, that is, incentives for innovation, is often seen as important. Much more controversial is the question of whether competition law should prevent redistribution through market power, leading in turn to the question of whether the total-welfare standard or the consumer-welfare standard should be applied. Although most economists would prefer the total-welfare standard, many of them accept the consumer welfare standard (as used by the European Commission). However, nearly all economists are reluctant to accept additional goals of competition policy such as economic freedom, fairness and justice, the protection of small and medium-sized firms, the international competitiveness of domestic firms and (with regard to the EU) economic integration.[1] The European Commission's interpretation of the goals of European competition policy is not entirely in line with this perspective, but it is also not so far away. Besides the specific goal of market integration, the EU competition rules are intended to protect 'effective competition' which 'brings benefits to consumers, such as low prices, high quality products, a wide selection of goods and services, and innovation'.[2] In the following, we will mainly discuss the goals of allocative and productive efficiency, dynamic efficiency and the problem of redistribution through market power.

2.2 Static Efficiency: The Concept of Efficient Allocation

Modern economic theory focuses on the optimal allocation of the resources of an economy. This is connected at the theoretical level with general equilibrium theory and normatively with the Pareto criterion.[3] The Pareto criterion is fulfilled if there is no possibility of increasing the well-being of any person in the economy without reducing that of any other person. Its normative attractiveness in economics stems from the widely held belief that

---

[1]   *See* for such overviews *eg* M de la Mano, 'For the Customer's Sake: The Competitive Effects of Efficiencies in European Merger Control' (2002) *Enterprise Papers* No 11; M Motta, *Competition Policy. Theory and Practice* (2004) 17; RJ Van den Bergh and PD Camesasca, *European Competition Law and Economics: A Comparative Perspective* (2006) 16; and W Kerber and U Schwalbe, 'Economic Foundations of Competition Law' in FJ Säcker, G Hirsch and F Montag (eds), *Competition Law: European Community Practice and Procedure – Article-by-article Commentary of the EC Competition Law* (2008) paras 1-8-93 to 1-8-109.

[2]   Guidelines on the assessment of horizontal mergers under the Council Regulation on the control of concentrations between undertakings, 5 February 2004, [2004] OJ C 31/7.

[3]   For the following, *see* any intermediate or advanced textbook in microeconomics, *eg* HR Varian, *Microeconomic Analysis* (3rd edn, 1992).

interpersonal comparisons of utility are not possible. This leads logically to the Pareto criterion, on which individuals can easily agree and which does not require interpersonal comparison of utility. Allocation theory assumes the existence of sets of factors of production (resources), production functions (technologies), products and preferences, which do not change. The goal of efficient allocation implies that the resources of an economy should be allocated to the production of products in such a way that the Pareto criterion is fulfilled for the whole economy: No person can be made better off through a reallocation of these resources without reducing the utility of another person. General equilibrium theory demonstrates that this requires the fulfilment of a number of marginal and total conditions. On the one hand, general equilibrium theory has succeeded in defining the concept of 'efficient allocation' (mathematically) precisely. On the other hand, it has also demonstrated that, for any economy, an infinite number of efficient resource allocations exists, depending on different initial distributions of these resources to the persons in the economy. Therefore, for different distributions, different allocations of resources are efficient.

The link between efficient allocation and competition is depicted by the first theorem of welfare economics: If the assumptions of the model of perfect competition are fulfilled by all markets (product and factor markets), the decentralized optimizing behaviour of all agents (persons, firms) will lead to an efficient allocation throughout the entire economy, that is, the Pareto criterion will be automatically fulfilled without the necessity for state intervention (Adam Smith's 'invisible hand of the market'). It is understandable why the model of 'perfect competition' (despite all its unrealistic assumptions) still has such a central position in economic theory. From the perspective of the goal of efficient allocation, it is an ideal form of the market and, even more generally, of organizing the entire economy. Consequently, the welfare-theoretical market failure theory (as the dominant theoretical basis for economic policy) is based upon the notion that any deviation from the assumptions of 'perfect competition' leads to some kind of allocative inefficiency and, hence, calls for some correction of the allocation through economic policy. From that welfare-theoretical perspective a number of economic policies (for solving different kinds of market-failure problems) are seen as necessary, and competition policy is only one of them. Therefore, in terms of the economic theory of allocation, competition is an instrument that has the sole task of bringing about allocative efficiency.

In competition policy, distinctions are often made between allocative and productive efficiency. Productive efficiency is fulfilled if in any firm the output is produced with the lowest amount of inputs or factors of production, that is, with minimal costs. Productive inefficiencies can result from the inability to exploit economies of scale, and so-called X-inefficiencies, due to the problem that managers might pursue goals other than profit maximization. This distinction plays a prominent role in the Williamson trade-off regarding the welfare assessment of mergers: It calls for a balance between an increase in productive efficiency through a merger (eg through economies of scale) and allocative inefficiencies that arise through larger market power ('deadweight loss').[4] However, it is misleading to view allocative and productive efficiency as two goals on the same level: Efficient allocation requires all firms to produce efficiently. Therefore the goal of productive efficiency is subsumed by the ultimate goal of efficient allocation. This does not preclude trade-offs between different kinds of specific efficiency effects (as in the Williamson trade-off).

It is important to note that 'allocative efficiency' is defined precisely in welfare-theoretical allocation theory and is closely linked to general equilibrium theory (elaborated by Arrow and Debreu in the 1950s) and the model of perfect competition. This efficiency concept is also referred to as static efficiency, because the set of products, production technologies, production factors and preferences are assumed as given and constant. They are not supposed to change as a result of competition. The mathematical models are static-equilibrium models, which do not consider dynamics (for dynamic efficiency see section 2.3). From this general-equilibrium concept of efficient allocation, conclusions can be derived for the optimal conditions in particular markets: Under certain assumptions the efficient solution is achieved through equilibrium prices at the intersection of the demand and supply curve (implying price = marginal costs and the maximization of the sum of consumer and producer surplus). However, the theory of 'second best' demonstrated that maximizing the surplus in a particular market need not lead to an efficient solution if there are, for example, effects on other markets.

From this theoretical perspective, a competitive market is only an instrument used to achieve efficient allocation. For many economists, it is hard to understand that there might be a real trade-off between competition and efficiency. From this welfare-theoretical perspective, it is plainly evident that efficiency is the ultimate goal, and if agreements between firms or mergers lead to a higher degree of efficiency, then they should be allowed. Balance between competition and efficiency effects, as is assumed in Article 81(3) or (as an efficiency defence) in merger control, does not make much sense. It might be necessary to balance the positive effects on efficiency of

---

[4]   OE Williamson, 'Economies as an Antitrust Defense: The Welfare Tradeoffs' (1968) 58 *Am Econ Rev* 18.

a certain business behaviour ('procompetitive effects') with negative effects on efficiency ('anticompetitive effects') but not between competition and efficiency.[5] If a conflict emerges between competitive markets (defined as a market structure with many competitors) and efficiency, then from this perspective a trade-off must always be made in favour of efficiency.

2.3   Dynamic Efficiency: Innovation

Since it is an undisputed empirical fact that technological progress is the most important determinant of long-term economic growth, there is also a widespread consensus that innovation and diffusion of new products and technologies are among the important results effective competition should bring about. This innovation dimension of competition is often linked to the term 'dynamic efficiency'. However, it is very important to understand that the term 'efficiency' in 'dynamic efficiency' does not have a comparably clear theoretical definition as the above-mentioned concept of allocative efficiency (or static efficiency). In the end, 'dynamic efficiency' does not mean much more than that it is normatively preferable that innovations be generated and spread. Although the question can be raised as to what the optimal amount and velocity of technological progress should be, the specific characteristics of innovation processes make it impossible to define such an optimum clearly. The main problems are the high uncertainty and unpredictability of innovation processes, which renders it impossible to know the outcome of research ex ante. Innovation processes cannot be treated as production processes (with predefined inputs and outputs), and, hence, they cannot be satisfactorily analysed as a pure problem of efficient allocation.[6] This is also the reason why the normative concept of 'efficient allocation' has been defined on the basis of given sets of products, production technologies, production factors and preferences. The whole dynamic dimension of the generation and spreading of innovations (and therefore the changing of products and production technologies as well as preferences) is theoretically excluded from the concept of allocative efficiency.

---

[5]   From a Chicago School perspective, the distinction between Article 81(1) and (3) was never clear, because if the net balance of efficiency effects is positive (according to Article 81(3)), then the argument would run that the agreements are not anticompetitive in the first place, and therefore should not be prohibited pursuant to Article 81(1) EC.

[6]   In general, G Dosi, 'Sources, Procedures and Microeconomic Effects of Innovation' (1988) 26 *J Econ Lit* 1120; RR Nelson, 'Recent Evolutionary Theorizing About Economic Change' (1995) 33 *J Econ Lit* 48; Kerber and Schwalbe, *supra* note 1, paras 1-8-66 to 1-8-78.

Since economic theory has not successfully integrated the innovation dimension into general equilibrium theory, the problem of technological progress and, therefore, dynamic efficiency remains, to a large extent, outside of mainstream neoclassical equilibrium theory. This is also the reason why innovation economics is largely influenced by approaches from evolutionary innovation economics. Schumpeter, who emphasized the importance of the entrepreneur and innovations for economic development, suggested the need to develop an alternative to traditional equilibrium theory.[7] For example, in modern innovation economics, variation-selection models (by analogy with biological evolution theory) are used to explain technological progress and economic growth.[8] In this tradition, a number of dynamic (or evolutionary) concepts of competition have been developed. These concepts see competition as a dynamic process of innovation and imitation[9] or as a knowledge-generating process of parallel experimentation ('competition as a discovery procedure').[10] This perspective vehemently criticizes the model of perfect competition (as an ideal form of competition). A well-known critique is that of Hayek that the model of perfect competition (with its knowledge assumptions) already presupposes the knowledge that is generated through the competition processes.[11] Particularly interesting is also the critique of Demsetz, who argued that perfect competition is not a theory about competition, which he sees as a rivalrous dynamic process, but a theory about the economic effects of perfect decentralization.[12]

---

[7] JA Schumpeter, *The Theory of Economic Development. An Inquiry into Profits, Capital, Credit, Interest, and the Business Cycle* (1934).

[8] RR Nelson and SG Winter, *Evolutionary Theory of Economic Change* (1982) and RR Nelson, 'Recent Evolutionary Theorizing about Economic Change' (1995) 48 *J Econ Lit* 48.

[9] JM Clark, *Competition as a Dynamic Process* (1961); E Hoppmann, 'Zum Problem einer wirtschaftspolitisch praktikablen Definition des Wettbewerbs' in HK Schneider (ed), *Grundlagen der Wettbewerbspolitik* (1968) 9; and JS Metcalfe, *Evolutionary Economics and Creative Destruction* (1998).

[10] FA Hayek, 'Competition as a Discovery Procedure' in FA Hayek (ed), *New Studies in Philosophy, Politics, Economics and the History of Ideas* (1978) 179; W Kerber, 'Wettbewerb als Hypothesentest: Eine evolutorische Konzeption wissenschaffenden Wettbewerbs' in K Delhaes and U Fehl (eds), *Dimensionen des Wettbewerbs: Seine Rolle in der Entstehung und Ausgestaltung von Wirtschaftsordnungen* (1997) 29; and W Kerber and NJ Saam, 'Competition as a Test of Hypotheses: Simulation of Knowledge-generating Market Processes' (2001) 4 JASSS No 3, http://www.soc.surrey.ac.uk/JASSS/4/3/2.html.

[11] FA Hayek, 'The Meaning of Competition' in FA Hayek (ed), *Individualism and Economic Order* (1948) 92.

[12] H Demsetz, *Economic, Legal, and Political Dimensions of Competition* (1982).

What is normatively meant by 'dynamic efficiency'? It is not as clearly defined as allocative or static efficiency. Rather, it is used loosely. Without wanting to discuss here different normative concepts that have been developed in evolutionary economics, the most convincing approach uses consumer preference as the normative criterion. Innovations can be seen as normatively positive when they allow a better fulfilment of consumer preference, that is, lead to an increase in their utility. However it is not possible to define what 'dynamic efficiency' in the sense of an optimal dynamic solution really means. In some respects, both static and dynamic effects of competition can be normatively measured by the criterion, namely the fulfilment of consumer preferences (which, however, are treated as constant). This can be seen as a consequence of the most fundamental normative approach in economics, namely normative individualism, the idea that all normatively relevant values in society derive from preferences (ie value judgments) of individual members of this society. If we use the term 'welfare' to mean that consumer preferences are fulfilled, then we can say that both allocative efficiency (static efficiency) as well as innovations (dynamic efficiency) increase the welfare of a society. This perspective on static and dynamic efficiency is widely accepted in economics. It also seems to be fairly compatible with the normative concept of 'effective competition' in EU competition policy, because 'low prices, high quality products, a wide selection of goods and services, and innovation' presumably reflect important preferences of the consumers.

To what extent do trade-offs exist between static and dynamic efficiency? The consensus is that perfect competition does not provide appropriate incentives for innovators, leading to discussions about the public-good character of innovation and the necessity of intellectual property rights to ensure incentives to innovate. However, the problem of potential trade-offs between static and dynamic efficiency is much more complex than this discussion suggests. Research about the determinants of innovation has shown that the conditions for the appropriation of innovation's advantages can be very complex;[13] often 'market imperfections' (heterogeneity, *tacit* knowledge' and limited imitability) can improve innovation activities. Another aspect of the relation between static and dynamic efficiency refers to the question of whether a competitive assessment, for example, of a merger, should only take into account the short-term effects on prices and quantities (as in merger simulations) or also consider the long-term effects on innovation. For example, there is considerable concern that in the 'more

---

[13]   G Dosi, 'Sources, Procedures and Microeconomic Effects of Innovation' (1988) 26 *J Econ Lit* 1120.

economic approach' of EU competition policy, the long-term effects of business behaviour and mergers on dynamic efficiency are neglected compared to short-term static-efficiency effects.[14]

2.4 Prevention of Redistributions through Market Power

Though there is a consensus that competition law should help increase welfare with regard to static and dynamic efficiency, some dispute has arisen about the aim of competition policy to prevent market participants from being exploited by firms with market power. Since the beginning of modern competition policy, the fight against cartels, monopolies and firms with market power has been largely motivated by the goal to impede the exploitation of individuals and firms on the opposite market side through market power, especially consumers through firms with market power on the supply side. Redistributions that are caused not by better performance but only through restraints of competition and market power should be prevented. However, the recent debate about the total-welfare standard versus the consumer-welfare standard and about the importance and design of an efficiency defence in merger control shows that this goal of preventing redistributions through market power is no longer undisputed – despite the clear pledge of the European Commission to uphold the consumer-welfare standard.

The difference between a total-welfare standard and a consumer-welfare standard is well known and can be explained easily. The total-welfare standard implies that in a particular market the sum of producer and consumer surplus should be maximized (total surplus).[15] Within the analytical framework of the Williamson trade-off analysis of mergers, the total-welfare standard asks whether additional producer surplus that might accrue through an increase in productive efficiency created by merger (eg by economies of scale) is larger than any additional allocative inefficiency (deadweight loss) that results from an increase of market power. However, it is not necessary to consider the distributional effects that turn a part of the former consumer surplus into market-power profits (and therefore into

---

[14] C Kirchner, 'Goals of Antitrust and Competition Law Revisited' in M Albert, D Schmidtchen and S Voigt (eds), *The More Economic Approach to European Competition Law, Conference on New Political Economy Vol 25* (2007) 7.

[15] A distinction can also be made between 'total surplus' (as the sum of consumer and producer surplus on a particular market) and 'total welfare' (as the sum of all welfare effects in the whole economy, which, in particular, would include additional welfare effects on other markets) (*see* PS Crampton, 'Alternative Approaches to Competition Law. Consumers' Surplus, Total Surplus, Total Welfare and Non-Efficiency Goals' (1994) 17 *World Comp* 55. In the following, we ignore welfare effects on other markets, and use the two terms as synonyms.

producer surplus): Such a redistribution between consumer and producer surplus does not affect total welfare as the sum of consumer and producer surplus.[16] If a consumer-welfare standard is used, then the assessment of mergers – within the price-quantity scheme – implies asking only whether the consumer surplus after the merger is larger or smaller than before the merger, irrespective of its impact on the surplus of the producers. This seems to lead to the simple assessment criterion of whether the market price after the merger is larger or smaller than before the merger.[17]

It is well known that applying the total-welfare standard or the consumer-welfare standard can lead to different results. In the case of merger control, there might be a number of mergers whose price-decreasing effects through efficiencies are smaller than the price-increasing effects of their additional market power (non-coordinated or coordinated effects) but whose gains in productive efficiency are larger than the additional allocative inefficiencies. In these cases, a consumer welfare standard would lead to a negative assessment of these mergers, even though they would increase total welfare. Consequently, the consideration of efficiencies in mergers can only impact their clearance under the consumer welfare standard if these efficiencies are very large – as stipulated in European merger control after its 2004 reform. Many economists cannot understand why merger control ignores the positive efficiency effects of many mergers and, therefore, also prohibits mergers that increase total welfare. Many economists would suggest using the total-welfare standard as the relevant normative criterion.[18] These economists readily admit that there might be distributional effects through mergers from consumers to producers, but assert that these redistributions should not be considered. A well-known position in the law and economics literature argues that analysis of legal rules and regulations should focus only on efficiency effects, whereas distributional effects should be dealt with through taxation and social policy.[19]

---

[16]   *See* OE Williamson, 'Economies as an Antitrust Defense: The Welfare Tradeoffs' (1968) 58 *Am Econ Rev* 18; J Farrell and C Shapiro, 'Horizontal Mergers: An Equilibrium Analysis' (1990) 80 *Am Econ Rev* 107; de la Mano, *supra* note 1; and Van den Bergh and Camesasca, *supra* note 1, at 31–35.

[17]   de la Mano, *supra* note 1, at 28. However de la Mano is right 'to emphasize that the price effect is only one of the several elements to be considered. . . . In fact, consumer welfare . . . is a multi-dimensional concept, including, together with prices, other aspects such as the quality of the product, the speed and the security of the supply etc.'

[18]   *See eg* K Heyer, 'Welfare Standards and Merger Analysis: Why Not the Best?' (2006) 2 *Comp Pol'y Int'l* No 2, 29.

[19]   L Kaplow and S Shavell, 'Why the Legal System is Less Efficient than the Income Tax in Redistributing Income' (1994) 23 *J Leg Stud* 667.

What is the result of a deeper analysis of the relationship between total welfare, consumer welfare and efficient allocation (static efficiency), as defined in section 2.2? Many economic texts give the misleading impression that total welfare is identical to allocative efficiency (as a Pareto-optimal allocation of resources in the entire economy), and that it is the consumer-welfare standard that additionally includes distributional issues. In welfare economics, it is clear that allocative efficiency says nothing about distributional questions. On the contrary, each 'efficient allocation' is defined based on a particular initial distribution of the resources of a society. If this distribution is changed, then the 'efficient allocation' changes as well. It is not possible to make any normative statement about the preferability of an efficient allocation A_1, based upon distribution D_1, compared to an efficient allocation A_2, based upon another distribution, D_2. This is also shown by the well-known conclusion in welfare economics that there are an infinite number of 'efficient allocations' in a society, and that the theory of efficient allocation cannot determine the 'optimal' efficient allocation (there is no so-called *optimum optimorum*). This is the result of standard welfare economics, which can be found in any advanced textbook on microeconomics.[20] It is also a logical consequence of the Pareto criterion itself: Since the Pareto criterion assumes that no interpersonal comparisons of utility are possible between different persons, no balancing is possible between positive effects on one person and negative effects on other persons.

The total-welfare standard is not compatible with the Pareto criterion, because it allows for redistributions between consumers and producers and, therefore, a balancing between positive and negative wealth effects between different persons. This implies that the total-welfare standard can be derived neither from the Pareto criterion nor from the goal of 'efficient allocation'.[21] It might be argued that the consumer-welfare standard can be derived from the Pareto criterion, because it stipulates that through mergers no one should be worse off, that is, the criterion that consumer surplus should not be reduced through a merger can be seen as an application of the Pareto criterion. The total-welfare concept corresponds to the so-called Kaldor-Hicks welfare criterion (principle of wealth maximization).[22] The

[20]   *See eg* Varian, *supra* note 3.

[21]   These problems do not depend on the aforementioned question of whether dynamic efficiencies should also be included or not.

[22]   For an explanation and critical discussion of the Kaldor-Hicks criterion and the wealth-maximization criterion, *see* RA Posner, 'Utilitarianism, Economics and Legal Theory' (1979) 8 *J Leg Stud* 103; RA Posner, 'The Ethical and Political Basis of the Efficiency Norm in Common Law Adjudication' (1980) 8 *Hofstra L Rev* 487; HB Schäfer and C Ott, *Lehrbuch der ökonomischen Analyse des Zivilrechts* (2nd edn,

Kaldor-Hicks criterion means that a state of society Z_4 is normatively better than Z_3 if those individuals who are better off in Z_4 are able to compensate those that are worse off in Z_4 to such an extent that the latter are not worse off than they would be in state Z_3. However such compensation need not be made. Regarding merger control, this means that those who benefit from a merger should be able to compensate consumers made worse off, but compensation need not be paid. If total welfare as the sum of consumer and producer surplus is increased by a merger, then the Kaldor-Hicks criterion is fulfilled, because the increase of producer surplus is larger than the reduction of consumer surplus.

In law and economics literature, the Kaldor-Hicks (or 'wealth maximization') criterion is the standard normative criterion for the economic analysis of legal rules. However, there is also much criticism with regard to the Kaldor-Hicks criterion. Besides a theoretical problem of inconsistency, the most important problem is that the Kaldor-Hicks criterion allows for all kinds of uncompensated redistributions between individuals or firms.[23] Whereas the Pareto criterion can easily be agreed on because it ensures that nobody is made worse off, it is not easy to argue why individuals should agree to a normative rule that allows society to reduce their wealth (without compensation) only on the basis of the argument that the gains of other persons or firms through policy measures outweigh their losses. The claim has been made that repeated application of the Kaldor-Hicks criterion can lead to a Pareto-superior situation, if all persons are both winners and losers in different situations.[24] However, this argument presupposes that the gains and losses are evenly distributed among the whole population. Somewhat along the lines of this reasoning is the

---

1995) 29–35; AM Feldman, 'Kaldor-Hicks Compensation' in P Newman (ed), *The New Palgrave Dictionary of Economics and the Law, Vol. II* (1998) 417; and LA Kornhauser, 'Wealth Maximisation' in P Newman (ed), *The New Palgrave Dictionary of Economics and the Law, Vol. III* (1998) 679. Note that in the case of actual payment of compensation, even the Pareto criterion is fulfilled. Therefore the Kaldor-Hicks criterion is also called a potential Pareto improvement test. For a very broad and deep critical analysis of economic efficiency with regard to the law, *see* H Eidenmüller, *Effizienz als Rechtsprinzi. Möglichkeiten und Grenzen der ökonomischen Analyse des Rechts* (1998). For a detailed application of the Pareto criterion and Kaldor-Hicks criterion to the discussion on total-welfare standard v consumer-welfare standard in merger control, *see* Van den Bergh and Camesasca, *supra* note 1, at 29.

[23]   T Scitovsky, 'A Note on Welfare Propositions in Economics' (1941) 9 *Rev Econ Stud* 77.

[24]   RA Posner, 'The Ethical and Political Basis of the Efficiency Norm in Common Law Adjudication' (1980) 8 *Hofstra L Rev* 487 and Schäfer and Ott, *supra* note 22, at 33–5.

widespread argument for the total-welfare standard in competition policy that many consumers might also be shareholders of firms under merger control, that is, that the increasing producer surplus through a merger ultimately might also accrue to the consumers. However, this presupposes certain unfulfilled assumptions about the distribution of wealth.

Despite the dominance of the Kaldor-Hicks criterion within the law-and-economics literature, a number of other normative concepts that limit the application of the total-welfare concept have also been discussed.[25] The total-welfare standard cannot be applied to many legal problems, because balancing the advantages of one person with the disadvantages of another is considered inappropriate (Abwägungsverbote).[26] Particularly interesting is the concept of 'liberal rights': 'If a person A, the owner of a liberal right, prefers social state x to state y, then state x should be better, independent of the preferences of all other members of society'.[27] This normative concept implies that if one person has a certain liberal right, he or she is allowed to decide according to his or her own preferences, even if the well-being of other persons or the total welfare of society is reduced. In such a case, society is not allowed to balance the positive effects on these persons with the negative effects on others. The most elementary rights of individual freedom (leading to core notions of private autonomy, private property, freedom of contract) have such characteristics, that is, their use is not allowed to be generally subjected to an overall balancing of the positive and negative effects on society. 'Voluntary consent' as an additional normative criterion, developed in constitutional economics, will be introduced in section 3. As a consequence, there are a number of other normative criteria in economics, besides the Pareto and Kaldor-Hicks criterion, leading to a more complex normative discussion of economics.

There are also many industrial economists who accept a consumer-welfare standard as a normative criterion – either as the result of a political decision or by relying on additional arguments. For example, there are arguments that a consumer-welfare standard might compensate for other advantages producers have, for example, through better possibilities of lobbying (rent-seeking advantages) or through information asymmetries between firms and competition authorities. Another practical argument is that the consumer-welfare standard is much easier to apply, because it is

---

[25]   For a broad overview, Schäfer and Ott, *supra* note 22, at 21–48.

[26]   *Id*, at 45.

[27]   *Id*, at 44 (translated by W Kerber); *see* in particular also AK Sen, 'The Impossibility of a Paretian Liberal' (1970) 78 J Pol Econ 152.

'only' necessary to estimate future market prices.[28] All of these arguments are somewhat pragmatic and do not justify the consumer-welfare standard very well. Another approach uses intermediate solutions between total welfare and consumer welfare that put different weight on consumer and producer surplus (weighted surplus standard). If consumer and producer surplus are weighted equally, a total-welfare standard is applied; if the weight for producer surplus is zero, then this corresponds to a consumer-welfare standard; also weights between 0 and 1 can be chosen, leading to intermediate solutions. An interesting variant is that the weighting factors might even depend on whether the product is an everyday or a luxury item. In the latter case, consumers might need less protection from market power, which would allow a shift of the normative standard to a total-welfare standard, whereas in the first case a consumer-welfare standard should prevail.[29] From the perspective of most economists, the crucial problem of these solutions is that it is unclear where the criteria for deciding on these distributional questions will come from.

2.5   Protection of Economic Freedom and other Goals

Other goals of competition policy, such as economic freedom, fairness and justice, protection of small and medium-sized firms, international competitiveness and economic integration (with regard to EU competition law) are

---

[28]   For this discussion, eg D Besanko and DF Spulber, 'Contested Mergers and Equilibrium Antitrust Policy' (1993) 9 *J L Econ & Org* 1; DJ Neven and LH Röller, 'Consumer Surplus vs. Welfare Standard in a Political Economy Model of Merger Control' (2000) *CEPR Discussion Paper* No 2620; BR Lyons, 'Could Politicians be More Right than Economists? A Theory of Merger Standards' [2002] *CCR Working Papers* 02-01; de la Mano, *supra* note 1, at 18–35; Motta, *supra* note 1, at 20–22; Van den Bergh and Camesasca, *supra* note 1, at 35–45; and J Gual et al, 'Report by the EAGCP: An Economic Approach to Article 82' (2006) 2 Comp Pol'y Int'l 111; important recent contributions to this discussion are SC Salop, 'Question: What is the Real and Proper Antitrust Welfare Standard? Answer: The True Consumer Welfare Standard', Statement before the Antitrust Modernization Commission, 11 April 2005, http://govinfo.library.unt.edu/amc/public_studies_ fr28902/exclus_conduct_pdf/051104_Salop_Mergers.pdf (accessed 31 January 2008); Heyer, *supra* note 18; J Farrell and M Katz, 'The Economics of Welfare Standards in Antitrust' (2006) 2 Comp Pol'y Int'l No 2, 1; DW Carlton, 'Does Antitrust Need to be Modernized?' (2007) 21 *J Econ Persp* 155.

[29]   *Eg* de la Mano, *supra* note 1, at 33; T Ross and RA Winter, 'The Efficiency Defense in Merger Law: Economic Foundations and Recent Canadian Developments' (2005) 72 *Antitrust LJ* 471; and L Bian and DG McFetridge, 'The Efficiency Defence in Merger Cases: Implications of Alternative Standards' (2000) *Can J Econ* 33, 97–318 for the so-called Hillsdown standard (used by Canada's competition tribunal in its *Hillsdown* decision).

usually viewed critically by most economists.[30] In German competition law (and, in the past, also in EU competition law), the protection of economic freedom is seen as an important goal of competition law. This goal of competition policy has been developed by economists as well. It can be traced back to ordoliberal concepts of competition policy and to Hoppmann's concept of 'freedom to compete' (*Wettbewerbsfreiheit*).[31] In competitive markets, consumers should be able to choose between different suppliers (freedom in the exchange process). Freedom of competition also encompasses the freedom of firms to decide on their action parameters (freedom in the parallel process). Market power might restrict both freedom of choice in the exchange process as well as freedom to decide on firms' action parameters in competition with other firms. From this perspective, competition law should protect the economic freedom of firms and other market participants. Although most economists view economic freedom as very important, so far no convincing solutions have been developed as to how to integrate an analysis of economic freedom with an industrial-economics approach to competition. Due to the absence of theoretical access to the concept of 'economic freedom', most economists either tend to think that it is somehow also encompassed by economic efficiency, that it should be ignored altogether or that other fields of law (outside competition law) should be used to protect economic freedom.[32]

Legal certainty aims to limit administrative costs, an important objective in any field of law. There is a broad consensus that these costs must be taken into account in competition law. However, most economists are not sufficiently aware that there might be large trade-off problems between the approach of analysing the effects of business behaviour (or mergers etc) upon consumer welfare on a case-by-case basis and the necessary administrative costs as well as the direct and indirect costs of legal uncertainty

---

[30]   *Eg* Motta, *supra* note 1, at 22–30, and Van den Bergh and Camesasca, *supra* note 1, at 39–53.

[31]   E Hoppmann, 'Zum Problem einer wirtschaftspolitisch praktikablen Definition des Wettbewerbs' in HK Schneider (ed), *Grundlagen der Wettbewerbspolitik* (1968) 9; W Möschel, 'Competition Policy from an Ordo-point of View' in A Peacock and H Willgerodt (eds), *Germany's Social Market Economy: Origins and Evolution* (1989) 142; D Gerber, *Law and Competition in Twentieth Century Europe: Protecting Promotheus* (1998); V Vanberg, 'Konstitution-enökonomische Überlegungen zum Konzept der Wettbewerbsfreiheit' (2001) 52 *ORDO* 37; M Hellwig, 'Effizienz oder Wettbewerbsfreiheit? Zur normativen Grundlegung der Wettbewerbspolitik' in C Engel and W Möschel (eds), *Recht und spontane Ordnung. Festschrift für Ernst-Joachim Mestmäcker zum achtzigsten Geburtstag* (2006) 231.

[32]   Van den Bergh and Camesasca, *supra* note 1, at 39–53.

resulting from case-by-case decisions. Up to this point, economics has failed to sufficiently analyse the problem of legal uncertainty.[33]

2.6   Conclusions

The discussion in this section should have helped to clarify the economic concepts of efficient allocation, static and dynamic efficiency, total welfare and consumer welfare. It has been shown that (1) these concepts have different meanings, (2) economics has major problems in dealing with distributional effects and (3) the economic discussion about the goals of competition law has mainly focused on the question of the total-welfare standard versus the consumer-welfare standard. In the following, a broader normative concept for deriving goals of competition law will be sketched. It is mainly based upon constitutional economics.

3   NORMATIVE FOUNDATIONS OF COMPETITION LAW: SKETCHING ANOTHER PERSPECTIVE

3.1   Starting Point: Normative Individualism, Constitutional Economics and Rules for the Market

The normative perspective of constitutional economics[34] starts with normative individualism, that is, the idea that all relevant values and goals in a society have to be derived from the preferences and values of individual members of that society. In contrast to traditional welfare economics, Buchanan (the most important representative of constitutional economics) argued that the decisive normative criterion is voluntary individual

---

[33]   The importance of 'legal certainty' can be translated into the direct and indirect costs of legal uncertainty. This might open the way for an economic analysis of this issue. *See* A Christiansen and W Kerber, 'Competition Policy with Optimally Differentiated Rules Instead of "Per se Rules vs. Rule of Reason"' (2006) 2 *J Comp L & Econ* 215, for an example of how to deal economically with the problem of legal uncertainty as to the question of rule of reason v per-se rules. *See*, for the problem of legal uncertainty in merger policy, also S Voigt and A Schmidt, *Making European Merger Control More Predictable* (2005).

[34]   *See* G Brennan and JM Buchanan, *The Reason of Rules. Constitutional Political Economy* (1985); JM Buchanan, 'The Constitution of Economic Policy' (1986) 77 *Am Econ Rev* 243; V Vanberg, 'Markets and Regulation: On the Contrast between Free-Market Liberalism and Constitutional Liberalism' (1999) 10 *Const Pol Econ* 219; and V Vanberg, 'Market and State: The Perspective of Constitutional Political Economy' (2005) 1 *J Inst Econ* 23.

consent.[35] By consenting to transactions or to mandatory rules of society, individuals reveal their preferences and legitimize contracts and mandatory rules. This notion is entirely compatible with notions of private autonomy and democracy as developed in the Western legal tradition. Consent as a normative criterion is very close to the Pareto criterion, because if as a result of policy at least one person is better off and no one is worse off, then it can be suggested that all persons can agree on the measure. In contrast, the fulfilment of the Kaldor-Hicks criterion is not sufficient to lead to the consent of all people involved, because it can leave some people worse off.

Constitutional economics succeeded in showing how the state, with its monopoly of legitimate power and its central functions (as protective state, productive state and redistributive state), can be derived consistently from the preferences of the members of a society.[36] Using the basic idea of society as a 'social contract', constitutional economics was able to show that the state can be seen as the result of a constitutional contract on which all members of society might agree under a 'veil of uncertainty', that is, under the hypothetical situation that no person in a society knows its strengths and weaknesses before consenting to the basic rules of this society. In an additional step, constitutional economics was able to justify the transition from the unanimity principle at the level of the most import-ant constitutional rules to other (more pragmatic) decision rules (at the post-constitutional level of normal legislation). Different kinds of major-ity rules can ensue, which balance the decision costs for requiring large majorities with the costs for minorities who might lose through majority decisions. An important implication of this approach is that there might be realms in which a simple majority rule is deemed acceptable, and there might be other realms involving certain basic rights and freedoms that are seen as part of the personal freedom (or property) of persons. Nobody should have the right to interfere in these protected domains, even if this would lead to positive welfare effects on other persons or the whole society.

Before deriving more specific conclusions for competition policy, some general implications of the constitutional-economics approach for the institutional framework of markets will be presented. Constitutional eco-nomics differentiates strictly between the rules (of a game) and the actions (of the players) within this game. Therefore the relevant question is: What is the appropriate set of rules for the market game? Institutional eco-nomics has demonstrated that different sets of legal rules (institutional set-tings) lead to different kinds of market processes – due to different sets of

---

[35]   Buchanan, *supra* note 34.
[36]   Brennan and Buchanan, *supra* note 34.

incentives. Changing the rules of the market implies a change of the market game, leading to different outcomes.[37] Based upon this constitutional-economics perspective, Vanberg argues that the decision on the rules for the market game can be seen as a 'constitutional' decision, and, according to the consent principle, this set of rules for the market should reflect the preferences of the citizens. As a consequence, Vanberg distinguishes 'constitutional liberalism', which acknowledges this normative and theoretical dimension of the institutional framework for markets, from 'free-market liberalism', which does not sufficiently take into account the fact that markets always work under a set of rules.[38] Of course, the institutional framework for markets and therefore the relevant set of legal rules for markets encompass a large number of different legal rules: rules that define property rights, contract law, consumer regulations, tort law, environmental law, corporate law, labour market regulations, rules on unfair business practices (as eg with regard to advertising) etc. Legal rules against private restraints of competition are only a small part of this entire set of rules with which firms have to comply in their business behaviour on markets.

What is different about this perspective of the normative approach in comparison to a welfare-economics approach? The decisive difference is that the preferences of citizens are viewed as the ultimate normative criterion. They should decide to what extent allocative efficiency and/or dynamic efficiency should be strived for, to what extent competition law should protect consumers from exploitation or competitors from being hurt through predatory strategies, and to what extent society is willing to sacrifice some 'total welfare' in order to prevent redistributions through market power. The task of economics is the analysis of the effects of legal rules with regard to these goals, including allocative and dynamic efficiency, consumer welfare or other goals, and the extent of trade-offs that might emerge.[39] However, this approach should not be identified with the often mentioned position that the goals of competition policy should be decided purely politically. Although the goals of competition policy will be determined politically through legislation, constitutional economics would claim that the outcome of these political decisions should reflect citizens' preferences. In the case of defective political processes, the goals of competition law might be distorted through the rent-seeking activities of

---

[37] W Kerber, 'Competition, Knowledge, and Institutions' (2006) 40 *J Econ Iss* 457.

[38] Vanberg, *supra* note 34. There is a close relationship to the ordoliberal concept of 'economic constitution' ('*Wirtschaftsverfassung*') that cannot be analysed here.

[39] *Kornhauser, supra* note 22.

interest groups. This is connected to the well-known discussion in constitutional economics (and public-choice theory) about the use of institutional reforms to make political processes more responsive to citizens' preferences. The constitutional-economics approach to the goals of competition law is a purely economic one: It argues that market rules are 'optimal' if they correspond to citizens' preferences (and values).[40]

3.2 Total Welfare, Consumer Welfare and Protected Rights: Some Tentative Conclusions from a Constitutional-economics Perspective

The arguments in this section should be viewed merely as suggestions as to how a deeper and more sophisticated normative analysis might be developed. Different sets of rules for competition lead to different kinds of competition. Economic theory has developed different concepts of competition. Although the most important one is still represented by the model of 'perfect competition', there is a broad consensus that this model is not able to capture all relevant dimensions of competition processes, such as, for example, the innovation dimension. Dynamic concepts of competition try to integrate innovation into their notion of competition (eg Schumpeterian competition or Hayek's 'competition as a discovery procedure'). However what kind of competition should be strived for and protected through competition policy is the result of a normative decision of the citizens. Their preferences should decide the kind of competition that prevails in the market game. For example, what 'effective competition' means in EU competition law is a normative question. If the European Commission defines 'effective competition' as competition that 'brings benefits to consumers, such as low prices, high quality products, a wide selection of goods and services, and innovation',[41] then this is a normative decision, and the relevant question is whether this corresponds to the preferences of the EU citizens. The following will demonstrate how a more specific discussion about appropriate goals of competition law might look from the perspective of the interests and preferences of the citizens.

First, it can be suggested that citizens would appreciate both an efficient allocation of resources and the generation and spread of innovations,

---

[40] 'Voluntary consent' as the ultimate normative criterion also leads constitutional economics to another interpretation of 'efficiency': Efficiency is achieved if the unanimity requirement, ie voluntary consent by all citizens, is fulfilled (Buchanan, *supra* note 34).

[41] Guidelines on the assessment of non-horizontal mergers under the Council Regulation on the control of concentrations between undertakings, 5 February 2004, [2004] OJ C 31, p 5.

because it is to be expected that both would increase their wealth. This implies that static and dynamic efficiency are important and that any potential trade-off between these two goals would be solved by the empirical question of the relative importance of static and dynamic efficiency for increasing the fulfilment of citizens' preferences. Much more difficult is the question of whether citizens would agree on an unconditional application of the total-welfare standard (Kaldor-Hicks criterion). Restrictive agreements, mergers and business practices of dominant firms would always be allowed if total welfare is increased, irrespective of any redistributive effects between the firms involved, the competitors, the firms in up- and downstream markets and the consumers. Firms and consumers would not be protected against redistributions through market power. Although the total-welfare standard would ensure that 'victims' of market power or (total welfare-increasing) predatory behaviour could be compensated, those without a claim for compensation would lose out. It is very doubtful whether a sound argument can be made that, in the long run, all individuals would win through the total-welfare standard, because they can be both winners and losers in different situations. Although this is an open research question, the assumptions that have to be made about the evenness of the chances of being a winner and a loser suggest that such an argument might only apply in a subset of cases. We also know from developments in other parts of the law (eg tort law) that citizens prefer to be protected against all kinds of negative effects on their individual wealth. Therefore it is very hard to imagine that citizens would be willing to give up all protection against the negative distributional effects of market power.

Beyond the question of whether citizens would accept any distributional effects through market power, the redistributional effects of the total-welfare standard can also lead to negative effects on total welfare. The application of the Kaldor-Hicks criterion leads to the situation that – due to non-compensated distributional effects – the private gains from business practices or mergers are larger than the net gain in total welfare. For example, in Williamson's trade-off model, the private gains from the merger are the sum of the additional productive efficiency through the merger and the part of consumer welfare that is changed into profits through additional market power, whereas the net gain in total welfare is only the difference between the additional productive efficiency and the additional deadweight loss. As a consequence, these redistributional effects can lead to wasteful overinvestment in the search for and implementation of activities (such as mergers and business practices) that will increase total welfare. Posner's argument about the danger of the dissipation of monopoly profits through the 'competition' of firms for a monopoly (or market power) position is an example of such an argumentation.[42] Such overinvestment, which is triggered by the private gains from redistributions, would lead to a waste of resources and, therefore, to a reduction of total welfare itself.

Although it can be expected that citizens would like to be protected against redistributions resulting from market power and therefore would reject a general application of the total-welfare standard, the question arises whether citizens, on the other hand, would agree on a pure consumer-welfare standard. At first sight this seems plausible, because all citizens are also consumers. However, on second thoughts, the citizens of a society are not only consumers but also owners of production factors such as, in particular, capital and labour, and are therefore interested in income from interest, wages and profits. From the perspective of the interests of the citizens it is not obvious why competition policy should only take into account the welfare effects of mergers and business behaviour on the citizens as consumers but not the welfare effects on the same citizens as owners of firms and production factors. The often mentioned argument against a consumer-welfare standard that the additional producer surplus (through efficiencies) in mergers also accrues to the 'consumers', and therefore should not be (entirely) neglected, goes along with this constitutional economics argument that, ultimately, all interests of the citizens – and not only their interests as consumers – are decisive for their consent. Therefore the normative asymmetry that holds that competition law is only about the protection of consumers' interests and that the interests of all other firms in upstream markets are irrelevant is hard to justify from a constitutional-economics perspective.

For example, an interesting question is whether competition and competition law should protect firms on the supply side of a market from the buying power of other firms. Whereas there seems to be a broad consensus that market power can be a problem on both market sides, this is no longer clear when viewed in terms of a pure consumer-welfare standard. Why should buying power that leads to a reduction of input prices (and therefore eventually to lower prices for consumers) be assessed negatively (if we assume that these market power-induced price reductions for suppliers do not lead to negative effects for consumers, like lower quality, less variety etc.)? If, for example, the crucial criterion for assessing a merger is the question of whether the prices for consumers increase or not, then all price-decreasing effects through any buying power that emerges through the merger would facilitate the clearing of the merger. Therefore the

---

[42]   RA Posner, 'The Social Cost of Monopoly and Regulation' (1975) 83 *J Pol Econ* 807, and Van den Bergh and Camesasca, *supra* note 1, at 28.

consumer-welfare standard tends only to protect against some of the distributional effects of market power, namely those that have a negative impact on consumers. It is not clear why the citizens as owners of capital and earners of wages in firms should not be interested in being protected against the negative distributional effects of market power through buying firms, which would deprive them of some of those earnings that would accrue to them under competitive conditions.

Therefore, neither a pure total-welfare standard nor a pure consumer-welfare standard seems to be the most appropriate solution. One possibility might be the application of intermediate solutions. Then preferences of citizens can determine the weight given to producer surplus in relation to consumer surplus ('weighted-surplus standard'). It would also be possible to use different weights with regard to different realms of competition policy. Although this is a first interesting step to a more differentiated approach, the normative problems seem to be much more complex. It is not easy to know how to proceed from here without getting into the swamp of vague concepts. This is precisely the point where much additional and interdisciplinary research is necessary. In the following, I would like to present some ideas that can be used to develop a much more precise and clear argumentation on the basis of this constitutional-economics perspective. The buying-power example suggests that it might be worthwhile to develop (also from an economic perspective) an approach under which competition law also has the task of protecting certain rights of market participants against market power and predatory behaviour. Such an approach of 'protected rights' might be directly in line with the recent *Courage* decision of the European Court of Justice,[43] which ruled 'that effective protection of the rights granted by the Treaty requires that individuals who have suffered a loss arising from an infringement of Articles 81 and 82 have the right to claim damages'. Also the Commission has started an initiative to promote private litigation through damages actions for breach of the EC antitrust rules, which uses the idea of rights that are protected by competition law.[44]

From a constitutional-economics perspective, it is not difficult to justify a normative position stipulating that each member of society should as a participant in markets have a set of rights that are protected against market power and predatory behaviour. Constitutional economics can show that members of society would agree on very differentiated solutions about the extent of such protection of their lives, their private property, their freedom of contract and their entrepreneurial freedom. It can be expected that they

---

[43]   Case C-453/99, *Courage v Crehan* [2001] ECR I-6297.

[44]   European Commission, Green Paper – Damages Actions for Breach of the EC Antitrust Rules, 19 December 2005, COM(2005) 672 final.

will greatly value the freedom to decide what to consume, what to produce and when to enter a market. Therefore private property, freedom of contract and basic rights of entrepreneurial freedom (including free market entry) should be especially protected ('economic freedoms'). The decisive point is that members of society might not be willing to accept interference with this basic set of rights, even if it might lead to an increase in overall consumer or total welfare. As discussed above with regard to the concept of liberal rights, the citizens of a given society can decide that there should be a (limited) set of rights whose value cannot be readily balanced against effects on the wealth of other persons.

In the same way as they choose their basic rights, the citizens may have preferences about what kinds of business practices should be accepted as 'normal' competitive behaviour, and what kinds of conduct are deemed as (perhaps 'morally') not acceptable, leading to 'infringements' of rights of competitors, buyers or sellers. Some of these preferences might be based on the widespread normative notion that the emergence of profits and losses in market competition should be linked somehow to firm performance ('competition on the merits'). In any society, citizens have more or less strong convictions about the question of whether the profits of firms or the income of others are justified. This is only partly a question of the 'inequality' of wealth distribution ('distributional justice'), but reflects more the dimension of 'commutative justice'. To a large extent the answer depends upon whether firms deserve their profits or losses due to their good or bad performance. If firms have been able to amass large profits because they have carried out successful strategies, lobbied for protective measures or built up positions of market power, then most citizens would view these profits as less justified than those that are the result of the innovation of new and better products or cost-decreasing production technologies. A logical consequence is that such considerations might be legitimate arguments in the discussion of the goals of competition policy from a constitutional-economics perspective.

In Germany, it was the ordoliberal legal scholar Franz Böhm[45] who, when working on the problem of unfair competition (*unlauterer Wettbewerb*), developed the idea that competition should be seen as a kind of contest in which competitors try to outstrip one another by offering good performance, and that consumers exercise the role of arbiters with regard to the relative quality of these performances. The central tenet of this concept of *Leistungswettbewerb* ('competition on the merits') was that

---

[45]   F Böhm, *Wettbewerb und Monopolkampf. Eine Untersuchung zur Frage des wirtschaftlichen Kampfrechts und zur Frage der rechtlichen Struktur der geltenden Wirtschaftsordnung* (1933).

the rules of this market game should be shaped so that only the overall quality of performance (merit) should determine market success.[46] This would imply that the competition rules for the market should ensure that profits and losses of firms (as a feedback mechanism from the market) reflect (at least to some degree) the relative quality of their performance for consumers, and not, for example, superior knowledge regarding rent-seeking activities or predatory strategies. The citizens of a society might view such an approach, which, in the theory of justice, corresponds to the concept of 'commutative justice', as normatively desirable.[47] Then all kinds of market-power profits through redistributional effects, which can emerge as a consequence of the application of the Kaldor-Hicks criterion (total-welfare standard), might be assessed as undesirable from the perspective of the preferences of the citizens. This would be a powerful argument against accepting the distributional effects of all kinds of market power, leading to an argument for protecting all market participants against these effects of market power and predatory behaviour.

The problem is that economics has not yet developed normative concepts that integrate the idea of protected rights for individual people or firms into their normative welfare-theoretical approach. The traditional efficiency approach (static and/or dynamic efficiency, consumer-welfare or total-welfare concept) is too crude to be capable of including this dimension.[48] From this welfare-theoretical perspective, freedom of contract and entre-preneurial freedom have no particular value of their own. They are only justified in so far as they help to achieve efficient allocation, total welfare or consumer welfare. Therefore they can be restricted or even abolished as soon as another institutional solution leads to an increase of total or consumer welfare. However, this result is not a necessary consequence of using an economic approach. From the general normative starting-point of 'normative individualism', it is no problem to derive the legitimization of sets

---

[46] This does not preclude the possibility that this concept of *Leistungswettbewerb* has also been abused for defending restraints of competition, especially in the German Act against Unfair Competition; *see* EJ Mestmäcker, *Der verwaltete Wettbewerb: eine vergleichende Untersuchung über den Schutz von Freiheit und Lauterkeit im Wettbewerbsrecht* (1984).

[47] For an application of the concept of 'corrective justice' to sanctions in competition law, *see* Van den Bergh and Camesasca, *supra* note 1, at 320–22.

[48] For the difficult relationship between 'liberal rights' and 'efficiency', *see* AK Sen, 'The Impossibility of a Paretian Liberal' (1970) 78 *J Pol Econ* 152; for a fundamental discussion of the relationship between fairness and welfare, see L Kaplow and S Shavell, *Fairness versus Welfare* (2002); critically LA Kornhauser, 'Preference, Well-being and Morality in Social Decisions' (2002) 32 *J Leg Stud* 303; and J Waldron, 'Locating Distribution' (2003) 32 *J Leg Stud* 277.

of protected rights of individuals and firms that are not subject to the question of whether they contribute to a total or consumer welfare. Rather it is itself a normative decision – based upon the preferences of the citizens – what sets of rights should be subjected to an efficiency test (consumer or total-welfare standard) and what set of rights should not allowed to be weighed in that way. As a consequence, it is possible to argue from an economic perspective as well that competition law should take into account the effects of restrictive agreements, mergers and business behaviour not only on consumer welfare but also on a set of protected rights of competitors and up- and downstream firms that might suffer losses through the infringement of these rights.

What might this imply for the discussion on the application of the 'more economic approach' to Article 82 of the EC Treaty on abusive behaviour of dominant firms? The Commission has stipulated that here as well the consumer-welfare standard should be the only normative standard. In the DG Competition Discussion Paper, it is argued that the aim of the application of Article 82 is the 'protection of competition on the market as a means of enhancing consumer welfare and of ensuring an efficient allocation of resources . . ... This means that it is competition, and not competitors as such, that is to be protected.'[49] The Commission is right to insist that competitors should not be protected from the consequences of the better performance of dominant firms. However, this does not necessarily require that the question of whether a certain behaviour is abusive should only be assessed according to its effects on consumers. It can also be argued that all firms in a market have certain protected rights whose infringement by dominant firms is prohibited as an abuse of Article 82.[50] The decisive point is the following: Is, for example, predatory pricing only prohibited because it might lead to a reduction of consumer welfare, or can certain (perhaps extreme) forms of predatory pricing also infringe the protected rights of competing firms (which would give the 'victim' a claim for

---

[49] DG Competition Discussion Paper on the application of Article 82 of the Treaty to exclusionary abuses, December 2005, http://ec.europa.eu/comm/competition/antitrust/art82/discpaper 2005.pdf (accessed 31 January 2008). For this discussion, also J Vickers, 'Abuse of Market Power' (2005) 111 *Econ J* F244, and Van den Bergh and Camesasca, *supra* note 1, at 247–99.

[50] It is unclear to me whether the following sentence in the Discussion Paper, *supra* note 49, para 54, can be interpreted in that way: 'Furthermore, the purpose of Article 82 is not to protect competitors from dominant firms' genuine competition based on factors such as higher quality, novel products, opportune innovation or otherwise better performance, but to ensure that these competitors are also able to expand in or enter the market and compete therein on the merits, without facing competition conditions which are distorted or impaired by the dominant firm'.

damages)? Therefore a crucial distinction can be made between protecting the competitors from the effects of the strong market position of dominant firms, which is a problematic concept,[51] and the protection of a certain (limited) set of rights of competing firms that accrue to them regardless of whether they are more or less efficient than the dominant firm.

The problem of whether Article 82 should also protect certain rights of market participants irrespective of their effects on consumer welfare cannot be discussed here in more depth. I primarily want to argue that an 'economic approach' to Article 82 does not require that only the effects on consumer (or total) welfare be taken into account. In addition, the effects on a certain set of protected rights which can be derived from the preferences of citizens can be considered. This can certainly also lead to additional trade-off problems. However, such a more general approach is still entirely compatible with economic theory. It might also be much more compatible with the recent approach of the EU regarding private enforcement of competition law: In so far as private enforcement is not only seen as a pure instrument for improving deterrence with regard to antitrust rules, the whole concept of private enforcement (with its remedies of damages claims for compensation and/or injunctions) is only defensible if the protection of the rights of consumers, competitors and firms in upstream and downstream markets and the protection against (at least some) distributional effects through infringements of antitrust rules are part of the goals of competition policy. The initiative of the Commission would be hard to defend from the perspective of a total-welfare standard. From the perspective of a consumer-welfare standard, it would not be easy to defend damages claims brought by competitors. However, from the perspective of constitutional economics which allows the legitimization of sets of rights for consumers, firms and competitors as market participants, this approach to private litigation is much more compatible.

4   CONCLUSIONS

The main point of this chapter is that the discussion on the normative foundations of competition law is not well developed. I have focused my critical analysis on the discussion in economics. I have tried to show that 'economic efficiency' – as it is usually defined – cannot be the final answer to this nor-

---

[51]   One rationale for such an approach is the attempt to impede a further worsening of the competitive structure of a market. The many problems with such an approach (*eg* the danger of assessing efficiencies negatively, leading to an 'efficiency offence') cannot be discussed here.

mative question. On the one hand, there are different concepts of efficiency, with their specific problems and deficits. On the other hand, the discussion in economics, which is narrowed down to 'total-welfare standard versus consumer-welfare standard', does not sufficiently grasp the complexity of the normative problems. In section 3, another approach based on constitutional economics was briefly sketched that allows for a broader normative discussion of the goals of competition law. The decisive difference is that here the preferences (and therefore also the values) of the citizens of a society are the relevant normative criterion from which the goals of competition laws should be derived. They should decide on the relative importance of applying a consumer-welfare standard, the extent of considering efficiencies and to what extent market participants should have rights against the (distributional) effects of market power and predatory behaviour (with damages claims through private litigation). This economic approach also implies that different societies can come to different conclusions about the appropriate goals of competition laws.

Our very preliminary discussion of the goals of competition law from this constitutional-economics perspective has demonstrated that it seems very improbable that citizens would consent to a total-welfare standard with its many entirely accidental distributional effects as a general standard. Presumably, they would prefer being protected from market power in the same way as they have preferences for their property to be protected, for example, through tort law. This does not rule out that in specific types of cases, for instance if the potential wealth losses are small, an application of the total-welfare standard might be defensible. It seems plausible that consumer welfare might be a very important normative criterion in competition policy, because all members of society are also consumers who benefit from such a standard. However, we have also seen that it is difficult to justify why consumer welfare should be the only relevant normative standard. One argument is the citizens' interests as owners of production factors and firms, which suggesst both an interest in protection against the negative distributional effects of buying power and predatory behaviour of (market dominant) competitors as well as some consideration of productive efficiencies in competitive assessments. From that perspective, it is normatively possible from an economic perspective also to defend the protection of certain rights of market participants as a goal of competition law. Even normative conclusions derived from concepts such as 'competition on the merits' or notions of fairness might be defensible, as long as these normative notions reflect widely held values of the citizens.

However, my argumentation here should not be taken to mean that I would like to recommend such a broad set of goals of competition law right now. Even if such goals are desirable from a normative perspective, a lot of additional concerns must be taken into account: additional administrative costs, trade-off problems and rent-seeking problems, to name only a few. My main claim is that we need much broader and deeper interdisciplinary discussion and research about the normative foundations of competition law. Neither 'efficiency' nor 'welfare' is a sufficiently clear and satisfactory answer.

7. Competition law should promote economic and social welfare by ensuring the freedom to compete – a lawyer's view

Roger Zäch*

1 INTRODUCTION

In connection with the subject of the role of economics in competition law, I will focus on the so-called more economic approach.

First of all, let me make clear that my critical view of some recent developments concerning the more economic approach refers to the application of the law. I will not talk in particular about making new law or amending existing law. I believe that it is important to differentiate clearly between the two functions: law making and application of law.

As far as legislating is concerned, the legislators, when developing or changing competition law, must – and this is quite obvious – have sound economic knowledge. Since competition is an economic phenomenon, the legislature must take appropriate economic theories into consideration; consequently they should use an economic approach. The reason is: There cannot be good law without good knowledge of the subject matter to which that law applies.

However, I also want to point out that the legislature has to respect some legal principles, for example the principle that legal provisions must be predictable.

This chapter deals with possible impacts of the 'more economic approach' in applying competition law. Recently, the EU enacted provisions that could lead to a tendency for restrictions of competition being appraised more and more by economic criteria, such as social or consumer welfare or, in short, under efficiency criteria.

* Prof. Dr., University of Zurich, Switzerland; Vice President of the Swiss Competition Commission.

Article 1(2) of Regulation 1/2003 and the Merger Regulation, paragraph 29 of the preamble, are relevant here and there is also some discussion about introducing the more economic approach into the area of control of conduct of dominant firms under Article 82.[1]

Furthermore, many academic scholars are proposing that the function and goal of competition law should no longer be that of ensuring the freedom to compete but rather the promotion of economic and social welfare.[2]

In the following short presentation I will argue that that proposition should not be supported: I will first show that the two different concepts of legal goals lead to two different ways of adjudicating restriction of competition (*infra* 2). I will then present arguments that may help to evaluate the concept of ensuring freedom to compete, the traditional concept (*infra* 3), and the concept of promoting economic and social welfare, the concept of the more economic approach (*infra* 4), before drawing a clear conclusion (*infra* 5).

2   TWO DIFFERENT LEGAL GOALS: ENSURING FREEDOM TO COMPETE OR PROMOTING ECONOMIC AND SOCIAL WELFARE?

According to the traditional concept, the goal of competition law consists in ensuring the firm's freedom to compete. The underlying rationale is that

---

[1]   DG Competition Discussion Paper on the application of Article 82 of the Treaty to exclusionary abuses, December 2005, http://europa.eu.int/comm/competition/antitrust/others/discpaper 2005.pdf.

[2]   M Amstutz and M Reinert, 'Vertikale Preis- und Gebietsabreden – eine kritische Analyse von Article 5 Abs. 4 KG' in W Stoffel and R Zäch (eds), *Kartellgesetzrevision 2003 – Neuerungen und Folgen* (2004) 77 *et seq,* with reference to supporting literature; against such tendencies: U Immenga and E-J Mestmäcker in U Immenga and E-J Mestmäcker (eds), *Wettbewerbsrecht, Kommentar zum Europäischen Kartellrecht* (4th edn, 2007) Introduction C paras 25–31; U Immenga and T Körber in U Immenga and E-J Mestmäcker (eds), *Wettbewerbsrecht, Kommentar zum Europäischen Kartellrecht* (4th edn, 2007) Art 2 FKVO, paras 12 *et seq,* 51 *et seq,* 204 *et seq* and 334 *et seq*; U Immenga, 'Ökonomie und Recht in der europäischen Wettbewerbspolitik' (2006) *ZWeR* 346–66; U Immenga, 'Europäisches Gemeinwohl und nationale Kartellverfahren' (2005) *EuZW* 353; W Möschel, 'Juristisches versus ökonomisches Verständnis eines Rechts der Wettbewerbsbeschränkungen' in E Keller et al (eds), *Festschrift für Winfried Tilmann* (2003) 716; E-J Mestmäcker, 'Die Interdependenz von Recht und Ökonomie in der Wettbewerbspolitik' in Monopolkommission (ed), *Zukunftsperspektiven der Wettbewerbspolitik* (2005) 19 *et seq*; D Zimmer,

freedom to compete leads to competition and competition leads to economic and social welfare.

This concept was confirmed by the Swiss legislature when it thoroughly revised the Cartel Act in 1995. When appraising agreements that restrain competition, under EC law the competition authority has to evaluate whether or not consumers will receive a fair share of the expected profits. This is stated explicitly in Article 81(3).

The Swiss legislature wanted to achieve the same result, though it did not enact an explicit provision for such 'consumer protection' as proposed by the government. In the legislature's view, it is the competitive process as such that will secure the interests of the consumer. Agreements to restrain competition are only legal, therefore, if they do not threaten or weaken competition in their relevant market.[3]

According to the more economic approach, however, the goal of competition law is to promote economic or social welfare. These two concepts have different outcomes when it comes to adjudicating a case of, for example, a resale price maintenance clause in a distribution contract. According to our traditional concept, a competition authority or a court has to decide on whether such a resale price maintenance clause leads to a restriction of the dealer's freedom to compete and thus has a negative impact on the competitive process. According to the new concept, however, a competition authority or a court has to decide whether such a resale price maintenance clause in a contract will lead to an increase or a decrease of economic or social welfare.

3 ENSURING FREEDOM TO COMPETE AS THE GOAL OF COMPETITION LAW – EVALUATION

In the European context, that is, in the law of the European Community and in German law, the goal of competition law traditionally consists in ensuring the freedom to compete. This concept has been succesfully applied for more than 50 years.

Due to long experience, it is possible today to assess quite precisely whether 'contractual' restrictions of the freedom to compete have a positive or a negative impact on the competitive process. In order to assess that

---

'Kommentar, Ende gut, alles gut? Bemerkungen zur 7. GWB-Novelle' (2005) *WuW* 715; M Dreher and M Adam, 'The More Economic Approach to Article 82 EC and the Legal Process' (2006) ZWeR 259–77; *see* also J Basedow, 'Editorial: Das Kartelldeliktsrecht und der "More Economic-Approach"'(2006) EuZW 97.

[3] Compare Article 81(3) EC Treaty, and Article 5(2) Swiss Cartel Act.

impact, in most cases it is sufficient to assess the remaining competition (*Aussenwettbewerb*) in the relevant market and the pressure of potential competition. Such assessments can – thanks to long experience – in general be made in a convincing way. So the concept of achieving economic and social welfare by ensuring in principle that firms have the freedom to compete is – as experience shows – a workable concept.

4 PROMOTING ECONOMIC AND SOCIAL WELFARE AS THE GOAL OF COMPETITION LAW – EVALUATION

In the following I will outline arguments that all run counter to the proposition that economic and social welfare should be the goal of competition law.

   (i)   This proposition disregards the constitutionally protected commercial freedom, which includes the freedom to compete.[4]
   (ii)   'Economic and social welfare' is a very open, wide-ranging and general term. Using it in a legal provision (where precision and clarity are – or should be – first priorities) would violate the legal doctrine of using only clearly definable legal terms. Using this vague concept would make decisions less predictable and thus raise legal uncertainty.
   (iii) This concept assumes that competition authorities or courts can *foresee* future economic outcomes. This is impossible.[5]
   (iv)   This concept limits the scope of laws against competition restraints: In most cases, it is not clear whether the particular behaviour of a firm will in the future enhance or reduce economic or social welfare.[6] In such cases, according to the advocates of this new concept, competition authorities should not intervene.[7] Non-intervention of competition authorities is not – as many may believe – neutral: not intervening or not deciding a case in most cases favours the firms because of whom most competition rules were designed, and in

---

   [4]   E-J Mestmäcker and H Schweitzer, *Europäisches Wettbewerbsrecht* (2nd edn, 2004) § 2 paras 74 and 81; Articles 27, 35 and 94 Swiss Federal Constitution.
   [5]   Dreher and Adam, *supra* note 2, at 270; Mestmäcker and Schweitzer, *supra* note 4, § 2 paras 90 *et seq*; *see* also U Schwalbe and D Zimmer, *Kartellrecht und Ökonomie* (2006) 397–405, concerning merger control; H-J Ruppelt, 'Kommentar: Nicht-horizontale Zusammenschlüsse besser als horizontale?' (2007) *WuW* 219.
   [6]   Amstutz and Reinert, *supra* note 2, 77 *et seq*.
   [7]   *Id.*

many other cases they are against those firms that consider their competitive process obstructed by competing firms. In addition, non-intervention may be against consumer interests.

5 CONCLUSION

The reasons outlined above, especially the consideration that competition law needs to ensure the freedom to compete instead of being used to evaluate possible future economic outcomes,[8] lead to the conclusion that *the creation and protection of the freedom to compete should remain the purpose of competition law.*

---

[8] Mestmäcker and Schweitzer, *supra* note 4, § 5 para 74; E-J Mestmäcker in U Immenga and E-J Mestmäcker (eds), *GWB* (3rd edn, 2001) Introduction, para 3; W Möschel, *supra* note 2, 716 seq; U Immenga, 'Editorial: Europäisches Gemeinwohl und nationale Kartellverfahren' [2005] *EuZW* 12/2005, 353.

8. Appropriation of the legal system by economic concepts: should conflicting goals be considered?

Anne Perrot*

1 INTRODUCTION

The primary objective of competition policy is to enhance consumers' welfare by favouring the development of competition on markets. This objective can take several dimensions: price competition is not the only goal of competition policy, which also favours other aspects of firms' behaviour, like diversity of products and differentiation through quality and innovation.

Some goals of competition policy are straightforward, with the aim of abolishing barriers to entry, preventing abuses of a dominant position, cartels and so on: these objectives are clearly at the core of the activity of competition authorities, and the tools used to achieve these objectives are well known: they consist mainly of pecuniary sanctions and injunctions to behave in compliance with some specified rules.

However, competition policy also often involves other dimensions of economic activity and consumer welfare. Very often the strategic behaviour of firms not only involves competitive actions, but also has consequences for other aspects of their economic activity, such as employment or the environment. Indeed, some goals (eg favouring both the environment and competitive behaviour) may be potentially conflicting.

A more straightforward objective of competition policy, on which most competition authorities now agree, is that of consumer surplus. Such an objective, for instance, avoids protecting competitors' interests directly and focuses instead on the efficiency of the competitive process. Despite this consensus, however, some problems may remain. For instance, this objective can indeed be considered either on a short-term or a long-

* Professor at the University of Paris I Panthéon-Sorbonne; Vice President of the Conseil de la concurrence, France.

term basis: some practices may benefit consumers or buyers in the short run, but may be detrimental in the long run. Considering these long-term effects, which are possibly in conflict with short-term ones, may be difficult even when the problem is confined to strictly competitive behaviour, but it is clearly an even more complex task when other fields are involved.

To illustrate this, many examples can be considered. As regards innovation, which is a long-term process, there is debate over whether competition policy can provide proper incentives to innovate or whether these objectives are in conflict. In addition, redistribution problems can occur due to a firm's competitive strategy. For instance, consumers as a whole may benefit from a merger, while 'poorer' ones suffer from this merger. Thus a merger may lead to redistribution problems that lie far beyond the scope of competition policy.

Some employment problems may also occur, since 'efficiencies' are sometimes obtained at the expense of jobs. In this respect, there may be a conflict of interests between employees and consumers, for instance again in the case of mergers. We will develop these examples further in what follows.

2   INNOVATION, IP AND COMPETITION POLICY

Intellectual property and competition policy both aim at promoting new products or services, but they use different tools. IP gives the innovator market power as the result of its innovation process, whereas competition policy would favour the spread of innovations, via the competitive process, once they have been achieved. Moreover, it is often the case that a particular innovation brings about many further ones: innovation often develops in clusters, each new service or product using the result of previous research. There is thus a clear conflict between the means used to provide proper incentives to innovate (market power, and often monopoly power) and the objective of encouraging more innovation, and a broader diffusion of the existing innovations.

Therefore the results of innovation often appear as essential facilities in terms of competition policy, that is, a good or a service owned by a monopoly and necessary for the production of other products. Theoretically, competition policy should only impose access to an essential facility when exclusive use of this facility by its owner is identified as an abuse of dominant position, since intervention amounts to forced access to a good or a service that is protected by IP rights. This may be justified if the essential facility is a costless by-product of the production process by itself. For instance, in the *Magill* case,[1] the good protected was the information TV channels have on their own TV programmes, and the firm seeking access was a publisher offering all the TV listings in the same magazine. The new service (the magazine offering a listing of all the TV programmes together) clearly requires access to the information over which TV channels have a monopoly, and it is a valuable product for consumers. In this case, where the essential facility does not result from a costly innovation process but from the natural consequence of a channel having access to information about its own TV programming, it was held that the essential facility should be open to the publisher. Also, in this case of a conflict between property rights and competition policy, the solution to the problem is quite straightforward.

A more delicate problem may occur in the case of specific investment, as in the case of *IMS Health*.[2] Here an innovator (a software firm) had invested in creating a new database. This product was based on a combination of geographical and commercial data, and allowed a better allocation of drugs between pharmacies for the pharmaceutical industry. Both pharmacies and the industry had specifically invested in this new database, which had led to a standardization of the format in which data had to be collected.

A competitor that wanted to launch a new database endowed with a better quality than the original one needed access to the core of the original database in order to offer its own product. In this case, again, access was given to the competitor by the Commission. However, this example is much more disputable than the previous one. Indeed, here again, the protection of innovation through intellectual property rights is clearly in conflict with the objective of competition policy: a short-term objective of maximizing the consumers' surplus leads to allowing the competitor to have access to the initial innovation, since consumers will then benefit from a better-quality product; but it also cancels out the incentives to innovate that should be provided to the potential innovators in this field, since this decision goes back on the commitment to protection of the innovator's (temporary) monopoly power over the innovation. In this case, competition policy prevailed over IP protection, but one can doubt whether this solution preserves sufficient incentives to innovate.

Besides this consideration, one may also wonder which market structures favour innovation.[3] This could indeed be an important element when com-

---

[1]   Joined Cases C-241 and 242/91 P, *RTE v Commission*, [1995] ECR I-743 ('*Magill*').

[2]   Case C-418/01, *IMS Health*, [2004] ECR I-5039.

[3]   R Blundell, R Griffith and J van Reenen, 'Market Share, Market Value and Innovation in a Panel of British Manufacturing Firms' (1999) 66 *Rev Econ Stud* 529.

petition authorities examine mergers. One might want to consider it when a merger concerns a highly innovative sector. However, the issue remains how to take it into account. Ambiguous results have come out of the empirical work carried out on the existing links between market structures and innovation. From the theoretical point of view, two effects are at work when one examines the links between market structure and innovation. First, competitive markets can generate high rates of innovation. The reason this holds is the following: in a very competitive market, firms want to escape the cancellation of their profits due to intense competition (the 'competition effect').

One way to escape it is to offer differentiated products, which can usually be obtained by product innovation; another is to lower costs, which can be done by process innovation. Therefore, it is the very low level of present profits that leads to more innovation under a competitive market structure. Second, the opposite may also be true: that concentrated market structures can be very innovative ones (the 'monopoly effect', in the Schumpeterian sense). This is due to the fact that a monopolist will more easily recover the costs of its investment in R&D than will a firm in a more competitive market. When considering market structures with an increasing degree of concentration, one first encounters markets within which the former effect dominates. Further up the scale this competition effect decreases, while the monopoly effect is not yet at work: this explains why empirically one obtains the result that oligopolies are less favourable to innovation. Then, when turning to more concentrated market structures, the monopoly effect appears and innovation increases again. This results in a U-shaped curve relating to market structure and the intensity of innovation.[4] It appears that the two extremes, both markets where competition is very intense and monopolies, favour innovation, a general result that is indeed very difficult to take into account when assessing the potential effect of a particular merger on innovation.

Let us now illustrate our point of view with the example of environmental policies.

3 CONFLICTS BETWEEN ENVIRONMENTAL AND COMPETITION POLICIES

Competitive market structures lead to low prices, higher demand and increased supply. However, competition is a drawback for the environment.

---

[4] P Aghion, N Bloom, R Blundell, R Griffith and P Howitt, 'Competition and Innovation: An Inverted-U Relationship' (2005) 120 *Qu J Econ* 701.

There are several reasons for this, such as increased pollution: if the production process is pollutive (ie pollution is a by-product of the good) or energy intensive, then the pollution level is higher under competitive market structures than under less competitive ones. If the good produced is in itself pollutive, the result is the same.

This reasoning is all the more valid in the case of exploitation of a common resource (the 'tragedy of the commons'). Indeed, a monopolist is in a better position to internalize the effects of its own behaviour on the resource: a monopolist will probably take into account the effect of its own behaviour on its present and expected profits. Thus it will not exhaust a given limited resource if this in turn will decrease its future profits. A monopolist is then better for the environment than are more competitive market structures. This principle has more general consequences: Consider two firms that are established on a river; assume the upstream firm pollutes the river and this reduces the quality of the environment (and thus productivity) of the downstream firm. A merger would solve the problem, since a single entity would internalize the effects of pollution and therefore the effects of the upstream pollution on the downstream production unit.

In brief, it can be said that competition policy aims at setting up more competitive market structures and these in turn lead to a higher level of environmental damage. This is due to the general mechanism at work in environmental problems, which is the impossibility of internalizing external effects. Therefore market mechanisms are very inefficient, which explains why a general result is that of conflict between competition and environmental policies.

Beyond this simple principle, other conflicts may arise.

As regards the quantitative evaluation of environmental damage, indeed, it is, first, sometimes difficult to take into account the direct effects of anti-competitive practices on consumer welfare; it is even more difficult in the case of environmental damage, since it is to be considered over the long term. Taking account of environmental issues in a competitive assessment would require measuring the environmental damage of a particular practice or market configuration and comparing it with an alternative situation in which the practice is prohibited or the market structure modified. This is a very difficult task. Moreover, difficulties arise concerning uncertainty and the issue of measurement. However, these are issues that may concern environmental policy itself, and not only the integration of environmental concerns into competition policy.

As already mentioned, competition policy is more apt to capture short-run than long-run effects. However, environmental effects of any behaviour on a market is in itself a long-run matter. Besides, the overall effects of a given, specific behaviour are difficult to assess.

Despite these difficulties, some convergence may exist between environmental and competition policies. Solutions to environmental problems do exist; they consist in general in creating markets where the problems are absent. Where markets exist, competition policy may be useful to guarantee a better functioning, less anti-competitive behaviour etc. For instance, when rights to pollute are created, competition policy can guarantee that firms do not collude in order to manipulate the price. Where the creation of pollution-reducing industries is the best solution to the environmental problem, then a better functioning of these industries may call for a rigorous application of competition policy. This shows that beyond the general principle according to which competition is bad for the environment, depending on the particular solution of an environmental problem, competition policy may be of interest as a means to improve the market mechanisms where necessary.

Let us now turn to the issue of employment.

4   EMPLOYMENT

Merger examination by competition authorities involves an 'economic assessment' of the merger: beyond its competitive effects, this overall evaluation usually includes the effect of the merger on employment.

Generally speaking, since competition increases output, it also increases employment in the sector concerned. It follows that restructuring in a given sector through mergers, disappearance of inefficient firms or other types of change in the organization of an industry may lead to a more efficient allocation of resources, lower prices, higher demand and finally increased employment.[5]

However, in the case of a particular merger, this may no longer be true. The efficiency gains emphasized by merging firms often involve elimination of inefficient duplication (by building a common accounting service, a joint commercial division etc). Of course, the efficiency gains that are taken into account in the assessment of the effects of a merger are not confined to economies of employment costs, but they involve such economies most of the time. This is why the 'local' effects of a particular

---

[5]   For an analysis of the impact of entry regulation on employment in the retail sector, M Bertrand and MF Kramarz, 'Does Entry Regulation Hinder Job Creation? Evidence from the French Retail Industry' (2002)107 *Qu J Econ* 1369; for a more general study, *see* P Askenazy, D Thesmar and M Thoenig, 'On the Relation between Organisational Practices and New Technologies: The Role of Time Based Competition' (2006) 115 *Econ J* 508.

merger on employment may be in contrast with the global, positive effects that are expected from restructuring a sector. This global effect may entail positive consequences on employment in that sector or in related ones. But it is hard to maintain that there will be efficiencies and at the same time that employment in the merging entity will not be reduced.

Should competition authorities take into account these short-run and long-run consequences of a merger (or more generally of any practice that it examines) on employment? Doing so would generate a number of delicate questions. First, competition policy should not be mixed up with employment policy, which pursues other objectives with other instruments. Distorting competition is rarely an efficient means to achieve other goals. Second, when competition authorities examine a merger, they have to anticipate the effect of the merger on competition, a prospective study that can be difficult in itself. Drawing conclusions on future employment would require detailed information on the future internal organization of the merging entity and on technologies that are not necessarily available at the moment of the assessment. Third, if such knowledge were available, taking into account the effects on employment would require a clear weighing of the various objectives, which is a political prerogative and certainly not the task of competition authorities. Indeed, the protection of employment can sometimes be obtained, in the short run, at the expense of a reduction in competition, that is, by sacrificing resources somewhere else in the economy. The task of balancing gains and losses cannot be in the hands of a competition authority.

5   CONCLUSION

To conclude, it is difficult for competition authorities to take into account objectives that are not strictly in line with short-term consumer surplus. Three main reasons justify that point of view. First, competition authorities have the relevant tools to measure the consequences of a practice or of a merger on the market equilibrium, but suffer from a lack of information on other aspects of a practice, like its effects on the environment or on employment. This lack of data makes it difficult to take into account these far-removed objectives.

Second, a general and well-known economic policy principle consists in using the tool that is the most appropriate to achieve a given objective. For instance, environmental policy should intervene at the relevant step of micro-decisions, that is, where these decisions involve environmental consequences. In the same spirit, employment policies are more relevant to the employment level and employment conditions than is competition policy, even if the latter has an impact on the job market.

Finally, of course, the most pertinent approach to dealing with the functioning of an economy as a whole would be, theoretically, a general-equilibrium one.[6] However, such an approach is impossible to manage in practice, and moreover this would require an objective weighing of the various costs and benefits of an action, which cannot be the role of a competition authority.

However, in many cases, competition policy may help to achieve closely related objectives. For instance, it may improve competitive mechanisms in the market for polluting rights or take into account the existence of incentives to innovate in some sectors.

---

[6] *See eg* R Griffith, R Harrison and G Macartney, 'Product Market Reforms, Labour Market Institutions and Unemployment' (2006) IFS Working Papers WP06/06, Institute for Fiscal Studies, London, http://eprints.ucl.ac.uk/2689/1/2689.pdf (accessed 31 January 2008).

9. Competition law and public policy: reconsidering an uneasy relationship – the example of Article 81

Heike Schweitzer*

1 INTRODUCTION

The development of an internal market with undistorted competition is one of the central fields of activity of the EU (Article 3(1)(g) EC), and has long been one of its seemingly uncontroversial goals. The debate about the relationship between this goal and other goals listed in Articles 2 and 3 EC that are not competition-related has been a reminder of the political tensions that the application of competition rules can raise at times. The battles surrounding the Draft Constitutional Treaty and later the drafting of the Lisbon Treaty have revealed how strongly these tensions are perceived by some Member States. Upon French initiative, the new Article 2 Treaty of the European Union (TEU), confirming the establishment of an internal market as one of the Union's goals, will no longer contain a reference to a 'system of undistorted competition' as was originally foreseen.[1] Although the British government in turn insisted on annexing a Protocol to the TEU which will specify that 'the internal market as set out in Article 2 of the Treaty on the European Union includes a system ensuring that competition is not distorted',[2] and the Protocol has formally the same legal

* Dr. iur., LL.M. (Yale), Professor of Law, European University Institute, Florence.

[1] The future Art 3(3) TEU will read in its relevant part: 'The Union shall establish an internal market. It shall work for the sustainable development of Europe based on balanced economic growth and price stability, a highly competitive social market economy, aiming at full employment and social progress and a high level of protection and improvement of the quality of the environment. It shall promote scientific and technological advance'.

[2] *See* sixth Protocol on the Internal Market and Competition.

status as Treaty provisions themselves, the implications of this drafting technique for the status of competition rules within the EU legal order are controversial[3] and will ultimately have to be explored by the European Court of Justice (ECJ).

While the negotiations surrounding the Lisbon Treaty reflect attempts to reduce the EU competition policy's weight vis-à-vis a growing diversity of EU policy goals, the European Commission's recent reforms in the area of competition policy are informed by a very different attempt to reconceptualize its goals. According to the Commission, the interpretation of EU competition rules should today mainly be driven by an efficiency criterion, namely the consumer-welfare goal. The formerly strong inter-linkage between competition rules and the market-integration goal should be weakened,[4] if not abandoned,[5] and the accompanying concept of freedom to compete given up. EU competition law should, according to this proposal, certainly not cede to conflicting political goals unrelated to the efficiency goal. Decision-making power should not be transferred to the political sphere. At the same time, the interpretation of competition rules is to some extent removed from its embeddedness in the EC Treaty's system of goals,[6] namely being de-coupled from the internal market goal, which has successfully driven the European integration process so far.

---

[3] For first comments *see* V Giscard d'Estaing, 'La boite à outils du traité de Lisbonne' (26 October 2007) *Le Monde*; C Lemaire, C Petite and M Waelbroeck, 'Competition Law and the Lisbon Treaty: What will be the Impact of the New Treaty on Competition Law?' (2008) *Concurrences* No 1, 16; A Riley, 'The EU Reform Treaty and the Competition Protocol: Undermining EC Competition Law', (2007) 28 *ECLR* 12.

[4] EU Commission, White Paper on Modernisation of the Rules Implementing Articles 85 and 86 of the EC Treaty, [1999] OJ C 132, p 1, executive summary, para 8: 'At the beginning the focus of its activity was on establishing rules on restrictive practices interfering directly with the goal of market integration. ... The Commission has now come to concentrate more on ensuring effective competition by detecting and stopping cross-border cartels and maintaining competitive structures'. *See* also O Odudu, *The Boundaries of EC Competition Law* (2006) 21: 'The formal completion of the internal market diminishes the extent to which integration as an ideological constituent of the concept of competition can be supported'.

[5] For a summary and discussion of the objections brought forward against the internal-market goal as a goal of competition policy, *see* R Wesseling, *The Modernisation of EC Antitrust Law* (2000) 80–82 and 85–8 (himself also critical with respect to the integration goal).

[6] For this embeddedness *see eg* Case C-6/72 *Europemballage Corporation and Continental Can Company v Commission* [1973] ECR I-215, paras 22–7: competition rules must be read in the light of the broader goals of the European Community.

This contribution traces these two diverging trends regarding the interface between competition-policy and public-policy goals by looking at the interpretation and application of Article 81 EC. In terms of doctrine, the debate is led on two levels: With regard to the interpretation of Article 81(1) the question is raised whether conflicting policy goals can delimit its scope. Article 81(3), with its broad and general terms, potentially provides an opening of EU competition law for the consideration of non-competition-related policy goals on the level of exemptions. The interpretation of Article 81(3) EC has gained new relevance since it was declared directly applicable by Article 1 of Regulation 1/2003.[7] While, under the former regime,[8] the Commission could regulate the competition-public policy interface case-by-case based on its monopoly for granting exemptions, the direct applicability of Article 81(3), that is, its enforcement by national competition authorities and courts, calls for more conceptual guidance. The difficulties in providing such guidance throw some light on the conceptual uncertainties associated with the recent reform of EU competition policy.

2 NON-COMPETITION GOALS IN THE INTERPRETATION OF ARTICLE 81(1)

The French initiative to confirm the EU's commitment to establishing an internal market while eliminating the reference to 'undistorted competition' can be read as an attempt to delimit the scope of EU competition rules where they conflict with other public-policy goals. Under the current regime of the EC Treaty, the ECJ has generally rejected such restrictive interpretations of Article 81(1). Only in a narrowly limited group of cases have public-policy considerations led the ECJ to exclude a certain restraint from the scope of Article 81(1). Two groups of cases can be distinguished.

One covers acts of self-regulation by collective bodies where the restraints on the freedom to compete are justified by a legitimate objective and are inherent in the organization and proper conduct of the regulated activity. The ECJ has inter alia accepted such exceptions with regard to the setting of rules of professional conduct by the Netherlands Bar (*Wouters*[9])

---

[7] Council Regulation (EC) No 1/2003 of 16 December 2002 on the implementation of the rules on competition laid down in Articles 81 and 82 of the Treaty, [2003] OJ L 1, p 1.

[8] Council Regulation No 17 (EEC), [1962] OJ P 13, 204.

[9] Case C-209/00 *Commission v Germany* [2002] ECR I-1577, paras 97 et seq ('*Wouters*'); *see* particularly para 110: '[A] national regulation such as the 1993

and in the sphere of sports (see inter alia *Meca-Medina*[10]). The rationale for this exception is an important, but limited one: In those cases where self-regulation by professional associations is regarded as legitimate in principle with regard to an act of state delegation or the nature of a given activity, the ECJ controls this self-regulatory activity according to the same criteria that it would apply to Member State regulation itself. It essentially transfers the exceptions to the free-movement rules to the sphere of Article 81. Where the conditions for an exception are met, Article 81(1) does not apply. The case-law on the analysis of legitimate self-regulatory activity under Article 81(1) does not justify the broader conclusion that free-movement rules and competition-law rules are generally converging[11] and that, therefore, the accepted justifications for violations of free-movement rules can equally be applied to justify restraints of competition.[12] Under a legal-policy perspective, the transfer of public-policy justifications recognized in

---

Regulation adopted by a body such as the Bar of the Netherlands does not infringe Article 85(1) of the Treaty, since that body could reasonably have considered that regulation despite the effects restrictive of competition that are inherent in it, is necessary for the proper practice of the legal profession, as organised in the Member State concerned'.

[10]   Case C-519/04 P *Meca-Medina and Majcen v Commission* [2006] ECR I-6991, paras 43–7. For a recent comment on the sports cases and their relevance from the perspective of competition law, *see* E Szyszczak, 'Competition and Sports' (2007) 32 *EL Rev* 95.

[11]   L Gyselen, 'The Emerging Interface between Competition Policy and Environmental Policy in the EC' in J Cameron, P Demaret and D Géradin (eds), *Trade and Environmental Law* (1994) 242: The Commission should operate an identical legality standard when assessing the compatibility with the Common Market of market-based or regulatory environmental action ('seamless web approach'). If competition policy were more generous than internal-market policy, companies in states with a strong regulatory tradition might collude. If competition law were stricter than internal-market policy, companies might put pressure on their authorities to regulate. For a careful and more cautious analysis of the alleged convergence, *see* KJM Mortelmans, 'Towards Convergence in the Application of the Rules on Free Movement and on Competition?' (2001) 38 *CML Rev* 613–49. Doubts with regard to a broad claim of convergence result inter alia from Case C-519/04 P *Meca-Medina and Majcen v Commission* [2006] ECR I-6991, paras 32–34, where the ECJ has found that the fact that certain sports regulations, since they are considered to be non-economic, do not fall within the scope of Article 39 or Article 49 EC does not automatically imply that those regulations do not fall under Articles 81 and 82 EC.

[12]   For such a proposition, *see* W-H Roth, 'Zur Berücksichtigung nichtwettbewerblicher Ziele im europäischen Kartellrecht – eine Skizze' in C Engel and W Möschel (eds), *Recht und spontane Ordnung. Festschrift für Ernst-Joachim Mestmäcker zum 80. Geburtstag* (2006) 413, 424, 426 *et seq* and 433 *et seq*. Against this proposition: Loozen, 'Professional Ethics and Restraints of Competition' (2006) 31 *EL Rev* 28.

the context of the free-movement rules to competition-law rules would significantly broaden the scope of justifications, and would imply the recognition of a general authority of private parties to self-regulate commerce and competition in the public interest. The Court of First Instance (CFI) has been unwilling to accept such a claim. In *Piau*,[13] it expressed serious doubts as to whether FIFA could assert general policing power and regulate the economic activity of sports agents. Since FIFA could not rely on an accepted public rule-setting competence, the CFI did not apply the *Wouters* test under Article 81(1), but rather performed an analysis strictly in accordance with the criteria of Article 81(3). In other words FIFA could not rely on the public-policy justifications accepted under the free-movement rules.

The second exception, established by the ECJ in *Albany*,[14] deals with collective bargaining. In *Albany*, the ECJ held that agreements concluded in the context of collective negotiations between management and labour, by virtue of their nature and purpose, fall outside the scope of Article 81(1) when the purpose of the agreement is to improve conditions of work and employment.[15] Some have concluded that the ECJ is now generally willing to engage in a balancing of EC Treaty goals to delimit the scope of Article 81(1). Such assertions clearly overstate the case. *Albany* reflects both the social importance of and Member States' traditional respect for collective bargaining agreements between employers and employees, the conclusion of which is also encouraged by Article 138f EC. Another example of the

---

[13]   Case T-193/02 *Piau v Commission* [2005] ECR II-209, paras 76–8: 'With regard to FIFA's legitimacy, contested by the applicant, to enact such rules, which do not have a sport-related object, but regulate an economic activity that is peripheral to the sporting activity in question and touch on fundamental freedoms, the rule-making power claimed by a private organisation like FIFA, whose main statutory purpose is to promote football . . ., is indeed open to question in the light of the principles common to the Member States on which the European Union is founded. The very principle of regulation of an economic activity concerning neither the specific nature of sport nor the freedom of internal organisation of sports associations by a private-law body, like FIFA, which has not been delegated any such power by a public authority, cannot from the outset be regarded as compatible with Community law, in particular with regard to respect for civil and economic liberties. In principle, such regulation, which constitutes policing of an economic activity and touches on fundamental freedoms, falls within the competence of the public authorities'.

[14]   Case C-67/99 *Albany International v Stichting Bedrijfspensioenfonds Textielindustrie* [1999] ECR I-5751.

[15]   *Id*, para 60: 'It therefore follows from an interpretation of the provisions of the Treaty as a whole which is both effective and consistent that agreements concluded in the context of collective negotiations between management and labour in pursuit of such objectives must, by virtue of their nature and purpose, be regarded as falling outside the scope of Article 85(1) of the Treaty [Article 81(1) EC]'.

ECJ's particular respect for the Member States' social-policy choices is the restrictive interpretation of the term 'undertaking', where Member States decide to structure their social systems according to the principle of solidarity. These decisions demonstrate that the ECJ is aware of the political sensitivity of competition law where Member States' fundamental social-policy choices are concerned. These decisions do not, however, stand for the proposition of a general balancing of the EC Treaty's policy goals in defining the scope of Article 81(1).[16]

Under the current EC Treaty regime, claims that such balancing should be performed are generally met by the argument that the competition rules themselves are firmly anchored in the European Community's system of goals, namely in Articles 3(1)(g) and 4(1) EC. The EC Treaty does not establish a hierarchy between the various goals mentioned in Articles 2 and 3 EC. The Community organs are therefore generally held to reconcile the various goals in implementing Community policies.[17] There are, however, limits to the mandate to consider conflicting goals. One of them is that conflicting goals cannot endow national authorities and courts or Community organs with discretion to disregard the lines drawn by the specific provisions of primary law that are mandatory and directly applicable. The application of directly applicable EU law must not be transformed into the exercise of political discretion and choice.

Eliminating the reference to undistorted competition in the list of the Union's goals in the Lisbon Treaty is an attempt to weaken this line of argument by degrading competition rules to the status of a mere instrument to achieve the superior goal of an internal market with balanced economic growth, full employment and social progress, a high level of protection for the environment and scientific and technological progress. An instrument may arguably have to cede where presumably better instruments, like direct policy intervention, are available. It is, however, highly doubtful whether such arguments would indeed be available to weaken the binding force of norms that continue to be mandatory, directly applicable and part of the 'acquis communautaire'.

---

16   For a narrow reading and critical comments on *Albany see* also P Camesasca and R Van den Bergh, 'Irreconcilable Principles? The Court of Justice Exempts Collective Labour Agreements from the Wrath of Antitrust' (2000) 25 *EL Rev* 492. For a detailed analysis of *Albany* and more general (potentially broader) conclusions to be drawn from it, *see* T Mühlbach, *Tarifverträge in der europäischen Kartellkontrolle* (2007).

17   In Germany, this mandate is termed 'praktische Konkordanz'; *see* H-P Ipsen, *Europäisches Gemeinschaftsrecht* (1972) 559–63.

3   NON-COMPETITION GOALS IN THE INTERPRETATION AND APPLICATION OF ARTICLE 81(3)

For practical purposes, the most important locus for the consideration of public-policy goals is thus Article 81(3), which provides for a possibility to declare Article 81(1) non-applicable when the economic benefits of the restriction of competition outweigh the harm caused.

The conditions for taking public-policy goals into account have fundamentally changed with the entry into force of Regulation 1/2003. Under the old system, the Commission, in its dual function as an enforcement agency endowed with a monopoly for granting exemptions under Article 81(3) and a policy-making institution, enjoyed broad discretion in applying Article 81(3). It included the possibility to take public-policy goals into account.[18] The Commission generally made cautious use of this power. In some cases, however, it allowed restrictive agreements fundamentally in opposition to the logic of competition policy (see *infra* 3.1). Under the new system, Article 81(3) is directly applicable, that is, national competition authorities and courts are to apply Article 81(3). This requires that Article 81(3) be clear and unconditional. Policy discretion is not compatible with a system in which Article 81(3) is directly applicable. The relevance of public-policy goals in the interpretation and application of Article 81(3) under the new regime is thus unclear (see *infra* 3.2).

3.1   Non-competition Goals in Article 81(3) Application before the Reform – Commission Practice and ECJ Jurisprudence

It is a general tenet of US antitrust law that restraints of competition are to be assessed in view of their pro- and anticompetitive effects. Public-policy goals, different from the public interest inherent in competition policy, are of no (direct) relevance in the application of Section 1 of the Sherman Act[19]

---

[18]   *See* for further discussion E-J Mestmäcker and H Schweitzer, *Europäisches Wettbewerbsrecht* (2nd edn, 2004) § 3 paras 75 *et seq*. For the interaction between the Commission's institutional role under Reg 17 and the recognition of its discretion to take public-policy goals into account, *see* also Roth, *supra* note 12, at 427.

[19]   *National Society of Professional Engineers v United States* 435 US 679, 688 (1978): 'Contrary to its name, the Rule [of Reason] does not open the field of antitrust inquiry to any argument in favor of a challenged restraint that may fall within the realm of reason. Instead, it focuses directly on the challenged restraint's impact on competitive conditions'.

– although they are, in some cases, considered implicitly where they can be linked to pro-competitive effects.[20]

Article 81(3) differs from the 'rule of reason' test under the Sherman Act, Section 1. It is frequently characterized as an efficiency defence: firms can justify restrictive agreements when the efficiency gains resulting from a restrictive agreement outweigh its anticompetitive effects. The ECJ has consistently stressed that advantages realized by the parties to the restrictive agreement are not sufficient, and not decisive, for an exemption under Article 81(3). An exemption will only be granted when an 'objective advantage' results, when, in other words, a public interest in the restrictive agreement can be said to exist with a view to the realization of the EC Treaty goals. The 'objective advantage' must go beyond the individual purposes that the parties to the restrictive agreement pursue and the gains they can realize, and at least part of the benefit must be passed on to the consumers.

Article 81(3), thus framed, provides for a public-interest exception to Article 81(1), although one related and generally restricted to the realization of economic benefits. In the vast majority of decisions in which the EU Commission has granted an exemption based on Article 81(3), the public interest lay directly in the realization of economic benefits like economies of scale or scope, the rationalization of production, conservation of resources, solving coordination problems, facilitation of product or process development and the like.

In a limited, but nonetheless significant number of cases, the EU Commission has taken broader non-competition goals into account, for example environmental goals,[21] cultural policy goals,[22] the protection of

---

[20] Quality improvements (*see NCAA v Board of Regents of the University of Oklahoma* 468 US 85, 114–15, 104 S Ct 2948, 2967, 82 L Ed 2d 70 (1984)), the protection of public health, consumer protection (*eg* measures to prevent false or misleading advertising – *see FTC v Algoma Lumber Co* 291 US 67, 79–80, 54 S Ct 315, 78 L Ed 655 (1934)) and even the goal of promoting socio-economic diversity in universities (*US v Brown University* 5 F3d 658, 62 USLW 2170, 1993-2 Trade Cases P 70, 358, 85 Ed Law Rep 1027) have thus been considered relevant by US courts under a rule-of-reason approach.

[21] Among others: Commission, *25th Annual Report on Competition Policy* (1995) para 85; Commission Decision 94/986/EC of 31 December 1994, Case No COMP/IV/34.252 – *Philips/Osram* [1994] OJ L 378, p 37; Commission Decision 2000/475/EC of 24 January 1999, Case no IV.F.1/36.718 – *CECED* [2000] OJ L 187, p 47, paras 55–7. For further references to relevant Commission decisions *see* Roth, *supra* note 12, at 417 note 26.

[22] Commission Decision 82/123/EEC of 25 November 1982, Case No IV/428 – *VBBB/VBVB* [1982] OJ L 54, p 36; upheld in Joined Cases 43/82 and 63/82 *VBVB and VBBB v Commission* [1984] ECR 19. For discussion of the consideration of

public health[23] and consumers,[24] but also employment policy,[25] regional policy and industrial policy goals.[26] The ECJ has generally endorsed the Commission's practice, and acknowledged that the Commission enjoyed broad discretion in applying Article 81(3),[27] including the authority to reconcile competition with 'objectives of a different nature', that is, with broader public-interest goals.[28]

While the Commission has generally used its discretion cautiously, and has been unwilling to sacrifice the core objective of protecting competition to conflicting public-interest goals,[29] some decisions have compromised

---

cultural goals in the application of Art 81 EC, *see* C Schmid, 'Diagonal Competence Conflicts between European Competition Law and National Regulation – A Conflict of Laws Reconstruction of the Dispute on Bookprice Fixing' (2000) 8 *ERPL* 155, 164.

[23]   *See* inter alia Commission Decision 97/770/EC of 6 October 1994, Case No IV/34.776 – *Pasteur Mérieux-Merck* [1994] OJ L 309, p 1, para 89; Commission Decision of 8 May 2007, Joined Cases No IV/36.957/F3 et al – *Glaxo Wellcome et al* [2001] OJ L 302, p 1, para 89.

[24]   For example in the form of protecting product safety, *see* inter alia Commission Decision No 75/73/EEC of 13 December 1974, Case No. IV/14.650 – *Bayerische Motorenwerke AG* [1975] OJ L 29, p 1, paras 23 *et seq*; Commission Decision 82/742/EEC of 29 October 1982, Case No IV/30.517 – *Amersham Buchler* [1982] OJ L 314, p 34, para 11.

[25]   Commission Decision 93/49/EEC of 23 December 1992, Case No IV/33.814 – *Ford/Volkswagen* [1993] OJ L 20, p 14, para 23; Commission Decision 94/296/EC of 29 April 1994, Case IV/34.456 – *Stichting Baksteen* [1994] OJ L 131, p 15, para 27. *See* also the relevant literature, eg: R Whish, *Competition Law* (5th edn, 2003) 153; G Monti, *EC Competition Law* (2007) 96–7.

[26]   For references and discussion *see* R Ellger in U Immenga and E-J Mestmäcker (eds), *Kommentar zum Europäischen Kartellrecht – Wettbewerbsrecht EG Teil* 1 (4th edn, 2007) Art 81, Abs 3, paras 318–28; Roth, *supra* note 13, at 417–24.

[27]   Case C-14/68 *Walt Wilhelm v Bundeskartellamt* [1969] ECR 1, para 5.

[28]   Case C-26/76 *Metro v Commission* ('*Metro I*') [1977] ECR 1875, para 21: 'The powers conferred upon the Commission under Article 85(3) show that the requirements for the maintenance of workable competition may be reconciled with the safeguarding of *objectives of a different nature* and that to this end certain restrictions on competition are permissible, provided that they are essential to the attainment of those objectives and that they do not result in the elimination of competition for a substantial part of the common market' (emphasis added). *See* also Joined Cases T-528/93, T-542/93, T-543/93 and T-546/93 *Métropole télévision SA v Commission* [1996] ECR II-649, para 118: '[I]n the context of an overall assessment, the Commission is entitled to base itself on considerations connected with the pursuit of the public interest in order to grant exemption under Article [81(3)]'.

[29]   *See* inter alia Roth, *supra* note 12, at 418: the Commission has attempted to link non-competition goals to the wording of Art 81(3) and has generally referred to non-competition goals merely in support of its decisions, without essentially basing its decisions on such goals.

competition-law goals to a certain extent.[30] Much-debated examples are the Commission's *Stichting Baksteen* decision, the *Ford/VW* case and the *CECED* decision:

- In the *Stichting Baksteen* decision[31] the Commission exempted a classic crisis cartel. It was held that the agreement, which provided for a coordinated closing down of plants and a compensation scheme among competitors, would improve production and promote technical and economic progress by leading to a closure of the least efficient production units, so that afterwards production would be concentrated in the more modern plants. Also, the coordination would allow the restructuring to be carried out in acceptable social conditions, including the redeployment of employees.[32]
- In the *Ford/Volkswagen* case[33] the Commission analysed a joint-venture agreement between VW and Ford and exempted the agreement under Article 81(3). According to its decision, all four conditions of Article 81(3) were met. It added that the joint venture would lead to the creation of 5,000 jobs and attract investment in disadvantaged regions of Portugal, and would thus promote a more harmonious development of the Community and the reduction of regional disparities.[34]
- In the *CECED* decision[35] the Commission exempted an agreement between most European manufacturers of washing machines according to which certain washing machines that consumed particularly high quantities of electricity were to be phased out. The agreement was clearly in violation of Article 81(1). The Commission exempted

---

[30] For a careful analysis of the relevant case-law, *see* G Monti, 'Article 81 and Public Policy' (2002) 39 *CML Rev* 1057. *See* also D Gasse, *Die Bedeutung der Querschnittsklauseln für die Anwendung des Gemeinschaftskartellrechts* (2000) 154 *et seq.*

[31] Commission Decision 94/296/EC of 29 April 1994, Case IV/34.456 – *Stichting Baksteen* [1994] OJ L 131, p 15.

[32] *Id*, at paras 26 *et seq.*

[33] Commission Decision 93/49/EC of 23 December 1992, Case No IV/33.814 – *Ford/Volkswagen* [1993] OJ L 20, p 14.

[34] According to the Commission's decision, this would not have been enough to make an exemption possible unless the conditions of Art 81(3) had been fulfilled, but it was 'an element which the Commission has taken into account' (para 36). Similarly, this point was also underlined by the CFI in its decision *Matra Hachette*, which confirmed the Commission's decision; see Case T-17/93 *Matra Hachette v Commission* [1994] ECR II-595, para 139.

[35] Commission Decision 2000/475/EC of 24 January 1999, Case No IV.F.1/36.718 – *CECED* [2000] OJ L 187, p 47.

the agreement under Article 81(3) due to its beneficial effects for the environment.[36]

3.2   Direct Applicability of Article 81(3) under Regulation 1/2003: The Need for Change in Considering Public-policy Goals

The most noticeable characteristic of the Commission's decisional practice with respect to considering public-policy goals in applying Article 81(3) under the old regime is the Commission's broad margin of discretion.[37] Under the new regime this feature cannot survive.[38] The direct applicability of Article 81(3) presupposes the absence of discretion in applying this norm.

The Commission, when proposing the new enforcement regime, was aware of the problem. The solution it suggested – in the White Paper preparing the reform,[39] as well as in later documents – was to remodel Article 81 along the lines of US antitrust law, that is, of Section 1 of the Sherman Act. According to the Commission's view, Article 81(3) was to be interpreted as a European rule of reason. Only pro-competitive effects were to be considered as potential justifications for competitive restraints. No room for public-policy considerations should remain.[40] It is this path that the

---

[36]   For a very critical comment *see* HR Basaran, 'How should Article 81 EC Address Agreements that Yield Environmental Benefits?' (2006) 27 *ECLR* 479–84.

[37]   Case T-29/92 *SPO v Commission* [1995] ECR II-289, para 288; confirmed by Case C-137/95 P *SPO v Commission* [1996] ECR I-1611, paras 38–46.

[38]   *See* Mestmäcker and Schweitzer, *supra* note 19, at § 13 para 77. Similarly J Koch, 'Die Einbeziehung nichtwettbewerblicher Erwägungen in die Freistellungsentscheidung nach Art. 81 Abs. 3 EG' (2005) 169 *ZHR* 625, 647. Against such a change in the interpretation of Art 81(3), U Everling, 'Querschnittsklauseln im reformierten europäischen Kartellrecht', in T Baums and J Wertenbruch (eds), *Festschrift für Ulrich Huber* (2006) 1073, 1088, with the claim that secondary law cannot change substantive primary law. Arguably, however, the discretionary element in Article 81(3) was always intertwined with the Commission's former enforcement monopoly, which was itself based on secondary law. In Case C-26/76 *Metro v Commission* ('*Metro I*') [1977] ECR 1875, para 21, the ECJ explicitly referred to the 'powers conferred upon the Commission under Article 85(3) [Article 81(3)]' – and thus to its powers under Regulation 17/62 – in finding that 'the requirements for the maintenance of workable competition may be reconciled with the safeguarding of objectives of a different nature and that to this end certain restrictions on competition are permissible'. Further on this point, JH Quellmalz, 'Die Justiziabilität des Art. 81 Abs. 3 EG und die nichtwettbewerblichen Ziele des EG-Vertrages' (2004) *WRP* 461, 467.

[39]   White Paper on Modernisation of the Rules Implementing Article 85 and 86 of the EC Treaty, [1999] OJ C 132, p 1, para 56.

[40]   White Paper on Modernisation of the Rules Implementing Article 85 and 86 of the EC Treaty, [1999] OJ C 132, p 1 para 57: The Commission emphasized its

Commission largely follows in its Guidelines on the application of Article 81 to horizontal cooperation agreements[41] and in its Guidelines on the application of Article 81(3).[42]

As a matter of legal policy there may indeed be much to recommend the rule-of-reason analysis developed under Section 1 of the Sherman Act,[43] according to which public-interest concerns can be considered only insofar as they translate into pro-competitive effects; this is particularly true in a system of decentralized enforcement in which the prohibition of competitive restraints is applied by national competition authorities and courts. De lege lata, however, Article 81 EC differs fundamentally from Section 1 of the Sherman Act in structure and content. According to its wording and in the understanding of the ECJ's case-law, it incorporates not a US antitrust-like 'rule of reason', but a public-interest defence, delimited by a proportionality principle. To change the character of Article 81(3) EC, that is, to transform it into a defence that is limited to showing that a restrictive agreement has overall pro-competitive effects, is not within the powers of the EU Commission. The Commission has the power to define competition policy, but it cannot alter the structure and content of the competition rules as incorporated in primary law. Article 81(3) thus continues to leave room for the consideration of public-policy goals as long as they can be said to contribute to improvements of production and distribution of goods or to advance technological and economic progress, whether or not these benefits can at the same time be shown to have pro-competitive effects. In describing the relevant economic benefits, Article 81(3) uses 'open' terms, the interpretation of which can potentially be

---

purpose to 'provide a legal framework for the economic assessment of restrictive practices and not to allow application of the competition rules to be set aside because of political considerations'.

41   [2001] OJ C 3, p 2, para 33.

42   EU Commission, Guidelines on the application of Article 81(3) of the Treaty, [2004] OJ C 101, p 97, para 33: 'The aim of the Community competition rules is to protect competition on the market as a means of enhancing consumer welfare and of ensuring an efficient allocation of resources. Agreements that restrict competition may at the same time have pro-competitive effects by way of efficiency gains. Efficiencies may create additional value by lowering the cost of producing an output, improving the quality of the product or creating a new product. When the pro-competitive effects of an agreement outweigh its anti-competitive effects the agreement is on balance pro-competitive and compatible with the objectives of the Community competition rules. The net effect of such agreements is to promote the very essence of the competitive process, namely to win customers by offering better products or better prices than those offered by rivals'.

43   Favouring such a reinterpretation of Article 81, inter alia, T Ackermann, *Art. 85(1) EGV und die rule of reason* (1997).

influenced by the broad range of policy goals set out in Article 2 and Article 3 EC.[44]

It is not easy to conceptualize, then, how Article 81(3) is to be applied by national competition authorities and courts as a matter of law, that is, without allowing these institutions to exercise policy discretion. In various areas of Community law, national courts are required to balance diverging policy goals – inter alia when applying the exceptions to the free-movement rules or Article 86(2) EC.[45] In these cases, the legal framework is, however, comparatively clearly circumscribed: courts analyse the legitimacy and proportionality of a clearly defined measure of public policy infringing upon free-movement rules or competition rules. In the context of Article 81(3), the measure that restricts competition results from private agreement, with no authority to define public policy. The benefit of the restriction for public policy must be established by the national court or competition authority itself. Within the limits of the wording of Article 81(3), the reference point is the broad set of public-policy goals set out in Articles 2 and 3 of the EC Treaty. Upon linking the restrictive effect to one of these policy goals, a national court or competition authority must, within the limits of the proportionality principle established by Article 81(3), decide whether a public interest of the Community outweighs the loss of competition that results. Absent a clear hierarchy of goals, a court or competition authority, in making such value judgments, acts no longer in the role of a judge, but enters the field of policy making.[46] It is against this background that US

---

[44]   This has been implicitly accepted by the Commission in its Guidelines on the application of Article 81(3) of the Treaty, [2004] OJ C 101, p 97, para 42: 'Goals pursued by other Treaty provisions can be taken into account to the extent that they can be subsumed under the four conditions of Article 81(3)'.

[45]   This has been emphasized by various authors in favour of the continuing possibility to consider conflicting public-policy goals in the application of Article 81(3) under the decentralized regime; *see* inter alia Roth, *supra* note 12, at 431; EM Fox, 'Modernisation: Efficiency, Dynamic Efficiency, and the Diffusion of Competition Law' in C-D Ehlermann and I Atanasiu (eds), *European Competition Law Annual 2000: The Modernisation of EC Antitrust Policy* (2001) 125; C Baudenbacher, 'The European Commission's Reform Proposal Seen from the Point of View of the EEA/EFTA Countries, the EFTA Surveillance Authority and the EFTA Court' in C-D Ehlermann and I Atanasiu (eds), *European Competition Law Annual 2000: The Modernisation of EC Antitrust Policy* (2001) 478. *See* also A Schaub, 'The Reform of Regulation 17/62: The Issues of Compatibility, Effective Enforcement and Legal Certainty' in C-D Ehlermann and I Atanasiu (eds), *European Competition Law Annual 2000: The Modernisation of EC Antitrust Policy* (2001) 245.

[46]   For a critical view of the ability of courts to make the value judgments required to consider public-policy goals within the framework of Article 81(3), *see* also Quellmalz, *supra* note 38, at 466: Courts would be able to handle non-

courts have declared their inability to consider public-policy goals in interpreting Section 1 of the Sherman Act.[47]

Is there a way to delimit and rationalize the public-interest dimension of Article 81(3) in a way that is compatible with the wording and structure of Article 81(3) and manageable for national courts? This question leads back to the distinction between the interpretation of competition rules in the light of the plurality of the goals of the EC Treaty, but within the limits drawn by the Treaty's provisions themselves on the one hand, and an open balancing of conflicting goals on the other.

In the light of this distinction, there are two groups of cases into which the EU Commission's practice under the old regime can be said to fall.

In the overwhelming majority of cases, the EU Commission has taken public-policy considerations into account in a complementary fashion: they have been referred to in order to specify the 'economic benefit' of restrictive measures, and thus the Community's public interest in granting exemptions under Article 81(3). Public interests were accepted as relevant to the extent to which they were not in direct and principled conflict with competition and did not jeopardize the working of the competitive system in its core. In such cases, the Commission has accepted that restrictive agreements may be a legitimate instrument to address imperfections of the market process – inter alia with regard to the protection of consumers, public health or the environment.[48] At the same time, those agreements did not challenge the fundamental policy choice in favour of the competitive process itself. The public-policy goals considered were complementary, not contradictory.

---

competition-related goals only if the goals themselves, but also the criteria for solving conflicts with different goals, were sufficiently specified.

[47]   *United States v Topco Associates* 405 US 596 (1972) (regarding exclusive territorial arrangements and their effects on intra-brand and inter-brand competition): 'Private forces are too keenly aware of their own interests in making such decisions [to sacrifice competition in one portion of the economy for greater competition in another portion] and courts are ill-equipped and ill-situated for such decisionmaking. To analyze, interpret, and evaluate the myriad of competing interests and the endless data which would surely be brought to bear on such decisions, and to make the delicate judgment on the relative values to society of competitive areas of the economy, the judgment of the elected representatives of the people is required'.

[48]   With respect to the relevance of the protection of the environment, *see* the Commission Guidelines on the applicability of Article 81 EC to horizontal cooperation agreements, [2001] OJ C 3, p 2, para 198, where the Commission justifies the exemption under Art 81(3) with respect to the benefits for individual purchasers who – although they have to buy more expensive products – will rapidly recoup the cost increase due to the lower running costs of the environment-friendly washing machines.

In a second group of cases – which includes the exemption of the crisis cartel or to some extent also the justification of the *Ford/Volkswagen* joint venture – the Commission has brought public-policy interests or instruments to bear that were in direct opposition to the core assumptions and principles of competition policy. When parties to an agreement in violation of Article 81(1) claim that restricting competition will protect employment or will allow for a coordinated restructuring of the industry, but also in a case in which restrictions of price competition are justified by a claim that price competition may confuse consumers, the underlying presumption is the superiority of planning over a competitive process with respect to resource allocation or consumer protection. Granting exceptions under Article 81(3) for such measures implies a value judgment that is in direct opposition to competition-policy rationales and hence implies policy choices that national competition authorities and courts are not authorized to take.[49]

4   CONCLUSION

In EU competition law – and, albeit less openly, also in US antitrust law – the relationship between competition-policy and public-interest goals is complex. Private restraints of competition can have economic benefits that relate to public-policy goals and bring about pro-competitive effects. Also, competition policy can never be isolated completely from other public-policy choices relevant to democratic societies.[50] Within the system of the EC Treaty, competition policy interacts to some extent with other policy

---

[49]   This line of reasoning is close to the reasoning underlying the refusal of US antitrust courts to consider public-policy goals within the rule-of-reason analysis; *see FTC v Indiana Federation of Dentists* 476 US 447, 106 S Ct 2009, 90 L Ed 2d 445 (1986): A group of dentists agreed to withhold x-rays from patients' insurers. The dentist's association argued that this was necessary to protect quality of care: since x-rays, standing alone, were no adequate basis for diagnosis of dental problems or for the formulation of an acceptable course of treatment, there was a danger that insurers would erroneously decline to pay for treatments that were in fact in the interest of the patient, and the patient would be deprived of fully adequate care. The Supreme Court found: 'The argument is, in essence, that an unrestrained market in which consumers are given access to the information they believe to be relevant to their choices will lead them to make unwise and even dangerous choices. Such an argument amounts to "nothing less than a frontal assault on the basic policy of the Sherman Act"'.

[50]   With regard to US antitrust law *see* H Hovenkamp, *Federal Antitrust Policy* (3rd edn, 2005) § 2.2, p 69. With a view to the EU *see* Monti, *supra* note 30, at 1059.

goals set out in Article 2 and Article 3.[51] The 'pure' view of competition policy oriented towards efficiency only incompletely reflects the reality of the plurality of legal institutions that frame the competitive process and influence it. Public-policy choices and value judgments are to some extent inherent both in balancing pro- and anticompetitive effects under Section 1 of the Sherman Act and in balancing effects restrictive of competition and economic benefits under Article 81 of the EC Treaty.

At the same time, competition-law norms cannot incorporate a balancing of all the goals set out in Articles 2 and 3 of the EC Treaty without losing their meaning and effectiveness. In a system in which Article 81(3) is directly applicable, a balancing of conflicting goals is impossible not only as a matter of policy, but also as a matter of law. In order to make Article 81(3) a clear and unconditional norm – a binding precondition for any EC Treaty norm that is directly applicable – Article 81(3) must be interpreted and applied with a clear reference to the overall goal of EU competition policy as set out in Article 3(1)(g): promoting a common market with undistorted competition. Where private restraints reflect a value judgment that private planning better protects public interest than the competitive process and that the former may therefore replace the latter, the limit for exemptions under Article 81(3) is reached. National competition authorities and courts can take public-policy interests into account only to the extent that they are not in direct opposition to the EC Treaty's fundamental decision in favour of open and competitive markets, and to the extent that practical concordance between competition and public-policy interests can be achieved within the framework delineated by the wording of Article 81(3).[52]

The same limitations apply to the EU Commission itself.[53] While the ECJ has accepted the Commission's competence to make discretionary policy choices in applying Article 81(3) under the old regime of Regulation 17/62,

---

[51] *See* AG Jacobs, Opinion on Case C-67/99 *Albany International v Stichting Bedrijfspensioenfonds Textielindustrie* [1999] ECR I-5751, 179: It is an established principle of interpretation that, with respect to EC Treaty provisions of equal ranking, no set of provisions can be implemented without taking into account other relevant provisions, and that no set of provisions may completely lose meaning. *See* also Everling, *supra* note 38, at 1081; Roth, *supra* note 12, at 425–7.

[52] Similarly J Koch, *supra* note 38, at 638.

[53] This is controversial. Some argue that the Commission, in decisions under Art 10 of Regulation 1/2003 and in block exemption regulations, can re-introduce, on a discretionary basis, the broader range of public-policy goals – *see* Quellmalz, *supra* note 38, at 466 *et seq*. See also Monti, *supra* note 30, 1096 *et seq* who proposes a revision of Art 81(3), namely the creation of a new para (4) under which the Commission has a monopoly to address public-policy questions. Rightly against such approaches: Roth, *supra* note 12, at 430.

this can no longer be true under the new regime of Regulation 1/2003. If Article 81(3) is directly applicable, this excludes the existence of policy discretion also on the part of the Commission itself.[54] The direct applicability of Article 81(3) presupposes that the direct addressees of this provision – the undertakings – are able to self-evaluate the legality of their conduct ex ante with sufficient certainty. Policy reservations on the part of the EU Commission would be incompatible with this requirement.

The Lisbon Treaty will most likely not change the legal framework developed here. It could, however, potentially enhance the Community institutions' discretion to compromise the binding force of competition rules by way of secondary law. Based on the envisioned revision, political attempts can be expected to exempt certain state measures, or even whole sectors of the economy to which special public interests attach, from the scope of the EC competition rules in the name of conflicting public-policy goals. If successful, the envisioned transformation of the system of undistorted competition into a pure instrument among others to achieve superior public goals could thus redefine the line between integration by law and integration by policy. The latter could easily result in disintegration, where national interventionism is protected in the name of public interest and national sovereignty.

Against this tendency, it is worthwhile recalling the indissoluble links between the system of undistorted competition and the project of European integration itself. Contrary to parts of the literature, the linkage between competition rules and market integration is not outdated – either legally or economically. The internal market is based on the protection of the fundamental freedoms, that is, of individual rights to participate in markets, from the exercise of which the competitive process results. The balance between the goal of an internal market and other public-interest goals is defined by the exceptions to the fundamental freedoms and to the competition rules. The balance of rules and exceptions at the same time determines the lines between EU and Member States' competencies. Through this system EU competition rules are integrated into the larger set of public-policy goals that the EU pursues. However these public-policy goals cannot challenge the space assigned to a system of undistorted competition within the EU. The internal market, the goal of economic integration, is to be achieved not by state or Community intervention, but by the forces of competition. Within their respective spheres of competence, Member States and the EU set the legal framework within which integration takes place, but they may not replace competition by alternative means. Under the revised European Treaties, this regime will likely persist, not unchallenged, but basically unchanged.

---

[54]   *See* also Roth, *supra* note 12, at 430.

PART III

Economic analysis and competition law in practice

10. Restrictive agreements and unilateral restraints: merging regimes on market power and exclusion

Thomas Eilmansberger*

1 INTRODUCTION

1.1 Scope of this Presentation

The title of this session is a bit ambiguous, for it can mean two things, namely (i) merging regimes regarding the assessment of market power on the one hand and exclusion on the other, or (ii) merging regimes on market-power-related exclusion. I took the liberty to choose the second variant, and I furthermore inferred from the first part of the title that the regimes mentioned in its second part are those in Article 81 and Article 82 EC. Also taking into account the overall theme of this conference, I reformulated the basic question of my presentation as follows: Does an increased role for economic analysis bring about a convergence of EC competition rules on cartels and dominant firms with regard to exclusionary practices? In addition, I will briefly examine whether a more prominent use of economic analysis has brought about, or might bring about, a merging of regimes with regard to the different exclusionary practices caught only by Article 82 EC.

1.2 What does an Increased Use of Economic Analysis Mean?

A discussion of the actual and potential effect of an increased use of economic analysis in competition law should first clarify the meaning and import of economic analysis in antitrust law. It is assumed here that economic analysis can influence the antitrust analysis of agreements and unilateral conduct in two largely beneficial ways but may, in addition, also assume a more controversial role.

* Prof. DDr., Law Professor at the University of Salzburg, Austria.

First, economic analysis means a stronger reliance on the concrete effects of the measure under investigation in order to determine whether this conduct falls under the prohibition, that is, creates competition concerns, in the first place. The relevant effects may be foreclosure effects regarding competitors or direct effects on consumer welfare (understood in the EC context as the welfare of final consumers).[1]

Second, an increased use of economic analysis leads to a more favourable view of positive economic effects ('efficiencies') as a redeeming virtue, that is, as defence or justification under Article 81(1) or Article 82 EC or as grounds for exemption under Article 81(3) EC.[2]

Third, economic analysis or insights, in particular macroeconomic doctrine, may have claimed, or will claim, some influence not only on the application and content of EC antitrust rules but also on the formulation of their ultimate goals. An example and consequence of this approach would be an even stronger focus on the immediate effect on consumer welfare (possibly also in the total-welfare sense) and a correspondingly weaker emphasis on 'structural' considerations. This is, however, a more controversial role for economic analysis, and it is not yet clear whether and to what extent it will be endorsed by the courts. In my view, this development should be resisted. Distortion of competition is predominantly a legal concept; it can and should not be shaped by economic theory.[3] The decision of the founding fathers to proscribe behaviour distorting competition is not subject to the proviso that this conduct is also economically inefficient or has a welfare-reducing effect.[4]

2   RELATIONSHIP BETWEEN ARTICLES 81 AND 82 EC

2.1   Preliminary Considerations

To somebody not familiar with EC competition law the title may suggest that, prior to the rise of economic analysis, Articles 81 and 82 EC con-

---

[1]   Case T-168/01 *GlaxoSmithKline v Commission* [2006] ECR II-2969, para 171.

[2]   *Eg* D Geradin, 'Efficiency Claims in EC Competition Law and Sector-specific Regulation' in H Ullrich (ed), *Evolution of European Competition Law: Whose Regulation, Which Competition?* (2006) 313.

[3]   *Cf* also T Eilmansberger, 'How to Distinguish Good from Bad Competition under Article 82 EC: In Search of Clearer and More Coherent Standards for Anticompetitive Abuses' (2005) 42 CML Rev 129.

[4]   Recently also AG Kokott, Opinion in Case C-95/04 P *British Airways v Commission* [2007] ECR I-2331, paras 68 and 85 *et seq*.

tained two separate regimes, also and in particular with regard to exclusionary practices. While there is some truth to that, it would, of course, be wrong to view Articles 81 and 82 EC as two autonomous and independent rules. This would be to ignore that the commonalities between these two norms have always been greater than the differences. These commonalities result from the shared objective of Articles 81 and 82 EC as pillars of the 'system ensuring that competition in the internal market is not distorted'. As explained by the court in *Continental Can*, Articles 81 and 82 EC merely safeguard this objective at different levels. While Article 81 EC concerns various forms of coordination of conduct between undertakings, Article 82 EC concerns unilateral activities potentially disturbing the goal of maintaining effective and undistorted competition.[5] As a consequence, there is an obligation to provide a harmonious and complementary interpretation. This means not only that outright conflicts are to be avoided but also that in the application of one norm the content and purpose of the respective other norm must properly be taken into account.[6]

An important manifestation of the common objective of Articles 81 and 82 EC is that these norms are essentially congruent as regards both their personal[7] and geographical scope.[8] As regards their material scope, there is a significant overlap, as both apply to bilateral practices.

At first glance, however, Articles 81 and 82 EC differ significantly – and this is where economic analysis could bring about some convergence of these two regimes – with regard to their basic normative content, that is, with regard to what they prohibit and accept as exemptions and justifications: Article 81 interdicts restrictions of competition but also provides for an efficiency-related exemption; Article 82 forbids abuses of a dominant position without providing for such an exemption.

---

[5] Case 6/72 *Europemballage Corporation and Continental Can Company v Commission* [1973] ECR 215, para 25.

[6] *Id*, para 25: 'In any case Articles 85 and 86 [Articles 81 and 82] cannot be interpreted in such a way that they contradict each other, because they serve to achieve the same aim'; *see* also Guidelines on the application of Article 81(3) of the Treaty [2004] OJ C 101, p 97, para 106: 'However, in the application of this concept it is necessary to take account of the relationship between Article 81 and Article 82. . . . Moreover, since Articles 81 and 82 both pursue the aim of maintaining effective competition on the market, consistency requires that Article 81(3) be interpreted as precluding any application of this provision to restrictive agreements that constitute an abuse of a dominant position'.

[7] Both norms address undertakings.

[8] With slight differences regarding the intra-Community trade requirement.

2.2   Potential for Convergence

As a result of their common purpose, the prohibitions in Articles 81 and 82 EC certainly coincide at a very fundamental level. Both provisions basically address foreclosure and exclusion on the one hand and exploitation of market power on the other. Nonetheless, a significant scope for a merging of regimes via economic analysis only exists (as the title of this presentation suggests) with regard to foreclosure and exclusion. With regard to exploitative practices, the two respective prohibitions are just too different: while Article 82 EC forbids the exploitation of already existing market power, Article 81 EC primarily addresses the creation of market power through coordination or collusion. The cartel prohibition is, therefore, necessarily much stricter in this respect. Furthermore, in the exploitation context economic analysis has only a very limited relevance to begin with; Articles 81 and 82 EC contain per-se prohibitions in this respect; exemptions are granted in exceptional cases only.

With regard to exclusionary practices, Articles 81 and 82 EC have at least a common objective and regulatory concern. This is to keep markets accessible and to protect the opportunities of competitors to succeed on the merits. Both rules accordingly apply to both variants of exclusionary practices, namely direct[9] and indirect foreclosure.[10] With regard to direct foreclosure, however, the scope for convergence between Articles 81 and 82 EC is again rather limited. This is because conduct directly excluding competitors typically consists of bilateral (or multilateral) horizontal concertation and is as such subject to a much stricter regime under Article 81 EC.

Relevant agreements or concerted actions such as collective boycotts, refusals to grant access to a jointly developed facility or a jointly developed standard, or coordinated predation, are, as a rule, dealt with under a per-se standard. Just as in the case of exploitative collusion, an anti-competitive object will normally be assumed[11] and effects therefore do not have to be established. In contrast, Article 82 EC prohibits unilateral conduct (refusal to deal, predatory pricing, certain rebate schemes, selective price cuts, certain variants of tying) under the condition, and to the extent, only that it actually

---

[9]   Which is the removal of competitive constraints through the elimination of rivals or denial of market access to them (relevant practices are *eg* predatory pricing or a refusal to share critical bottleneck input).

[10]   Which is the hindrance of rivals to succeed on the merits by influencing and ultimately reducing the demand for their products (*eg* through exclusivity agreements).

[11]   Most recently, Case T-168/01 *GlaxoSmithKline v Commission* [2006] ECR II-2969, para 119.

excludes rivals or at least has a commensurate potential to do so; consequently, there has always been some economic analysis in which both the exclusionary effect and (at least in some cases) a corresponding intent was examined. This analysis may have been superficial in many cases and can be expected to become more thorough and sophisticated in the future. This development, however, will not lead to a merging of regimes, but on the contrary to a further separation of relevant standards under Articles 81 and 82 EC. There is scope for convergence only on the justification level. If an agreement is exempted under Article 81(3) because of the efficiencies it generates, this exemption should also shield it from the application of Article 82.[12]

The following analysis will therefore focus on exclusionary vertical practices, that is, single-branding agreements, rebate schemes and tying.[13] It must be preliminarily noted, however, that with regard to these practices as well, limitations on the merging of regimes exist due to the diverging normative content of Articles 81 and 82 EC. With regard to these practices, Article 82 EC contains the stricter standard. Under this rule, exclusionary vertical arrangements are judged under an exploitative standard as well. Agreements concluded by dominant firms must also pass a fairness test (for which economic analysis is of course largely irrelevant). Single-branding obligations that are forced upon the buyer and are not adequately compensated for can be abusive even in the absence of any foreclosure effect. In fact, this applies to any restriction of the commercial freedom of action of the customer.[14] Furthermore, vertical practices by dominant firms must not be discriminatory. Article 82(c) EC prohibits the application of dissimilar conditions to equivalent transactions with trading partners to the extent that this distorts secondary line competition. This is an important additional hurdle (not found in Article 81 EC) for rebate schemes (especially loyalty rebates).[15]

---

[12]   Case T-193/02 *Piau v Commission* [2005] ECR II-209; DG Competition Discussion Paper on the application of Article 82 of the Treaty to exclusionary abuses, December 2005, available at http://ec.europa.eu/comm/competition/antitrust/art82/discpaper 2005.pdf (accessed 31 January 2008).

[13]   Exclusive distribution, restrictions of parallel trade and other inter-brand restrictions will not be dealt with because they do not as a rule raise serious exclusion or foreclosure concerns.

[14]   T Eilmansberger, in G Hirsch, F Montag and FJ Säcker (eds), *Münchener Kommentar zum Europäischen und Deutschen Wettbewerbsrecht (Kartellrecht), Part I* (2007) Art 82, para 226; W Möschel, in U Immenga and EJ Mestmäcker (eds), *Wettbewerbsrecht, EG/Teil 1* (4th edn 2007) Art 82, para 149; H Schröter, in H Schröter, T Jakob and W Mederer (eds), *Kommentar zum europäischen Wettbewerbsrecht* (2003) Art 82, para 194; EJ Mestmäcker and H Schweitzer, *Europäisches Wettbewerbsrecht* (2nd edn, 2004) § 17, paras 53 *et seq.*

[15]   Commission Decision 88/518/EEC of 19 October 1988, Case IV/30.178 – *Napier Brown/British Sugar* [1988] OJ L 284, p 41, paras 74 *et seq*; Case C-163/99

3 ECONOMIC ANALYSIS IN THE CONTEXT OF ARTICLE 81 EC

In a comparison of the two regimes regarding the use and impact of economic analysis, Article 81 EC is clearly the point of reference. Economic analysis has always played a role in the competition-law assessment of agreements, and it saw its role altered and further increased as a result of modernization efforts undertaken at a comparatively early stage. Originally, economic analysis (in the form of a recognition of efficiencies) was predominantly carried out at the exemption level. Article 81(3) EC has always been viewed as a platform where pro- and anti-competitive effects of restrictive agreements could be weighed against each other. Precisely because of this comprehensive interpretation of Article 81(3) EC,[16] the role of economic analysis in the interpretation and application of Article 81(1) EC was somewhat limited for a long time.

As was mentioned above, the scope for an economic-analysis-driven convergence between Articles 81 and 82 EC is somewhat restricted: economic analysis plays no or only a minimal role with regard to restrictions by object, where it is neither necessary for establishing the infringement nor of any significant relevance for exemption or justification purposes. As most exclusionary horizontal agreements constitute such restrictions by object and are accordingly subject to a per-se analysis, the focus naturally shifts to indirectly foreclosing vertical agreements, more specifically to single-branding obligations such as non-compete clauses and exclusive purchasing agreements. For those agreements, in particular single-branding

---

Portugal v Commission (*'Portuguese Airports'*) [2001] ECR I-2613, paras 552 *et seq*; Commission Decision 95/364/EC of 28 June 1995, *British Midland-Zaventem* [1995] OJ L 216, p 8, para 16; Case T-83/91 *Tetra Pak v Commission* (*'Tetra Pak II'*) [1994] ECR II-755, para 221; Joined Cases 40–48/73, 50/73, 54–56/73, 111/73, 113 & 114/73 *Suiker Unie and Others v Commission* [1975] ECR 1663, para 522; Commission Decision 2000/74/EC of 14 July 1999, Case No IV/D-2/34.780 – *Virgin/British Airways* [2000] OJ L 30, p 1, para 109; confirmed by Case T-219/99 *British Airways v Commission* [2003] ECR II-5917, para 240; Commission Decision 93/82/EEC of 23 December 1992, Joined Cases No IV/32.448 and IV/32.450 – *Cewal, Cowal and Ukwal* [1993] OJ L 34, p 20, para 85; Commission Decision 91/299/EC of 19 December 1990, Case No IV/33-133-C – *Soda-ash/Solvay* [1991] OJ L 152, p 21, para 62; Case 85/76 *Hoffmann-La Roche v Commission* [1979] ECR 461, paras 89 *et seq*; Case 322/81 *Nederlandsche Banden Industrie Michelin v Commission* (*'Michelin I'*) [1983] ECR 3461, para 72; European Commission, *XIX. Report on Competition Policy 1989*, para 50.

[16] Under a narrower interpretation, Article 81(3) EC would only apply to net restrictions of competition believed to better (than competition between the parties) attain certain economic or non-economic goals.

agreements, economic analysis has long been established as a central evaluation tool also at the prohibition level. This was a fairly natural development: as these practices constitute normal commercial conduct, they cannot be presumed to be restrictive of competition by object and can thus restrict competition only by effect. That, of course, requires an effects-based analysis, the relevant effect being the foreclosure of rival suppliers. The central, though not exclusive, parameters in this analysis are the nature of the product (final products or intermediate products), market foreclosure thresholds (total tied share of the market and percentage attributable to firm), and the market share of the parties (in particular of the supplier).[17]

4   ECONOMIC ANALYSIS IN THE CONTEXT OF ARTICLE 82 EC

4.1   Preliminary Remarks

With regard to direct foreclosure or exclusion, an economic analysis has, at least to some extent, always been carried out under Article 82 EC. But there is certainly scope for a greatly increased role in particular for an effects-based application and interpretation of this rule. However, as mentioned above, there is little scope for convergence because of the much stricter standard for such conduct under Article 81 EC. I shall therefore now focus on indirect exclusion, that is, vertical, customer-related practices such as exclusive dealing, rebate schemes, tying and bundling.

Also with regard to these practices, however, the normative content of Articles 81 and 82 EC differs significantly, with Article 82 EC setting the stricter standard. As mentioned above, under this provision, exclusionary arrangements are also judged under an exploitative standard. Agreements concluded by dominant firms must pass a fairness test (for which economic analysis is completely irrelevant) as well. Single-branding obligations forced upon the buyer that are not somehow 'remunerated' are abusive even in the absence of any foreclosure effect. More generally, any restriction of the commercial freedom of action of the customer would be caught

---

[17]   Case C-234/89 *Delimitis v Henninger Bräu* [1991] ECR I-935; Case C-214/99 *Neste Markkinointi Oy v Yötuuli Ky* [2000] ECR I-11121; Commission Regulation (EC) No 2790/1999 of 22 December 1999 on the application of Article 81(3) of the Treaty to categories of vertical agreements and concerted practices [1999] OJ L 336, p 21; Commission Notice – Guidelines on vertical restraints [2000] OJ C 291, p 1; Commission Notice on agreements of minor importance which do not appreciably restrict competition under Article 81(1) of the Treaty establishing the European Community (de minimis) [2001] OJ C 368, p 13.

by the fairness standard even in the absence of foreclosure.[18] Furthermore, vertical practices by dominant firms must not be discriminatory either.[19]

4.2 Bilateral Conduct: Exclusive Purchasing and Non-compete Obligations

4.2.1 Application of the basic prohibition and relevant effects

With regard to single-branding arrangements, the decisional practice is not quite coherent yet. In older cases, exclusive dealing was considered prohibited per se.[20] Although the courts never explicitly retreated from this position, the Commission in its more recent cases did in fact apply a more effects-based approach[21] and, perhaps even more significant, its analysis in this respect was double-checked by the courts.[22] The often articulated contention that under Article 82 EC effects are largely ignored by the courts and the Commission[23] is thus exaggerated. Rather, the reverse seems true: those effects were at times assumed too readily, for instance when it was merely pointed out that the conduct had such a tendency.[24]

In its Discussion Paper, the Commission now explicitly acknowledges that the abusiveness of single-branding should be assessed under an effects-based analysis,[25] and in the recent *Tomra* case, that approach appears to have

---

[18] *See supra* note 14.

[19] *See supra* note 15.

[20] *Eg* Case 85/76 *Hoffmann-La Roche v Commission* [1979] ECR 461; Joined Cases 40–48/73, 50/73, 54–56/73, 111/73, 113 & 114/73 *Suiker Unie and Others v Commission* [1975] ECR 1663. For a detailed account of the development of the decisional practice and case-law under Article 82 EC *see* R O'Donoghue and AJ Padilla, *The Law and Economics of Article 82 EC* (2006) 357–9.

[21] Commission Decision 98/531/EC of 11 March 1998, Joined Cases Nos. IV/34.073, IV/34.395 and IV/35.436 – *Van den Bergh Foods* [1998] OJ L 246, p 1; Commission Decision 89/22/EEC of 5 December 1988, Case No IV/31.900 – *BPB Industries* [1989] OJ L 10, p 50.

[22] Case T-65/98 *Van den Bergh Foods v Commission* [2003] ECR II-4653, para 160; Case T-65/89 *BPB Industries and British Gypsum v Commission* [1993] ECR II-389.

[23] *Eg* P Lugard, 'Eternal Sunshine on a Spotless Policy? Exclusive Dealing under Article 82 EC' [2006] *Eur Comp* J 163, 179.

[24] Case T-219/99 *British Airways v Commission* [2003] ECR II-5917, para 293; confirmed by Case C-95/04 P *British Airways v Commission* [2007] ECR I-2331; Case T-203/01 *Michelin v Commission* ('*Michelin II*') [2003] ECR II-4071, para 239.

[25] Discussion Paper, *supra* note 12, at para 145. The incidence, *ie* the extent to which the dominant company is applying the single-branding obligation or rebate system in the market, is the same as its tied market share, ie that part of its market share sold under the single-branding obligation or rebate system. The potential negative effects will in general depend on the size of the tied market share. In case the

already been applied in practice.[26] This clarification is certainly welcome. If the only charge directed against the dominant firm is foreclosure (and not unfairness or discrimination), an effects-based analysis showing a corresponding foreclosure potential is simply inevitable. A per-se approach would not be justified. Proof of an actual impact on the market structure is evidently not necessary,[27] but a plaintiff in an abuse case should be required to prove that, under the concrete market circumstances, the practice at issue is capable of generating such an effect.[28] In the case of the systematic employment of such practices by a dominant firm, a (rebuttable) presumption that these have the requisite foreclosure potential may be appropriate.[29]

In this context, it must be emphasized that the effect to be proven is a structural one. The underlying rationale is not to preserve a market structure displaying a certain degree of competition (or even to protect certain competitors), but to safeguard the basic conditions under which the competitive process unfolds, and to defend the possibilities for competitors to succeed on the merits. That has always been the position of the European Courts. Already in *Continental Can*, the ECJ defined exclusionary abuse by reference to the impact of the conduct 'on an effective competition structure'.[30] A reference to the potential 'to influence the structure of a market'

---

dominant company does not apply the single-branding obligation or rebate system to a good part of its buyers but only selectively, the Commission will investigate whether or not these selected buyers are of particular importance for the possibilities of entry or expansion of competitors.

26   Commission Decision of 29 March 2006, Case COMP/E-1/38.113 – *Prokent-Tomra*,   http://ec.europa.eu/comm/competition/antitrust/cases/decisions/38113/decision_en.pdf (accessed 31 January 2008), *see* also Press Release IP/06/398; F Maier-Rigaud and D Vaigauskaite, 'Prokent/Tomra, a Textbook Case? Abuse of Dominance under Perfect Information' (2006) Comp Policy Newsletter No 2, 19.

27   Case T-219/99 *British Airways v Commission* [2003] ECR II-5917, para 297 ('the fact that the hoped-for result is not achieved is not sufficient to prevent a finding of abuse of a dominant position within the meaning of Article 82 EC'); also Case T-24–26/93 and 28/93 *Compagnie maritime belge v Commission* [1996] ECR II-1201, para 149.

28   Also AG Kokott, Opinion in Case C-95/04 P *British Airways v Commission* [2007] ECR I-2331, paras 71–3.

29   Guidelines on vertical restraints, *supra* note 17, at para 148: 'It is for these reasons that for final products at the retail level, significant anti-competitive effects may start to arise, taking into account all other relevant factors, if a non-dominant supplier ties 30% or more of the relevant market. For a dominant company, even a modest tied market share may already lead to significant anti-competitive effects. The stronger its dominance, the higher the risk of foreclosure of other competitors'.

30   Case 6/72 *Europemballage Corporation and Continental Can Company v Commission* [1973] ECR 215, para 26.

can also be found in the landmark definition of abuse in *Hoffmann-La Roche*.[31]

It is thus necessary to carefully define and assess those effects that can rightfully be termed structural. The loss of business to a dominant firm is as such not a relevant effect. Even dramatic changes in respective market shares do not constitute a structural effect as this does not normally hinder rivals from successfully competing for future business. Rather, a lasting change in the dynamics and conditions of competition is required. Such a lasting, structural effect can concern the supply side as well as the demand side of the market. Each type of market-structure effect needs to be assessed under a different standard.

Relevant supply-side effects would be the elimination, exit-inducing intimidation or entry deterrence of (potential) competitors, and the resulting reduction of horizontal competitive restraints. That is obviously an effect that is rather difficult to achieve, even for a dominant firm. On this presumption, it should be possible to screen out many cases, especially alleged pricing abuses. Meeting competition through, for example, price cuts under this approach only merits further investigation under Article 82 EC if it has the potential to actually bring about those effects. If a selective price cut can realistically only achieve the maintenance or increase of market shares, the conduct should not be considered abusive.

Pertinent demand-side structural effects are lasting alterations of demand patterns of consumers. This effect, which also goes beyond the exclusionary effects inherent in any successful sales transaction, can be brought about by practices influencing or determining the future purchasing behaviour of consumers on a given market, for example, by rebate systems or long-term purchasing or supply arrangements. It is suggested that those effects should be assessed under the methods and standards developed for Article 81 EC to evaluate foreclosure effects of agreements.[32] Loyalty-inducing practices employed by dominant firms, however, should only be considered abusive (and not merely restrictive of competition under Article 81) if these arrangements bring about such a foreclosure effect by themselves. Where, instead, only the cumulative effect of the dominant firm's arrangements and its competitor's similar arrangements cause the foreclosure, only Article 81 EC applies.

It is furthermore submitted that a business practice (potentially) bringing about such a structural change should be considered abusive only if it

---

[31]   Case 85/76 *Hoffmann-La Roche v Commission* [1979] ECR 461, para 91.

[32]   In its Guidelines on vertical restraints, *supra* note 17, at para 148, the Commission proposes to analyse single-branding arrangements of normal and dominant firms under a uniform standard.

can be shown that it also aimed to achieve that result. As one is dealing with normal business practices here, there is a presumption that such practices are employed for normal, that is, innocent, commercial reasons. Even in the absence of Article 2 of Regulation 1/2003,[33] the burden of proof should thus be borne by the competition authority or the plaintiff. Furthermore, it must always be open to the firm to rebut evidence suggesting anti-competitive motives. This can be done by showing, firstly, that the practice did indeed make economic sense for the firm and did so irrespective of whether it would have caused the alteration of the market structure (eg the exit of a competitor) or not; and, secondly, that it was also proportionate in that respect, that is, there was no competition-friendlier alternative. Arguably, the relevance of the objective, purpose or strategic aim of the business practice explains a number of modern approaches to identifying abuse practices, such as the sacrifice test or the objective-justification test (employed regularly by the Commission in its decisional practice). More importantly, the case-law of the Courts also regularly relies on intent.[34]

If the relevance of intent is accepted, Article 82 EC contains a more lenient standard than Article 81 EC. As a consequence, an agreement can be condemned only under Article 81 EC if such an intent cannot be proven. An example would be an exclusive purchasing or supply agreement concluded as a result of a bidding procedure. As the terms of such contracts are typically determined by the other party, no anti-competitive intent on the side of the dominant firm can be assumed. Those agreements would thus only be subject to scrutiny under Article 81 EC.

4.2.2 Justification and efficiencies
At the justification level, a variant of economic analysis has occasionally been accepted by the Commission. Microeconomic arguments have in some cases been accepted in the form of an objective-justification defence, that is, as a means to distinguish anti-competitive practices from performance-based competition.[35] The objective justification was probably

---

[33] Regulation 1/2003 of 16 December 2002 on the implementation of the rules on competition laid down in Articles 81 and 82 of the Treaty [2003] OJ L 1, p 1.

[34] Case 27/76 *United Brands v Commission* [1978] ECR 207, para 189; Case C-62/86 *AKZO v Commission* [1991] ECR I-3359, paras 71 ff; Joined Cases 40–48/73, 50/73, 54–56/73, 111/73, 113 & 114/73 *Suiker Unie and Others v Commission* [1975] ECR 1663, para 518; Case 322/81 *Nederlandsche Banden Industrie Michelin v Commission* ('*Michelin I*') [1983] ECR 3461, para 71; Case T-65/89 *BPB Industries and British Gypsum v Commission* [1993] ECR II-389, para 120; Case T-203/01 *Michelin v Commission* ('*Michelin II*') [2003] ECR II-4071, para 56.

[35] This criterion is regularly used by the Commission to identify exclusionary abuses; recently *eg* in Commission Decision 2004/33/EC of 27 August 2003, Case

not supposed to be an efficiency defence in the sense of Article 81(3) EC (better product; more efficient production etc). In the Discussion Paper, however, the Commission does propose to take efficiency-related arguments into consideration with regard to the analysis under Article 82 EC. While this position appears to be at odds with the case-law of the ECJ (which so far has denied the relevance and applicability of Article 81(3) EC to dominance abuses),[36] it does find support in the recent *Laurent Piau* judgment by the CFI.[37] It is submitted that this is persuasive. If an agreement, under the standards of Article 81(3) EC, is considered to create relevant efficiencies, and if the dominant position of one of the parties to the agreement has also been properly taken into account in the analysis under Article 81(3) EC,[38] there is no reason why this should not also be

---

No COMP/37.685 – *GVG/FS* [2004] OJ L 11, p 17 para 145. *See* also J Faull and A Nikpay, *The EC Law of Competition* (2nd edn, 2007) paras 4.182–4.185; O'Donoghue and Padilla, *supra* note 20, at 227–35.

[36]   After its suggestion in Case 85/76 *Hoffmann-La Roche v Commission* [1979] ECR 461, para 120, that exclusive purchasing agreements might benefit from individual exemptions under Article 81(3) EC, the Court consistently rejected the applicability of this defence under Article 82. *See* Case 66/86 *Ahmed Saeed Flugreisen and Silver Line Reisebüro GmbH v Zentrale zur Bekämpfung unlauteren Wettbewerbs e.V.* [1989] ECR 803, para 32; Joined Cases C-395/96 P and C-396/96 P *Compagnie maritime belge v Commission* [2000] ECR I-1365, para 135; Case T-51/89 *Tetra Pak Rausing SA v Commission* [1990] ECR II-309, para 27; Case T-65/89 *BPB Industries and British Gypsum v Commission* [1993] ECR II-389, para 75; *see*, however, Case C-95/04 P *British Airways v Commission*, [2007] ECR I-2331, para 86, where an efficiency defence was, in substance, accepted.

[37]   Case T-193/02 *Piau v Commission* [2005] ECR II-209, para 119: 'Consequently, although the Commission wrongly considered that FIFA did not hold a dominant position on the market for players' agents' services, the other findings contained in the contested decision, namely that the most restrictive provisions of the regulations had been deleted and that the licence system could enjoy an exemption decision under Article 81(3) EC, would accordingly lead to the conclusion that there was no infringement under Article 82 EC and to the rejection of the applicant's arguments in this regard. Therefore, despite the error in law made by the Commission in taking the view that Article 82 EC was not applicable, its application could not, in any event, have resulted in a finding of an abuse of a dominant position based on the other findings that had rightly been made from the examination of the regulations. Thus, the lawfulness of the rejection of the complaint on the ground of lack of Community interest in continuing with the procedure is not affected'.

[38]   *See* Guidelines on vertical restraints, *supra* note 17, at para 135: 'The last criterion of elimination of competition for a substantial part of the products in question is related to the question of dominance. Where an undertaking is dominant or becoming dominant as a consequence of the vertical agreement, a vertical restraint that has appreciable anti-competitive effects can in principle not be exempted. The vertical agreement may however fall outside Article 81(1) if there is an objective justification, for instance if it is necessary for the protection of relationship-specific

considered relevant under Article 82 EC (not least because it disproves intent).[39]

An interesting and controversial aspect in this context is the burden of proof. Under Article 81(3) EC, relevant efficiencies need to be proven by the undertakings claiming them. The question now is whether this also applies if these efficiencies are invoked to defend the dominant undertaking against abuse charges under Article 82 EC. At first sight, this may appear problematic, as under Article 82 EC this would have to be part of the proof of the infringement, and, in this respect, the burden of proof according to Article 2 of Regulation 1/2003[40] is on the competition authority or claimant. It is submitted, however, that this would be an overly literal application of that rule, which would not be in keeping with the general principle (of which presumably Article 2 Regulation 1/2003 is also an expression) that each party is obligated to prove all facts triggering the legal rules and principles that it invokes.[41] Furthermore, in cases concurrently caught by Article 81 EC (ie all restrictive agreements), the burden-of-proof rule in Regulation 1/2003 regarding Article 81(3) EC applies at any rate. For dominant firms, this is certainly not an unreasonable burden, as the evidence with regard to these efficiencies (and with regard to the legitimate motivation of a business practice) is usually controlled by them.

5   PRACTICAL CONSEQUENCES

As mentioned before, a convergence of regimes is not possible as far as direct foreclosure is concerned. The relevant standards in Article 81 and Article 82 EC are too different: Article 81 protects the freedom of parties to autonomously determine their conduct with regard to prices, output, customers etc; and it protects this freedom with a per-se prohibition of all restrictive arrangements. As a consequence, a restrictive agreement should be dealt with under Article 81 EC exclusively even if it might conceivably also run foul of Article 82 EC in that it creates and abuses a collective dominant position. There is scope for convergence only at the justification level.

---

investments or for the transfer of substantial know-how without which the supply or purchase of certain goods or services would not take place'.

[39]   *See* Discussion Paper, *supra* note 12, at paras 172–6.

[40]   Regulation 1/2003 of 16 December 2002 on the implementation of the rules on competition laid down in Articles 81 and 82 of the Treaty [2003] OJ L 1, p 1.

[41]   In this sense also E Paulis, 'The Burden of Proof in Article 82 Cases', Fordham Conference 2006, http://ec.europa.eu/comm/competition/speeches/text/sp2006_014_en.pdf (accessed 31 January 2008).

An Article 81(3) EC exemption should be relevant under Article 82 EC as well.

With regard to indirect foreclosure, that is, single-branding agreements, the adoption of a more effects-based approach under Article 82 EC would bring about a merging of regimes.[42] If relevant practices were to be judged by an identical standard under both regimes, this would have one important practical consequence: the analysis could concentrate on Article 81 EC only. If the cartel prohibition does not apply because a significant foreclosure effect cannot be established or because the foreclosure effects are more than compensated for by efficiencies taking the form of better products, distribution or production, the agreement – at least as far as its exclusionary quality is concerned[43] – should also be considered unproblematic under Article 82 EC. If, on the other hand, a relevant foreclosure effect has been established under Article 81 EC, and an exemption under Article 81(3) EC denied, there is no need to apply Article 82 EC any more. In such a case, the application of Article 82 EC does not present any added value for sanctioning purposes either. A cumulative application of fines under both provisions is correctly excluded even by the Commission,[44] and sufficiently harsh and deterrent fines can also be imposed for an infringement of Article 81 EC alone.[45] In the case of a merging of regimes, therefore, Article 82 EC would be displaced or, to use the German expression, 'consumed' by Article 81 EC at least as far as exclusion is concerned. For competition authorities and plaintiffs in private actions, this has one obvious advantage: they would no longer need to establish dominance in the sense of Article 82 EC in these cases.

6   CONVERGENCE OF RULES FOR UNILATERAL CONDUCT

6.1   Fidelity Rebates

Loyalty-enhancing rebate schemes are unilateral practices and therefore only subject to Article 82 EC. Consequently, a convergence of relevant

---

[42]   Also M Albers, 'Der "*more economic approach*" bei Verdrängungs-missbräuchen: Zum Stand der Überlegungen der Europäischen Kommission', http://ec.europa.eu/comm/competition/antitrust/art82/albers.pdf (accessed 31 January 2008) 11.

[43]   It must be borne in mind that under Article 82 exclusionary conduct is also judged under a fairness and non-discrimination standard.

[44]   Commission 89/93/EEC of 19 October 1988, Case No IV/31.908 – *Flat glass* [1989] OJ L 33, p 44, paras 84 *et seq*.

[45]   Article 23(2) Regulation 1/2003.

standards under Articles 81 and 82 EC is obviously not possible. The more interesting issue is whether a mutatis mutandis application of the foreclosure standards and principles applied to bilateral single-branding arrangements is possible or advisable. This specific kind of indirect convergence, however, is limited by the fact that rebate schemes under Article 82 EC are not only subject to a foreclosure standard but also to a fairness,[46] as well as to a non-discrimination, requirement, the latter being particularly important for loyalty rebates.[47]

Like exclusive dealing agreements, rebate schemes were initially treated under a rather strict standard. In fact, the ECJ regarded fidelity rebates as a variant of an exclusive purchasing arrangement.[48] In contrast to single-branding agreements, loyalty-enhancing rebate systems were never prohibited per se, though. In view of the varied character of such schemes, that would not have been possible. The economic analysis employed in this context, however, was not about the economic effects or justifications of fidelity-enhancing rebates. Rather, it was focused on the question of whether the rebate scheme under investigation was in fact loyalty-enhancing, that is, whether and to what extent it created significant switching costs and a corresponding suction effect. A thorough assessment of the foreclosure effect on (potential) competitors, possibly in conjunction with other rebate schemes and exclusivity arrangements, has not been carried out yet. For instance, in *Michelin II* a foreclosure effect was simply assumed,[49] or

---

[46] Recently, Case T-203/01 *Michelin v Commission* ('*Michelin II*') [2003] ECR II-4071.

[47] *See* Case C-163/99 *Portugal v Commission* ('*Portuguese Airports*') [2001] ECR I-2613, paras 52–3; Commission Decision 95/364/EC of 28 June 1995, *British Midland-Zaventem* [1995] OJ L 216, p 8, para 16; Case T-83/91 *Tetra Pak v Commission* ('*Tetra Pak II*') [1994] ECR II-755, para 21; Joined Cases 40–48/73, 50/73, 54–56/73, 111/73, 113 & 114/73 *Suiker Unie and Others v Commission* [1975] ECR 1663, para 52; Commission Decision 2000/74/EC of 14 July 1999, Case No IV/D-2/34.780 – *Virgin/British Airways* [2000] OJ L 30, p 1, para 109; Case T-219/99 *British Airways v Commission* [2003] ECR II-5917, para 240; Commission Decision 93/82/EEC of 23 December 1992, Joined Cases Nos IV/32.448 and IV/32.450 – *Cewal, Cowal and Ukwal* [1993] OJ L 34, p 20, para 85; Commission Decision 91/299/EC of 19 December 1990, Case No IV/33–133-C – *Soda-ash/Solvay* [1991] OJ L 152, p 21, para 62; Case 85/76 *Hoffmann-La Roche* [1979] ECR 461, paras 89 *et seq*; Case 322/81 *Nederlandsche Banden Industrie Michelin v Commission* ('*Michelin I*') [1983] ECR 3461, paras 87–91.

[48] Case 85/76 *Hoffmann-La Roche v Commission* [1979] ECR 461, paras 89 *et seq*.

[49] Case T-203/01 *Michelin v Commission* ('*Michelin II*') [2003] ECR II-4071, para 57: 'More generally, as the applicant submits, a rebate system which has a foreclosure effect on the market will be regarded as contrary to Article 82 EC if it is

only assessed with regard to the individual customer.[50] The reasoning of the CFI,[51] according to which these measures were aimed at foreclosure and were thus also likely to achieve that effect, therefore appears a bit facile. A somewhat more thorough foreclosure analysis would have been advisable. In *British Airways*, a relevant market foreclosure effect prima facie seemed obvious. Not only was the rebate scheme applied across the board. Owing to its continuous application, it also provided a permanent incentive to every distributor to increase its business with British Airways.[52] But even this particular rebate scheme was not really exclusionary, because it put pressure on resellers only at the margin, and it is unclear whether these volumes were crucial for the viability of competition. At best, it can be presumed that this rebate scheme created an impediment to rivals' growth, and thus produced at least some indirect foreclosure effect. But also, in this case, the two Courts' analysis of the effects of the rebate scheme focused on the question of whether it was loyalty-enhancing with regard to co-contractors,[53] but was rather cursory with regard to the more

---

applied by an undertaking in a dominant position. For that reason, the Court has held that a rebate which depended on a purchasing target being achieved also infringed Article 82 EC'.

[50]　Case T-203/01 *Michelin v Commission* ('*Michelin II*') [2003] ECR II-4071, para 60: 'In determining whether a quantity rebate system is abusive, it will therefore be necessary to consider all the circumstances, particularly the criteria and rules governing the grant of the rebate, and to investigate whether, in providing an advantage not based on any economic service justifying it, the rebates tend to remove or restrict the buyer's freedom to choose his sources of supply, to bar competitors from access to the market, to apply dissimilar conditions to equivalent transactions with other trading parties or to strengthen the dominant position by distorting competition'.

[51]　Case T-203/01 *Michelin v Commission* ('*Michelin II*') [2003] ECR II-4071, para 241.

[52]　This also seems to be the position of AG Kokott, Opinion in Case C-95/04 P *British Airways v Commission* [2007] ECR I-2331, para 95: 'What determines whether rebate and bonus schemes are likely to have a foreclosure effect on the market, however, is – as already mentioned – an overall assessment of all the circumstances of the particular case. As the Commission has correctly pointed out, what counts is not just the duration in absolute terms of the reference period in which turnover must be achieved, but also how far back the relevant period for comparison lies. One cannot exclude the possibility that even a system in which reference is made month by month to periods lying one year back will, on account of the continual incentive it gives to increase turnover, result in a *long-term binding* of the contractual partner to the dominant undertaking, making it hard for him to switch to the competition'.

[53]　Case T-219/99 *British Airways v Commission* [2003] ECR II-5917, paras 270–78; Case C-95/04 P *British Airways v Commission*, [2007] ECR I-2331, paras 78 *et seq*.

fundamental question of whether there was indeed a relevant foreclosure effect.[54]

The lack, or misdirected focus, of effects-based analyses in the assessment of rebates has been widely criticized in the literature.[55] This critique is in principle justified, and – as is evidenced by the Discussion Paper – has also been accepted by the Commission. The crucial question, however, is what the relevant effect should be in the rebates context. Two possibilities exist in this regard.

First, the relevant effect could be indirect foreclosure, that is, the impediment to growth or market access brought about by the binding of a portion of consumer demand. This would mean that foreclosure tests applied to other single-branding obligations would have to be applied mutatis mutandis. In my view, this approach is problematic. Given that rebate schemes have a much lower binding force in the first place[56] and also considering that they may have a much shorter duration, a very high degree of general foreclosure and a fairly widespread application of the rebate scheme would be required to attain the same foreclosure effect as an exclusive purchasing obligation imposed on important customers. Furthermore, a quantification of this effect appears almost impossible.

Second (and in view of these shortcomings in my opinion clearly preferably), the relevant effect could be direct foreclosure or exclusion, with the test to be applied mutatis mutandis accordingly being the predatory pricing test. The decisive question in that case would be whether the rebate, like a predatory price, completely denies the competitor access to

---

[54] However AG Kokott, Opinion in Case C-95/04 P *British Airways v Commission* [2007] ECR I-2331, para 46: 'It further needs to be examined whether the relevant rebate or bonus scheme as a whole is capable of making it difficult or impossible for the dominant undertaking's competitors to have access to the market, or for its contractual partners to choose between various sources of supply or business partners'.

[55] *Eg* D Geradin, *supra* note 2; J Kallaugher and B Sher, 'Rebates Revisited: Anti-Competitive Effects and Exclusionary Abuse under Article 82' (2004) 25 *ECLR* 263, 268; D Waelbroeck, 'Michelin II: A Per Se Rule against Rebates by Dominant Companies?' (2005) 1 *J Comp L & Econ* 149; D Ridyard, 'Exclusionary Pricing and Price Discrimination Abuses under Article 82: An Economic Analysis' [2002] 23 ECLR, 286; R O'Donoghue, 'Over-regulating Lower Prices: Time for a Rethink on Pricing Practices under Article 82 EC' in CD Ehlermann and I Atanasiu (eds), *European Competition Law Annual 2003: What is an Abuse of a Dominant Position?* (2006) 371, 372.

[56] They do not foreclose in the way exclusive dealing does. While the latter effectively excludes rivals from that portion of demand, a rebate scheme only establishes a strong economic incentive to maintain the business relationship with the dominant firm.

certain customers or, more generally, to a certain portion of the market. If I understand it correctly, this indeed seems to be the approach advocated in the Discussion Paper,[57, 58] and it also appears to have been applied in the recent *Tomra* decision.[59] The crucial question under this test is whether the price for the amount of the customer's purchases perceived by the dominant firm to be contestable by rivals[60] would be cost-covering in itself, or whether it would be cost-covering only if the rebate were cross-subsidized by non-contested sales.[61] This price would have to be calculated by a deduction of the full rebate; that is, by an allocation of the rebate to that quantity.[62] Although that may be counter-intuitive,

---

[57]   Discussion Paper, *supra* note 12, at para 139: 'The main possible effect of single branding obligations and rebate systems is foreclosure of the market to competing suppliers and potential suppliers, which maintains or strengthens the dominant position by hindering the maintenance or growth of residual or potential competition (horizontal foreclosure)'. *See id*, para 146: 'If competitors are competing on equal terms for all the customers and for each individual customer's entire demand, then a rebate scheme is unlikely to have a foreclosure effect unless the effective price under the rebate scheme, calculated over all sales by the dominant company to its customer(s), is found to be predatory (*see* section 6 on predatory pricing)'.

[58]   *Cf* O'Donoghue and Padilla, *supra* note 20, at 397.

[59]   *See supra* note 26.

[60]   The dominant position (more precisely, factors such as capacity constraints on other suppliers, the 'must stock item' quality of the dominant firm's products) will typically ensure that most buyers will purchase most of their requirements from this dominant supplier even in the absence of any loyalty-enhancing rebate (*see* also Discussion Paper, *supra* note 12, at para 152).

[61]   Discussion Paper, *supra* note 12, at para 153: 'The rebate enables the dominant supplier to use the inelastic or "non contestable" portion of demand of each buyer, i.e. the amount that would anyhow be purchased by the buyer, as leverage to decrease the price for the elastic or "contestable" portion of demand, i.e. the amount for which the buyer may prefer and be able to find substitutes'.

[62]   Discussion Paper, *supra* note 12, at para 154: 'In case this effective price is below the average total cost of the dominant company, it will be very difficult and possibly even impossible for as efficient competitors to compete with the dominant company for this part of demand. In case the effective price is above cost this may make it possible for efficient competitors (in the long run) to match the dominant company's offer, but it may exceptionally still work as a disincentive on expansion or entry by competitors. The main reason to take ATC as the cost benchmark below which the rebate system is considered to lead to an exclusionary effective price is that the leveraging between the "non-contestable" and the "contestable" portion of demand allows the rebate system to operate without a profit sacrifice and thus to operate for a long time. The customer may not derive a direct benefit from the rebate system as the rebate may only bring the average price down to the level existing without the rebate system'.

duration is not a relevant factor in this test.[63] As the Commission convincingly argues in its Discussion Paper,[64] the crucial question instead is whether the rebate system – by using the inelastic or 'non-contestable' portion of demand of each buyer as leverage to decrease the price for the elastic or 'contestable' portion of demand – denies rivals market access by hindering them from supplying commercially viable amounts to individual customers.[65]

The adoption of a predation-oriented standard as suggested in the Discussion Paper would lead to a certain 'demerging' of standards for single-branding practices such as exclusive purchasing and non-compete agreements on the one hand, and rebate schemes on the other (with the latter then being judged under a somewhat more lenient standard). This, however, would be a welcome development, since it permits the application of similar standards to ultimately similar practices and would thus strengthen the inner coherence of abuse-control law. One such similar practice is bundled discounts, where the customer gets a discount on the dominant (tying) product if she also purchases the competitive (tied) product. In the Discussion Paper, the Commission now suggests basically the same approach for rebates and these practices, namely the allocation of the rebate to the competitive product and a subsequent determination of whether the resulting price is in itself cost-covering, that is, a predatory pricing test.[66] This is convincing because these practices are indeed very comparable: secure amounts in rebate schemes equal the dominant (tying) product in the tying scheme; and the contestable amount equals the competitive (tied) product. The common principle to be applied to both types of pricing practices should be that it must remain possible for rivals to compete also for the competitive amount or product only.

---

[63] Also Maier-Rigaud and Vaigauskaite, *supra* note 26; F Maier-Rigaud, 'What has Time got to Do with it?' MPI Collective Goods Preprint 2005/3, http://papers.ssrn.com/sol3/papers.cfm?abstract_id=666722#PaperDownload (accessed 31 January 2008); *see* however *eg* Case 322/81 *Michelin v Commission* ('*Michelin I*') [1983] ECR 3461, para 81; Case T-203/1 *Michelin v Commission* ('*Michelin II*') [2003] ECR II-4071, para 88; Kallaugher and Sher, *supra* note 55, at 263; L Gyselen, 'Rebates: Competition on the Merits or Exclusionary Practice', in CD Ehlermann and I Atanasiu (eds), *European Competition Law Annual 2003: What is an Abuse of a Dominant Position?* (2006) 285; O'Donoghue, *supra* note 55.

[64] Discussion Paper, *supra* note 12, at para 153.

[65] Also Maier-Rigaud and Vaigauskaite, *supra* note 26.

[66] O'Donoghue and Padilla, *supra* note 20, at 505.

6.2   Tying and Bundling

Tying is only caught by Article 81 EC if there is a horizontal agreement between competitors to tie or bundle,[67] and such agreements are under normal circumstances prohibited per se. An individual tying agreement or practice adopted by a particular firm could thus only fall under Article 82 EC. Given the different scope of Articles 81 and 82 EC and the per-se condemnation of horizontal tying agreements, economic analysis cannot bring about a merging of regimes with regard to tying and bundling. Economic analysis, however, may achieve more coherence in the application of Article 82 EC to the different variants of this practice. In fact, economic analysis may further the understanding and acceptance that tying and bundling are or can be too fundamentally different to be assessed under the same standard. These two types of conduct offend against Article 82 EC in different ways, and they can also foreclose the market in different ways. It is therefore necessary, as a matter of coherence, to apply the right tests for identifying these different foreclosure effects, but also to apply the appropriate justification standards.

The three main variants to be distinguished in this context are the following.

First, there is genuine tying. This is a (if not the classic) leveraging abuse whose characteristic feature is that market power is used as a lever to force the buyer to also purchase a separate product. The three main sub-variants are contractual tying (the tying product is sold on the condition that the buyer also purchases the tied product), technical tying (interfaces restrict the use of secondary products made by rivals) and economic tying, that is, pure bundling (the two products are sold as a package only).

The second variant is mixed bundling, in which the buyer receives a discount for purchasing both products.

The third variant would be pure bundling without an associated price increase for the addition or integration of an additional product (otherwise it would be economic tying). Under Article 82 EC, the respective standards are still a bit unclear. This applies in particular to bundling.

For genuine tying, a per-se approach appears to have mostly been used in the decisional practice.[68] A possible explanation for this is that the

---

[67]   *See* also G Grill, in CO Lenz and KD Borchardt (eds), *EU- und EG-Vertrag* (4th edn, 2006) Art 81, para 34; *see* however H Schröter, in H von der Groeben and J Schwarze (eds), *Kommentar zum Vertrag über die Europäische Union und zur Gründung der Europäischen Gemeinschaft, Teil 2* (6th edn, 2006) Art 81, para 175.

[68]   *See eg* Commission Decision 88/138/EEC of 22 September 1987, Joined Cases No. IV/30.787 and IV/31.488 – *Eurofix-Bauco v Hilti* [1988] OJ L 65, p 19;

Commission – with the possible exception of *Microsoft*[69] – has only pursued rather clear-cut cases so far. In the Discussion Paper, however, the Commission now advocates an effects-based approach with regard to both tying and bundling.[70] This is in my view problematic, not only because tying is also an exploitative abuse,[71] but also because genuine tying is a leveraging offence,[72] which should be considered abusive irrespective of any foreclosure effect.[73] The crucial test thus is whether there are really two separate products involved. This should be a very dynamic, and consumer-demand-driven, concept, and it is in the context of this test that efficiencies created by tying could possibly be taken into account.

Mixed bundling is a sort of market structure abuse, that is, an abuse based on manipulating the dynamics of competition by foreclosing rivals from a significant portion of the market. The relevant effect is direct foreclosure and the test to be applied should accordingly be a predation test:[74] Does the price for the second product still cover (fully distributed) costs

---

Commission Decision 88/518/EEC of 19 October 1988, Case IV/30.178 – *Napier Brown/British Sugar* [1988] OJ L 284, p 41, Commission Decision 92/163/EEC of 24 July 1991, Case No IV/31.043 – *Tetra Pak II* [1992] OJ L 72, p 1; Commission Decision 2002/180/EC of 5 December 2001, Case No IV/37.859 – *De Post-La Poste* [2002] OJ L 61, p 32.

[69] Commission Decision of 24 May 2004, Case No COMP/C-3/37.792 – *Microsoft* [2007] OJ L 32, p 3

[70] Discussion Paper, *supra* note 12, at paras 182 *et seq.*

[71] The argument made in US jurisprudence and writing that tying is merely an alternative way of reaping the monopoly profit does not hold in the EU context because of the explicit prohibition of excessive prices.

[72] Where dominance, instead of superior business performance, is used to conquer a separate market.

[73] In such cases, a foreclosure effect will exist in most cases anyhow, but this likely foreclosure effect should be considered the reason and not the condition for the prohibition of tying arrangements; *see* also Eilmansberger, *supra* note 14, at Art 82, para 283; Schröter, *supra* note 14, at Art 82, para 240; Schröter, *supra* note 67, at Art 82, para 239; W Weiß, in C Calliess and M Ruffert (eds), *EUV-EGV, Kommentar* (3rd edn, 2007) Art 82, EG para 65; Möschel, *supra* note 14, at Art 82, para 203. For a different view, *see* M Dolmans and T Graf, 'Analysis of Tying Under Article 82 EC: The European Commission's Microsoft Decision in Perspective' (2004) 27 *World Comp* 225, 232.

[74] Commission practice has been strict so far; *see* Commission Decision 96/546/EC of 17 July 1996, Case No IV/35.337 – *Atlas* [1996] OJ L 239, p 23; XXVIth *Report on Competition Policy 1996*, pp 158, 159 – *IRI/Nielsen*; XXVIIth Report on Competition Policy 1997, pp 173, 174 – *Digital Equipment*. However, its Discussion Paper, *supra* note 12, at paras 189–95, now also includes a predation-like, cost-based test, but reliance on long-run incremental cost (LRIC), which is probably better than full distributed cost (FDC) because it measures profitability and intent, but is harder on less diversified rivals.

after the full discount has been deducted?[75] That appears to be the position of the Commission taken in its Discussion Paper.[76]

Pure bundling without price increase for the integration of an additional product or service does not present a leveraging issue either, because there are no additional sales. This is again a market-structure abuse. A per-se approach is thus excluded.[77] The structural effects, however, are different from those relevant in connection with mixed bundling. If the addition or integration of the secondary product does not entail a significant price increase, the purpose of this measure is obviously not to distort competition in the market for this secondary product (though this may have disastrous effects there as well), but to strengthen the market position of the dominant firm somewhere else. This might be the market for the dominant product,[78] or the markets adjacent to the bundled product.[79]

In the context of tying and bundling as well, a more diligent economic analysis will lead to a more differentiated analysis, and to a certain 'demerging' of standards. At the same time, however, this should bring about more coherence with other practices, giving rise to the same or sufficiently similar competition problems.

---

[75]   It has been suggested that to address the concern that rivals could not even match cost-covering prices for the second (competitive) product because the defendant's anti-competitive conduct prevented them from reaching an efficient scale, the test could be formulated so as to focus either on the costs of the defendant or those of the plaintiff. For example, the test could require the plaintiff to show that, to match the defendant's bundled discount, it would have been forced to price below its cost (DA Crane, 'DoJ/FTC Hearings On Loyalty Discounts', http://www.antitrustreview.com/files/DoJ-FTC%20Hearings.doc, accessed 31 January 2008).

[76]   Discussion Paper, *supra* note 12, at para 192. A bundle may be discounted in various ways. In the simplest case, a bundle AB consisting of two products A and B has a separate price that is lower than the sum of the stand-alone prices of A and B. In that case, the incremental price of product B is measured as the price of the bundle AB less the stand-alone price of product A. *See* also Crane, *supra* note 75: 'Another way of stating this is that a bundled discount is not unlawful unless the "effective price" of the competitive product is below cost, taking into account the discounts on the non-competitive products that consumers would forgo by buying the two products individually instead of in the package'. *See* also O'Donaghue and Padilla, *supra* note 20, at 505.

[77]   *See* also O'Donoghue and Padilla, *supra* note 20, at 510 *et seq.*

[78]   A relevant effect could therefore be predation if after the addition of the secondary product, the package is not cost-covering any more.

[79]   This type of abusive bundling appears to have been realized by Microsoft with the Media Player software: The Windows operating system is used as a sort of launch vehicle to disseminate the Media Player so widely that Microsoft would receive an immediate advantage, and is likely to become the dominant player, on markets for software written for such audio and video software.

7 CONCLUSION

The increased use of economic analysis has led, and should continue to lead, to more convergence between Articles 81 and 82 EC. Real scope for convergence, however, exists in certain areas only. As regards the application of Article 82 EC solely, a stronger reliance on effects-based rules may have the opposite effect, namely a more differentiated analysis and therefore a sort of 'demerging' of regimes, that is, a separation of the relevant tests. This, however, is a good development, because there may be a bit too much convergence (though not necessarily coherence) at the moment. This applies in particular to the tests applied to exclusive dealing, rebates, tying and bundling.

11. Convergence of competition law prohibitions: foundational issues

Michal S Gal*

1 INTRODUCTION

The increased role of economic analysis in competition law raises a host of interesting issues regarding the goals and foundations of competition law as well as their effects on competition rules. One such issue, addressed by Professor Eilmansberger in his comprehensive and thoughtful chapter, relates to the convergence of the prohibitions on restrictive agreements and unilateral restraints in light of a more economics-oriented approach that strives to increase consumer welfare.[1] The first part of this chapter addresses some of the issues raised in Professor Eilmansberger's chapter and goes a bit beyond it, mostly supplementing rather than contradicting it. Yet, as the language of the Treaty of Rome indicates, EC competition law is based on at least one additional foundation: fairness in market relations, which is sometimes viewed as contradictory to pure economic considerations. Accordingly, the second part of this chapter offers some preliminary thoughts with regard to the role of fairness in EC competition law at its incipiency and its relationship with the more economics-oriented approach.

---

* LL.B., LL.M., S.J.D. Associate Professor, Haifa University School of Law; Global Hauser Visiting Professor, NYU School of Law. Many thanks to Adi Eyal for most thoughtful comments. The second part of this chapter is part of the author's ongoing research on the subject of fairness in competition law. For this part, the author would like to thank Professors Drexl, Engel, Fikentscher, Hellwig, Mestmäcker, von Weizsäcker, and Möschel for most helpful discussions on the subject and Eran Fish and Benjamin D. Ullrich for superb research assistance. Many thanks to the Max Planck Institute for Research on Collective Goods, and especially Professors Hellwig and Engel for their wonderful hospitality while conducting this research. The research was supported by a grant from the GIF, the German-Israeli Foundation for Scientific Research and Development.
1 T Eilmansberger, 'Restrictive Agreements and Unilateral Restraints: Merging Regimes on Market Power and Exclusion', Chapter 10 in this volume.

2 CONVERGENCE BROUGHT ABOUT BY A MORE ECONOMICS-ORIENTED APPROACH

2.1 A Suggested Dichotomy

Let me begin my comments by suggesting a dichotomy: between convergence of logic and convergence of application. The former relates to the normative foundations of the prohibition while the latter relates to the actual rules applied in practice. Convergence on the former does not necessarily lead to convergence on the latter – it might well be that legal prohibitions converge with regard to the logic and rationale on which they are based, but still might be applied differently because the factual situation requires different legal solutions. I suggest that this is true with regard to the provisions regulating multilateral and unilateral conduct: while economic analysis brings about more convergence with regard to their rationales, there is less convergence on their application, because they relate to different factual settings. This distinction, in my view, explains most of the differences that are observed in practice, as elaborated below.

2.2 Exploitative Practices

Professor Eilmansberger makes a preliminary point that in exploitative practices there is not much convergence between the provisions of Articles 81 and 82. I would like to argue that such a convergence – of logic and, to some extent, also of application – already exists and is, at least in some sense, built into the system. This is because the prohibition against cartels is indirectly designed to limit market power, which enables exploitation in the first place. Prohibiting cartels that harm competition indirectly deals with exploitative practices. Furthermore, one of the conditions for approving a restrictive agreement is that consumers receive a 'fair share of the benefits'.[2] This condition was interpreted as requiring, inter alia, that the joint venture not exploit its newly created market power by charging exploitative prices. Most decisions focus on benefits to consumers in the form of lower prices or a more competitive industry in the long run. In *Synthetic Fibres,* for example, the Commission regarded as a benefit to consumers the fact that the agreement would result in a healthier, more competitive industry in the long run.[3] In addition, should the agreement create a dominant position for its parties, it will also be subject to the prohibition on exploitative practices

---

[2] Article 81(3) EC.
[3] Commission Decision 84/380/EEC of 4 July 1984, Case No COM/IV/30.810 – *Synthetic fibres* [1984] OJ L 207, p 17, paras 39–41.

included in Article 82 through the application of the doctrine on collective dominance.[4] Accordingly, although Article 81 does not directly deal with exploitative practices, it does deal with it indirectly. Thus there is already some convergence on the issue of exploitative practices.

Yet, in accordance with modern economic thinking, there is a basic conceptual difference with regard to exploitative practices between a joint venture and a dominant firm, and thus convergence on exploitative practices should never be complete. This difference is better acknowledged in the US, but has had some effect on European competition-law thinking as well.[5] In the case of a dominant firm, there exists a market-dynamics-based argument for exploitation that does not exist – at least not to the same extent – in the case of a joint venture. In the words of the US Supreme Court in *Trinko*: 'The opportunity to charge monopoly prices – at least for a short period – is what attracts "business acumen" in the first place; it induces risk taking that produces innovation and growth. To safeguard the incentive to innovate, the possession of monopoly power will not be held unlawful unless it is accompanied by an element of anticompetitive conduct.'[6] Such a consideration might be weaker in the case of some joint ventures, because they are not so much a product of market Darwinism and unilateral achievements, but rather they result from a change in the market structure by a joint decision of their members. Moreover, given that the approval of the joint venture by the competition authorities might strengthen it by enabling it to adopt legal measures to overcome the internal forces that might otherwise break it down, the argument that by prohibiting exploitative pricing we are taking away the fruits of the market struggle and thereby reducing the incentives of firms to compete might in some joint ventures be weaker than in the case of a monopoly. To sum up, there exists a difference in logic in regulating exploitative prices of restrictive agreements and dominant firms. Yet this difference is one of degree rather than an absolute one – it requires that we generally place fewer limitations on high prices charged by dominant firms than on those charged by joint ventures.

---

[4]   *Eg* Joined Cases T-68/89, T-77/89 and T-78/89 *Società Italiano Vetro v Commission* [1992] ECR II-1403; JT Lang, 'Oligopolies and Collective Dominance in Community Antitrust Law', in BE Hawk (ed), *International Antitrust Law and Policy* (2002) 269.

[5]   The UK Guidelines on abusive practices, for example, take into account this dynamic consideration in determining whether a price is abusive or not. For the different trans-Atlantic views on excessive pricing, *see* MS Gal, 'Monopoly Pricing as an Antitrust Offense in the U.S. and the EC: Two Systems of Belief about Monopoly?' (2004) 49 *Antitrust Bull* 343.

[6]   *Verizon Communications Inc. v Law Offices of Curtis v Trinko Ltd* 540 US 398 (2004).

2.3 Exclusionary Practices

Turning to exploitative practices, on a general level of abstraction the prohibitions contained in both Articles are quite similar in terms of the impact of economic thinking on the scope of the law and the rules of application. Both prohibitions attempt – at least in theory – to differentiate between the 'hard-core' cases, in which harm to competition is so evident that there is no justification to spend additional resources in order to verify their harm, and all other cases, in which economic teachings demonstrate that harm is not so evident, so that such cases should be analysed individually in order to verify their actual impact on the market. In the former case, the law uses economic analysis as a basis and rationale for the creation of legal presumptions of harm. This concept is apparent both in Article 81 (especially in the case law that interprets its provisions), as well as in Article 82 (in the wording of the law and the interpretation and application of the examples enumerated therewith).

When one moves beyond this level of normative abstraction, however, there is much to be said for the legal convergence of the two Articles. Not necessarily one towards the other, but rather both in a similar direction, which attempts to carve out more carefully those cases in which harm to competition is so self-evident that there is a justification for a legal presumption of harm. Although in recent years there has been a move – in the courts and the Commission – to base legal rules on more rigorous economic analysis, both Articles still need more careful 'carving out' of legal prohibitions. Currently, both Articles are much too wide in their scope of application and much too harsh, in some cases, in the legal presumptions they apply. For example, the per-se prohibition of agreements whose 'object' is to limit competition is much too wide to be justified on economic grounds.[7] Similarly, the legal presumptions of abuse included in Article 82 are also often interpreted much too broadly. There is, accordingly, still much scope for convergence.

Let me focus on those cases whose 'object' is assumed to be the limitation of competition and which are therefore subject to a per-se prohibition. While Professor Eilmansberger does not believe there is much room for convergence on such issues, given that economic analysis has so far not been applied to them, in my view, such prohibitions exhibit probably the most important scope for convergence. Economic analysis is most important *not* in those cases in which economic analysis has already for some time shaped the legal

---

[7] *Eg* V Korah, 'EEC Competition Policy – Legal Form or Economic Efficiency?' (1986) 39 *CLP* 85; C Bright, 'EU Competition Policy: Rules, Objectives and Deregulation' (1996) 16 *OJLS* 535.

rules, but rather in those cases in which such analysis has so far encountered a closed door. The Treaty does not specifically provide which types of conduct have an 'object' of limiting competition. Rather, the scope of this prohibition is determined by the courts and is informed by the purpose of the Treaty. Thus there is no unbreakable legal barrier to economic analysis in order to shape the scope of the prohibition. When, on its face, the agreement seems to have a wider object than simply fixing prices or controlling production, then a per-se prohibition should not apply. In fact, some EC cases can be interpreted as applying such a rule. As Bellamy and Child point out, where joint ventures are involved, the Commission has relied entirely on the 'effects' test.[8] Indeed, in cases in which the agreement is primarily intended to achieve some pro-competitive purpose, it seems difficult to regard the agreement as having 'the object' of restricting competition.

It is noteworthy that the requirement that the 'object' of the agreement not be a restriction on competition is much easier to change by interpretation than other legal requirements. For example, Article 81(3) requires, as one of the conditions for approving a joint venture, that it not afford the undertakings concerned the ability to eliminate competition in respect of a substantial part of goods or services. This condition is an inefficient one, as it might prevent welfare-enhancing joint ventures just because they concentrate the market even further. Yet it is much more difficult to overcome without changing the wording of the law. Accordingly, convergence in such cases would be much more difficult.

2.4   Identification of Abusive Conduct

I also want to consider the thought-provoking suggestions of Professor Eilmansberger to change the requirements for finding an abuse of a dominant position. The identification of abusive behaviour is one of the most difficult questions in competition law, as it often cannot be easily distinguished from competitive conduct that benefits consumers in the long run. Professor Eilmansberger proposes to cancel some requirements and add others in order to move the analysis closer to an effects-based one. He suggests cancelling the requirement that the conduct be fair and that it not be discriminatory, and adding the following requirements:

- The plaintiff should prove that, under the concrete market circumstances, the practice at issue is capable of generating a foreclosure effect.

---

[8]   C Bellamy and G Child, *European Community Law of Competition* (5th edn, 2001) 2-099.

- Proof should focus on the structural effect, in the sense that the basic conditions under which the competitive process unfolds (and which define the dynamics of competition) be protected from manipulation by the dominant firm. A lasting change in the dynamics and conditions of competition is required.
- A business practice with the potential to bring about a structural change should be considered abusive only if it can be shown that it aimed at that result.

Let me respond to each of these considerations in turn.

Elimination of fairness considerations   Fairness is squarely included in Article 82, which provides that when a dominant firm sets 'unfair prices and trade conditions' it will be considered an abuse. However, fairness considerations do not necessarily come into play in all other types of abuse. Indeed, most exclusionary practices – as differentiated from exploitative ones – do not require that the conduct be 'unfair' in order to be considered abusive. Thus there is no real need to eliminate this condition so that it will not stand in the way of an efficiency-based economic analysis of exclusionary practices. But even if fairness were a condition in all abusive practices (and one can argue that it underlies all the Treaty's provisions), it is not apparent that fairness would necessarily clash with the prohibition of exclusionary practices. Rather, under some theories of fairness, it may converge with efficiency considerations. One can maybe learn by analogy from the interpretation of the requirement in Article 81(3) that consumers receive a 'fair share'. In *REIMS II*,[9] for example, the Commission acknowledged that prices might rise for some consumers, but it was satisfied that other benefits – for example the elimination of cross-subsidization in the postal sector that would allow for more competition in one sector and improved service standards – were sufficient to offset the higher-price effects. Accordingly, fairness considerations did not stand in the way of a more efficient industry. I shall return to this point later.

Elimination of the non-discrimination requirement   Indeed, discrimination might increase welfare. This is the case, for example, where discrimination allows the dominant firm to supply its product to more consumers, rather than set one price that might not enable some consumers to meet their demand. Yet the non-discrimination requirement was one of the most important principles on which the Treaty was founded. Indeed, in the

---

[9]   Commission Decision 1999/695/EEC of 15 September 1999, Case No IV/36.748 – *REIMS II* [1999] OJ L 275, p 17.

earliest drafts of the Treaty, a wide discrimination prohibition based on nationality was included in the competition section.[10] This prohibition was later abandoned, not because it was considered to be unimportant, but because the general prohibition against discrimination was deemed to be wide enough to include cases of anti-competitive discriminatory conduct.[11] Thus the discrimination prohibition is a basic tenet of the Treaty. It is note-worthy that some of the Treaty's requirements reduce the scope of the pro-hibition, for example by requiring that discrimination place the trading parties 'at a competitive disadvantage'.[12] This requirement might be inter-preted to limit the cases that fall under the prohibition to those in which dis-crimination creates an advantage not otherwise enjoyed by the competitor. Yet it might still prevent some types of efficiency-enhancing conduct from taking place. However, given the general goals of the Treaty, it seems that a non-discrimination requirement will not be easily removed or limited.

Proof of capability to generate anti-competitive consequences   Professor Eilmansberger suggests that the plaintiff should not be required to prove the anti-competitive consequences in a specific case, but rather to prove the potential of such conduct to generate anti-competitive harm. I gener-ally agree with this suggestion. This is because in many cases it might be extremely difficult to prove that the conduct did indeed have anti-competitive effects, and thus placing such a burden on the plaintiff might create too high a hurdle to prevent abusive conduct. For example, it might well be that the abusive conduct was stopped in its incipiency, or that market conditions changed materially and unexpectedly after the conduct was contemplated, so that it did not actually have the effect that it would have had otherwise. At the same time, however, when the effects of a certain type of conduct involve a high degree of uncertainty and require a more case-specific analysis, such a detailed analysis should be required. Also, specific harm should be proven in private civil damage cases.

Proof of structural effects   As Professor Eilmansberger shows, European courts have focused on structural effects, to ensure that the prohibition cap-tures those cases in which the dynamics of competition are harmed in the long run. This requirement is a sound and important one, precisely because the line between use and abuse is often blurred and we wish to prohibit only those cases in which harm to competition is evident.

---

[10]   R Schulze and T Hoeren (eds), *Dokumente zum Europäischen Recht, Vol. 3: Kartellrecht (bis 1957)* (2000) documents 54, 64 and 68.
[11]   *Id*, documents 70 and 71.
[12]   Article 82(c) EC.

Intent requirement[13]   Many jurisdictions require anti-competitive intent to misuse market power as a fundamental underpinning of a violation.[14] Intent, however, is an uncertain indicator, as competitive conduct is also motivated by the immediate objective of winning sales from competitors and gaining monopoly profits. Exclusionary purpose thus follows almost inevitably when there is use of market power. For example, a firm must anticipate that by exploiting economies of scale it would eliminate rivals. It would be surprising if the firm did not do so with that end in mind, as elimination of rivals is a natural consequence of expanding production to reduce costs. Moreover, even if a dominant firm had no specific anti-competitive intent (or such intent could not be proven), the exclusionary practice should still be prohibited. Otherwise the goal of abuse-of-dominance provisions, to limit the creation of artificial barriers to competition, would be inhibited. The assumption that a firm intends the results of its conduct does not add much to the analysis. The focus should thus be on the economic effects of a conduct rather than on its intent. Nonetheless, proof of pro-competitive purpose may be useful in proving the legitimacy of the conduct by a monopolist. Also, the lack of anti-competitive intent should be factored into the remedies granted. Otherwise, the unclarity regarding the legal status of many types of conduct, given the case-specific analysis required, might reduce the incentives of firms to become dominant or of dominant firms to engage in pro-competitive conduct.

3   THE ROLE OF FAIRNESS AT THE TREATY'S INCEPTION

3.1   The Concept of Fairness in Competition Law in General

Let me now turn to the issue of the role of fairness in EC competition law. In recent years, competition-law analysis has generally focused on efficiency: whether or not the legal rules increase economic efficiency in the market. The debate has largely centred on what sort of balance between the different types of efficiencies – allocative, productive and dynamic efficiency – should be achieved, and whether the existing prohibitions achieve such goals. Yet the historic and philosophical roots of competition laws reveal

---

[13]   This paragraph builds upon MS Gal, *Competition Policy for Small Market Economies* (2003) chapter 3.

[14]   *Eg* Sections 78 and 79 Canadian Competition Act 1986; *Spectrum Sports v McQuillan* 506 US 447, 113 S Ct 884 (1993).

another element that shaped the ideology and the legal tools included in them: the concept of fairness. In fact, from the earliest times until very recently, competition law has been chiefly a response to calls for fairness in economic relationships, rather than a vehicle for promoting economic efficiency. Even when fairness is not specifically referred to in the law, courts sometimes apply it to justify their decisions, either directly or indirectly. The question is thus what role fairness plays in competition law, and whether it will not stand in the way of the convergence that the first part of this chapter focused upon.

Despite the fact that many jurisdictions refer to fairness in their competition laws, what fairness is and what it means in the context of competition law is still an open question. Fairness is not a single-valued concept. Rather, it is a flexible one that can incorporate different meanings, depending on the ideology and the goals that are sought to be achieved. Fairness ties into deep notions of morality and justice, often stemming from different religious, sociological and political concepts of how societal interactions should be conducted. For example, fairness can relate to distributive justice, to ensure that all consumers will be granted a relatively equal share of the welfare pie created by trade and that the dominant firm does not charge supra-competitive prices. Alternatively, fairness might relate to the creation of equal conditions among producers that compete in the market, even when one firm has a strong comparative advantage over its competitors. Fairness is thus derived from the perceived rules of the market game and may vary among cultures and time periods. It is part of one's jurisculture. In this sense, fairness has 'nationality', in contrast to economic terms, which generally have no cultural dimensions or geographic boundaries.

The meaning of fairness in market relationships thus goes to the heart of the competition-law doctrine, to its goals and its conceptions. It shapes the dialogue between law and economics in the antitrust sphere. Yet, surprisingly, such questions have not been analysed in depth. One of the only accounts is Professor Gerber's article, which serves as an excellent starting point.[15] What I seek to do in my current research is to attempt to answer these questions in depth. The first step, on which I would like to report briefly herewith, focuses on the ideological roots that shaped EC competition law at its inception.

---

[15]   DJ Gerber, 'Fairness in Competition Law: European and U.S. Experience', Paper presented at a Conference on Fairness and Asian Competition Laws, 5 March 2004, Kyoto, Japan, http://www.kyotogakuen.ac.jp/%7Eo_ied/information/fairness_in_competition_law.pdf (assessed 31 January 2008).

3.2 The Treaty of Rome

The concept of fair competition is an important foundation of the Treaty. The Treaty's preamble refers to fair competition when stating that 'the removal of existing obstacles calls for concerted action in order to guarantee steady expansion, balanced trade and *fair competition*' (emphasis added). In addition, both competition Articles refer to fairness. Article 81 requires, as one of the conditions for approving a restrictive agreement, that it grant consumers a *fair* share of the benefits generated by it. Article 82 provides that the setting of *unfair* prices or trading conditions by a dominant firm is considered abusive.

Why, then, did the framers of the Treaty refer to fairness in all the provisions that related to competition law, and what did they mean by that? Let me start by pointing to a few relevant historical facts. Previous supranational treaties did not mention fairness considerations. The Havana Charter (which was never ratified but was meant to be an international agreement) and the European Coal and Steel Community (ECSC) Agreement did not mention fairness considerations. Indeed, the Treaty of Rome is the first supranational agreement on competition to include such a concept.

Moreover, the first drafts of the Treaty did not mention fairness. The wording of Article 82 is especially interesting. Following a laconic first draft, some of the Member States required that examples of abuse be included in the Treaty, and thus an example was given of 'setting prices and trade conditions' by a dominant firm.[16] This formula was, of course, very problematic, as it was wide enough to include any economic conduct by the dominant firm. It was thus limited in later drafts, by including the requirement that such prices and trade conditions be 'unfair'.

Another fact of historical importance is that the only Member State that had a viable competition law when the Treaty was signed was Germany. Although the German Competition Law was only enacted a few months before the Treaty (previous German competition laws did not have much effect on the market), debates regarding the scope of the legal prohibitions to be contained in it lasted quite a few years and were well known to the German public and – more importantly for our purposes – to the German delegates who negotiated the Treaty. In fact, due to his relative understanding of competition-law issues, Hans von der Groeben, a German delegate who later became the first Commissioner for Competition, was chosen to lead the negotiating team that was to agree on competition

---

[16]   Schulze and Hoeren, *supra* note 10, documents 54, 59 and 64.

provisions. The German law contained a reference to fairness in its provisions.[17] Indeed, the Germans were the ones to suggest the inclusion of fairness considerations in the Treaty, and their suggestion was accepted by all.[18] The Messina Conference's Committee on the Common Market, which started the negotiations on the Treaty, agreed that the goal of the future European competition rules should not only be to ensure effective competition, but also fair competition.[19]

So – what are the ideological roots that shaped the concept of fairness, and what did the Treaty's founding fathers mean when they referred to fairness? Several normative foundations are worth mentioning.

The first, and probably the most important of all, is the German ordoliberal concept of economic constitution.[20] Ordoliberal theories were developed by the Freiburg School of German academics before and immediately after the Second World War. Against the backdrop of economic and social chaos and amassed power, the ordoliberals attempted to create a tolerant and humane society that would protect human dignity and personal freedom while creating a framework for the well-functioning of the market. The ordoliberal ideology stressed the need for an economic constitution that would limit the convergence of private economic power in the interest of a free and fair political and social order. Competition was regarded as a constituent element of the liberal order of the community. Such an order includes the freedom to autonomously decide on economic activity, to freely choose one's partner in an economic transaction and to have the discretion of making offers to those partners and entering into an agreement with them. Cartels and dominant firms were regarded as limiting these options. Thus, the ordoliberals posited the need to regulate the conduct of such firms by requiring them to act in a manner consistent with a competitive economic model. They also stressed the goal of fairness, which was understood as protecting the individual's economic freedom of action as a value in itself against any impairment of market power. This applied both to consumers as well as to competitors, to exploitative practices as well as

---

[17]   Article 26(2) of the German Act against Restraints of Competition 1957 states that '[m]arket dominating enterprises . . . may neither directly or indirectly unfairly (*"unbillig"*) hinder another enterprise in a business activity which is customarily accessible to enterprises of the same kind, nor without justifiable cause directly or indirectly treat it differently from other enterprises . . .'.

[18]   Schulze and Hoeren, *supra* note 10, documents 54, 59 and 64.

[19]   H von der Groeben, *Deutschland und Europa in einem unruhigen Jahrhundert: Erlebnisse und Betrachtungen* (1995) 275.

[20]   For materials on ordoliberal thinking, *eg* A Peacock and H Willgerodt (eds), *Germany's Social Market Economy: Origins and Evolution* (1989); A Peacock and H Willgerodt (eds), *German Neo-Liberals and the Social Market Economy* (1989).

to exclusionary conduct that harmed the economic opportunity of consumers and competitors. This led some ordoliberals to suggest that dominant firms had to act 'as if' they were operating in a competitive market. It is this concept of fairness that to a large degree shaped German thinking in the 1950s on fairness in market relationships and that influenced their negotiators of the Treaty.

The second theoretical root is the civil-law concepts of just price and usury, according to which a price that exceeds a certain limit is unlawful. The idea of imposing restrictions on certain forms of conduct of economically dominant firms can be traced back to Roman times, where sanctions were imposed on individuals or groups who 'cornered' a market and used the power achieved in that monopoly position to drive up prices for consumers.[21] This idea influenced medieval thinking. During medieval times the concepts of 'just price' and 'usury'[22] emerged, which were both rooted in Canonical law, and established the proposition that a price can be 'unjust', as determined by the legal system. The charging of 'unjust' prices was labelled morally wrong and abhorrent to the religious tenets of society.

The prohibition against usury was based on the biblical prohibition of taking biting interest from the defenseless poor. It applied to situations in which the parties did not have equal bargaining power and one side exploited the need, carelessness or inexperience of the other in order to gain a pecuniary advantage that disproportionately exceeded the value of the performance granted in return. Usury was perceived as unjust and dishonest conduct, and therefore intrinsically unlawful. Banning it thus limited the ability to achieve private gain based on exploiting the economic weaknesses of others.[23] The doctrine of just price was also based on exploitation of market conditions. The just-price doctrine was linked to the medieval concept of social hierarchy and corresponded to a reasonable charge that would enable the producer to live and to support his family on a scale suitable to his station in life, but not to gain more and better his situation.[24] These doctrines must be understood in the light of medieval life. Medieval producers and consumers had limited options to trade. This is why it was important that the monopolist, who had the *ability* to take more, had a special responsibility to act in a fair manner and not exploit his power.

---

[21] DJ Gerber, 'Law and the Abuse of Economic Power in Europe' (1987) 62 *Tulane L Rev* 57, 60 *et seq*, notes 10 *et seq*.

[22] *Eg* B Nelson, *The Idea of Usury* (2nd edn, 1969); J Noonman, *The Scholastic Analysis of Usury* (1957).

[23] *Id.*

[24] *Eg* R de Roover, 'The Concept of the Just Price: Theory and Economic Policy' (1958) 18 *J Econ Hist* 418.

These concepts were incorporated into the Corpus Juris Civilis, which served as a basis for law and legal education throughout much of Europe from the 11th century until well into the 19th century. These ideas on unfair prices helped set the stage for the concept of abuse, which builds upon the idea that legal processes can determine whether a price is fair.

A third source, which is tied to the second, is the civil-law concept of good faith in contractual relationships. The European doctrine of *bona fide* has its roots in Roman law and is part of the French *Code civile* that was also applied in the Benelux countries. It is also part of German and Italian law. The doctrine is based on the idea that parties to an agreement should act in good faith towards one another, not exploiting the weaknesses of the other to their advantage.

The last source that I would like to mention is the ideas of a social contract that were prominent in France as well as in other European countries. Under some theories, fairness was understood as part of an implied contract between all market players (including producers, consumers and the public authorities) regarding the 'rules of the game' in the marketplace, which are set in accordance with the societal values that exist at the time. One such possible social contract is based on an agreement that every producer is allowed to become a monopolist, but is not allowed to enjoy profits beyond some preset limit or to use his power to exclude other, more efficient producers. The State creates a setting for the game by creating and enforcing property rights and contractual obligations and by limiting the creation of artificial barriers to competition. On what basis could such a social contract be justified? One possible basis is a conceptual agreement between all relevant players prior to the beginning of the game and before each player knows what role he will be playing in it.[25] To justify the fairness requirements one must therefore assume that even a successful monopolist might have chosen to prohibit unfair conduct if asked ex ante, before he knew whether he would be a producer, and if so how successful he would be.

It was with those different and sometimes conflicting notions of fairness that the framers of the Treaty came to the negotiating table. However, even if they did not share the exact concept of fairness in market relationships, fairness played an extremely important role in the framing of the Treaty. Moreover, the flexibility of the concept was what made it easier to accept a supranational competition law.

---

[25]   Such ideas are nowadays linked to John Rawls. Yet ideas of a social contract that are created behind a 'veil of ignorance' were prominent much earlier. As Rawls himself observes, 'the notion of the veil of ignorance is implicit . . . in Kant's ethics'; J Rawls, *A Theory of Justice* (1971) 140 *et seq*.

As already mentioned, fairness is a highly flexible notion. Apart from a few core cases in which all would agree that the conduct was 'unfair', it does not necessarily tie its enforcer to one concept of market relations. It is broad enough to be used either in a command-and-control model as the French envisaged, or in a more hands-off model as the Germans envisaged. This fact had several important implications. First, it enabled the framers not to commit to one economic or legal view of market relationships, but rather to fill the prohibitions with different content as the law evolved. It must be remembered that the Treaty's negotiators were administrators – albeit high-level ones – who wanted primarily to create the general framework, so it could start operating, and then enable it to evolve as it developed. Indeed, the documents surrounding the negotiations of the Treaty were, until recently, not publicized. This was done purposefully, so as not to tie the Commission and the courts to the views held by members of the negotiating teams. Second, fairness served an additional purpose, as the Treaty was intentionally designed so that it would be very difficult to change its provisions. Including fairness in the law allowed a change in views without requiring a change in the wording of the law.

In addition, fairness has legitimizing power – who could object to fairness in market relationships? It thus made it much easier to pass a competition law when the law was deemed to promote fairness. Furthermore, fairness is even more important in a supranational relationship than in a national one. Countries may well be more willing to concede their power to a central institution if it is perceived as operating under fair procedures and applying fair rules. Fairness reduces fears of exploitation and abuse by foreign companies. Moreover, whereas in a domestic context fears of abuse can be at least partly addressed by redistribution through the tax system and by national-champion arguments, such arguments have no relevance in a supranational context. Fairness thus becomes much more important when one moves beyond an organic unity. To conclude, it seems that fairness served its mission well, as it contributed to the enactment of the Treaty and to its success.

4   CONCLUSION

An economics-oriented approach that furthers efficiency and consumer welfare seems to be emerging as a major guiding light of EC competition law. Yet such an approach still has a long way to go in order to shape EC competition rules. As was argued in this chapter, there are still many options for convergence – mostly convergence of application but sometimes also convergence of logic – of the different competition-law prohibitions included in the Treaty, towards a more economics-oriented approach.

Still, economic efficiency is not the only value advanced by the Treaty. Fairness considerations are squarely included in all of its competition-law provisions. This chapter has thus attempted to sketch some of the notions that shaped the concept of fairness at its inception. While fairness is a flexible concept and was not tied down to one set of societal values, it may well be argued that the concept of fairness held by the framers of the Treaty might have clashed with economic efficiency, at least to some extent. This is because limitations on prices charged by dominant undertakings might limit dynamic motivations to become dominant by investing in better productive technologies or in the creation of better products. Yet, as argued, fairness served its goal well and was essential for shaping an agreement on competition rules, even if it was later difficult to apply in practice.

The question still remains what fairness in EC competition law means today. Does it, indeed, clash with efficiency, and if so, to what extent? My initial intuition is that fairness does not have to clash with efficiency, as both can be interpreted as ensuring that markets are kept open in the sense that no artificial barriers to the entry or expansion of more efficient competitors are created by incumbents. This notion of fairness fits well with current philosophies of market relations. Yet it should be determined whether it serves well the legacy of the Treaty's framers. This study is beyond the scope of this chapter. It is the focus of my current research, on which I hope to report in future publications.

12. Efficiencies in merger analysis: alchemy in the age of empiricism?

Thomas L Greaney*

1 INTRODUCTION

One is hard-pressed to find in law an undertaking more fraught with uncertainty than the application of the efficiencies defence in merger analysis. Generalist fact finders (judges) and politically attuned government officials (prosecutors and regulators) are charged with two Herculean tasks: (1) predicting the outcome of organic changes in business enterprises and (2) comparing the magnitude of those changes to the equally uncertain amount of harm to future competition that the transaction will cause. Given the enormous, perhaps intractable, uncertainty of this inquiry, it is therefore paradoxical that many of the strongest advocates for strengthening the role of efficiencies analysis in merger reviews are self-described proponents of bringing a 'new empiricism' to antitrust analysis.[1]

This chapter focuses on the tensions inherent in incorporating an efficiencies defence (or evaluating efficiencies as part of the appraisal of mergers) and maintaining the rigour and impartiality promised by proponents of the 'empirical' approach. This argument should not be misconstrued as a brief for abandoning the efficiencies inquiry altogether. Rather, it is, first, an appeal for candour (and humility) by those undertaking the inquiry; and second, it is a brief for constraining discretion by imposing

---

* Chester A. Myers Professor, Saint Louis University School of Law.
[1] For example, former FTC chairman Timothy Muris has contended that merger law should not rely on presumptions and economic theory alone. Questioning presumptions that increased concentration harms competition, 'without specific evidence relating to the precise characteristics of the industry under review . . . the current state of empirical work does not justify the conclusion . . . that challenged mergers are likely to increase price.' *See* TJ Muris, 'The Government and Merger Efficiencies: Still Hostile after all these Years' (1999) 7 *George Mason U L Rev* 729 (contending the government give more weight to efficiencies in those cases lacking clear factual evidence underpinning the presumption of a competitive concern).

more clearly delineated presumptive rules of law on judges and insisting on greater transparency by agencies in deciding whether to challenge mergers.

2 EFFICIENCY ANALYSIS IN AMERICAN MERGER CASES: A BRIEF HISTORY

The tenor of early antitrust treatments of efficiencies in merger cases ranged from suspicion to outright disfavour. Prompted by Supreme Court dicta, courts occasionally went so far as to view efficiencies as an aggravating rather than a mitigating factor. Whether based on legislative history, the belief (in the words of Judge Learned Hand) that 'great industrial consolidations are inherently undesirable', empathy for small producers and entrepreneurs, or worries about the political and social risks of concentrated power, suspicion warranted legal rules foreclosing consideration of efficiencies as a grounds for mergers. Today this outlook may seem quaint and long outmoded. The US federal enforcement agencies (the Department of Justice and the Federal Trade Commission) have explicitly recognized efficiencies as a possible defence to otherwise anticompetitive mergers for at least 30 years. Moreover, the triumph of the 'efficiency school' in informing the interpretation of the Sherman Act and shaping its doctrinal landscape for assessments of restraints of trade is indisputable.

Yet when one examines the case law and prosecutorial decisions in the American merger context, one finds that *in practice* efficiencies analysis follows a curious pattern. Despite protestations of the centrality of the issue for sound economic analysis, the case law in the US fails to reveal a single case in which efficiencies alone persuaded a court to permit an otherwise anticompetitive merger to go forward. It is not the case, however, that efficiency claims have simply failed to capture the attention of judicial fact finders. Indeed, conscious avoidance offers a better explanation. A well-recognized pattern of courts and the FTC is that efficiencies are cited as an 'add on' justification for finding that a merger was otherwise benign and the absence of efficiencies is noted only to support other findings that a merger will lessen competition. Whether courts are overwhelmed or intimidated by the task at hand or view the efficiencies question as intractable or not worth the considerable resources needed to appraise it accurately, one cannot escape the conclusion that courts do not place the issue at the forefront of issues they need to carefully explore.

At the same time, one finds considerable enthusiasm for the task expressed by federal enforcers and their staffs of economists when examining mergers informally, especially at the clearance stage. For at least two decades, Assistant Attorney Generals at the Department of Justice and FTC Commissioners have taken pains to give assurances that they do indeed take efficiencies into account at the evaluation stage in making the decision whether to challenge a merger. Moreover, they are quick to point out that the efficiencies defence has been outcome-determinative in a number of decisions to allow concentrative mergers to go forward. The casual observer might find this a curious state of affairs. At the investigatory stage, even with modern disclosure and discovery tools available after 'second requests' for information are filed under the Hart-Scott-Rodino law, enforcers lack detailed economic evidence about claimed economies that are produced in litigation. There is little doubt that the quantum of evidence, quality of sources, and, as discussed below, standards for evaluation are markedly different at the clearance stage than after an adversarial hearing. Yet that is where the defence has its most impact, while fully litigated adversarial proceedings never result in determining the outcome of cases.

3 THE PATH AND INFLUENCE OF ECONOMIC THINKING ON EFFICIENCY ANALYSIS IN MERGER CASES

The economic underpinnings for explicitly incorporating efficiencies into merger analysis can be traced to Oliver Williamson's influential article '*Economies as an Antitrust Defense: The Welfare Tradeoffs*', which threw down the gauntlet for enforcers: 'If neither the courts nor the enforcement agencies are sensitive to [efficiency] considerations, the system fails to meet a basic test of economic rationality. And without this the whole enforcement system lacks defensible standards and becomes suspect.'[2] Assumptions about demand elasticities and other factors led many to adopt working assumptions that rectangles (surpluses resulting from efficiencies) were likely to be larger than triangles (deadweight welfare losses) in conducting the welfare trade-off. At a minimum, the possibility that in a not insignificant proportion of cases empirical examination by courts would reveal that efficiencies outweighed potential harms led a chorus of academics and politically appointed agency heads to support adding an efficiencies defence to Clayton Act jurisprudence.

---

[2] OE Williamson, 'Economies as an Antitrust Defense: The Welfare Tradeoffs' (1968) 58 *Am Econ Rev* 18.

Although it remains influential and is frequently cited, the Williamsonian model has been sharply criticized for a variety of shortcomings both conceptual and practical. As to estimating effects in homogeneous product markets, analysis based on assumptions of uniform price setting is largely unrealistic given that firms negotiate prices with customers and other market realities are ignored. In addition, the simplified trade-off model assumes that the merger takes place in a perfectly competitive market; when applied to markets already distorted by pre-existing market power, the potential reductions in social welfare from deadweight losses are greater.[3] Economists have noted that other important qualifications include the need to account for 'dynamic efficiencies'. Roberts and Salop have noted that efficiencies in some industries diffuse readily and that factor has important implications for trade-off analyses.[4] Further, ideally the trade-off calculus would include some measure of a merger's impact on the incentives (and hence probability) of inducing greater or lesser innovation. Finally and perhaps most critically, the model needs to be refined and qualified for application to heterogeneous products.

4   FEDERAL GOVERNMENT MERGER GUIDELINES

Revising an explication of their merger enforcement policies (albeit not committing themselves to adhering strictly to them in litigation), the FTC and Department of Justice issued an important amendment of their Merger Guidelines in 1997.[5] Notably, they recognize efficiencies as a defense to an otherwise objectionable merger only if of specified quality and sufficient magnitude to ensure that the post-market price will not increase. The guidelines enunciate first, a three part test to determine whether claimed efficiencies are 'cognizable': they must be (1) analytically valid, (2) verifiable and (3) merger specific. Those efficiencies clearing this hurdle will then be balanced (after a fashion) against the anticompetitve effects of the merger to determine the merger's net impact on price.

---

[3]   PE Areeda and H Hovenkamp, *Antitrust Law*, Vol IVA (2006).
[4]   GL Roberts and SC Salop, 'Efficiencies in Dynamic Merger Analysis' (1996) 19 *World Comp* 5.
[5]   US Department of Justice and Federal Trade Commission, Horizontal Merger Guidelines, 2 April 1992 (revised 8 April 1997), http://www.usdoj.gov/atr/public/guidelines/hmg.htm (accessed 31 January 2008).

5 UNCERTAINTIES IN APPLYING EFFICIENCY ANALYSES

Efficiency analysis poses an almost endless number of conundrums and real world difficulties in application. This chapter next surveys some of the principal uncertainties that are particularly likely to undermine the hopes for an empirical foundation for efficiency appraisals. The claim advanced is that the problems associated with efficiency evaluations are distinct from and more severe than those encountered in other areas of antitrust inquiry, while also being less susceptible to empirical verification.

5.1 Uncertainties Inherent in Ex Ante Evaluations

Virtually all merger challenges are brought before the fact. The ex ante evaluations required for analysing efficiencies confront multiple sources of uncertainty. Beyond the obvious difficulties inherent in foreseeing any future events, several problems peculiar to the posture of these inquiries should be noted. In many respects, the information needed to make an informed prediction is unavailable because it is unavailable to the parties themselves. In a yet-to-be consummated merger, the parties may be restricted in the degree to which they can share information, or may be unwilling to do so before consummation for business or legal reasons. Because the realization of efficiencies may be contingent on the presence of a variety of conditions within the merging firms, many important facts are unknowable ex ante. For example, corporate 'culture', learning curves, personality conflicts, impediments to knowledge transfers, and a host of other factors may limit the magnitude and feasibility of synergistic benefits flowing from a merger.

The procedural aspects of merger analyses also tend to impede acquisition of information that can be relied upon to support reliable predictions. The merging parties are the source of the most useful information, but have clear incentives to shade or conceal full disclosure of damaging proof. A central problem is that efficiencies claims lack adversarial perspective. In the case of pre-merger clearances, the assertions of efficiencies savings do not undergo the scrutiny afforded by litigation (testimony under oath, cross-examination, etc). Even in litigated cases, information is uniquely problematic because efficiency claims usually involve matters of internal resource allocation and capabilities specific to the merging parties. Hence, benchmark testing of claimed efficiencies is often not possible. Likewise, the experience of third parties (competitors and customers) is insufficient either because the circumstances of the merging firms is sui generis or they lack access to specific information that can rebut the self-interested claims of the merging parties. Finally, even if made fully available, internally generated estimates of efficiencies may lack reliability. Behavioural economists studying mergers have found that cognitive biases of corporate decision makers may underlie mistaken estimates of benefits from mergers.[6]

The lessons of failed mergers reinforce the argument that efficiency claims of merging parties are inherently imprecise. A large literature examining the high percentages of unsuccessful mergers underscores the uncertainty the corporations themselves face in ascertaining the likelihood of realizing hoped-for cost savings from mergers.[7] The business consulting literature reveals that a substantial number of merger transactions, perhaps more than half, do not achieve the shareholder benefits that were predicted. These studies suggest, first, that information on potential efficiencies is impacted and not easily interpreted. They also lend support to the behaviouralists' claims that managers of takeover firms overvalue targets' potential to realize synergies and other efficiencies. In sum, the spotty track record in evaluating efficiencies ex ante of those who have enormous financial stakes in the reliability of those outcomes counsels caution in relying on the accuracy of generalist judges and prosecutors undertaking similar investigations.

5.2   Uncertainties Flowing from the Applicable Economic Standard

The most sharply contested 'economic' issue regarding efficiencies, the choice of the applicable welfare standard, is one that ultimately turns on critical normative judgments by the decision maker. A long-running debate over the appropriate economic standard to be applied in antitrust law, and specifically in merger analyses, focuses on whether an aggregate economic welfare standard (or 'total surplus' standard) or a consumer surplus standard should apply. The aggregate economic welfare standard condemns mergers that decrease the aggregate welfare of consumers (ie buyers) plus producers (ie sellers and their competitors), without regard to any wealth transfers. In contrast, the consumer welfare standard would condemn conduct if it actually reduces the welfare of buyers, irrespective of its impact on sellers. Thus, under the consumer surplus standard, efficiencies count only if there is evidence that enough of the efficiency benefits would be passed through to consumers so that consumers would benefit from the

---

[6]   ME Stucke, 'Behavioral Economists at the Gate: Antitrust in the 21st Century' (2007) 38 *Loy U Chi L J* 513.

[7]   *See* RE Caves, 'Mergers, Takeovers, and Economic Efficiency: Foresight vs. Hindsight' (1989) 7 *Int'l J Ind Org* 151.

conduct.[8] The Federal Merger Guidelines and case law for the most part adopts the consumer standard, recognizing efficiencies only if they are sufficient to ensure that post-merger prices will not increase.

The choice of the appropriate welfare standard is usually not outcome-determinative on the efficiencies issue, but it may be in several cases. The first involves the treatment of fixed cost savings. Mergers that are found to cause price increases or lessen quality or innovations may sometimes result in an allocative efficiency loss that is less than production efficiency benefits arising from fixed cost savings. In this case, the consumer welfare standard would suggest condemnation of the merger because prices would rise, while the aggregate welfare standard would not. The welfare standard could also matter when the efficiencies from a merger involve a reduction in marginal cost that is not passed on to consumers sufficiently to prevent prices from rising. Such an agreement would be considered harmful under a consumer welfare standard, because price would rise. But if the production cost savings exceeded the allocative efficiency loss, the merger would not be considered harmful under an aggregate welfare standard.

Even where real cost savings can be demonstrated, they do not necessarily lead to lower prices. Further, the propensity of efficiencies to do so may vary significantly, with the theory of the claimed effect on competition arising out of the merger. In cases involving unilateral effects, even substantial reductions in marginal cost may not be sufficient to generate price declines if firms behave as is supposed by some common oligopoly models. And in cases involving coordinated effects, demonstrated efficiencies could under some circumstances lead to *higher* prices, such as in the case of imperfect industry coordination, where the effect of efficiencies may be to enhance threatened punishment facing a 'maverick' competitor that otherwise would constrain industry prices.

5.3 Which Efficiencies Count?

An admixture of economic and pragmatic considerations underlie legal determinations as to which efficiencies will gain recognition in antitrust merger analyses. The Federal Merger Guidelines list several criteria for efficiencies that will be 'cognizable'. First, they must be 'merger specific',

---

[8] Fundamentally, the consumer surplus can be seen as a kind of entitlement under the policies endorsing competition through the antitrust laws. Professor Lande, for example, argues that legislative history and the logic of competitive markets imbue in consumers a right to receive the consumer surplus flowing from competition. RH Lande, 'Chicago's False Foundation: Wealth Transfers (Not Just Efficiency) Should Guide Antitrust' (1989) 58 *Antitrust LJ* 631.

that is, they must be likely to be accomplished through the merger and unlikely to be accomplished in the absence of the merger or through other means having fewer anticompetitive effects. A second criterion is that efficiencies be 'verifiable'. By this, the Guidelines intend that merging parties must substantiate their claims in a manner that permits the agencies to verify the likelihood, magnitude and cost of the efficiencies, the manner in which they will enhance incentives and abilities to compete, and the reasons why they are merger specific. Although both of these tests may be justified on theoretic and pragmatic grounds, they add to the uncertainty of the efficiencies evaluation process because they add complexity, lack precision and ultimately permit considerable discretion in their application by judges and prosecutors. To take one example, subsumed in the inquiry as to merger specificity are questions of whether internal expansion or joint ventures are feasible alternatives to merger. Other inquiries cascade from these questions: what are the minimum scale requirements? Are there capacity limits in the market that would make internal expansion unprofitable?

The Guidelines also list favoured and disfavoured efficiencies, stating that efficiencies result from shifting production so as to enable the merging firms to reduce the marginal cost in the former category and procurement, management, or capital cost in the latter. It is noteworthy that the Guidelines' categorization differs in detail and selection from those identified by leading treatises on antitrust law.[9] Further, many commentators (including Timothy Muris, former chairman of the FTC) assert that there is no economic or pragmatic basis for disfavouring certain efficiencies. At the same time, there is widespread agreement that informal practice by the FTC and DOJ departs significantly from this analysis, as federal officials have acknowledged that consideration of all efficiencies is commonplace.

A central tension in the categorization approach is that some of the most economically salient efficiencies rank among the most difficult to predict or to measure. As a former FTC Commissioner stated, '[i]nnovation or managerial economies are probably the most significant variable in determining whether companies succeed or fail – or in determining whether certain

---

[9]   Several prominent commentators have endorsed a categorization approach that classifies efficiencies based on their relative importance and susceptibility of proof and contemplates that antitrust tribunals should, as a matter of law, limit the defense according to these classifications. For example, Professor Areeda and his co-authors proposed that economies of scale and scope should generally be recognized, while economies in distribution, promotion and R&D, which present relatively weak cases for consideration, should be subject to more rigorous analysis. Others, such as managerial economies and savings in capital cost, procurement, or overhead, should generally not be recognized.

more specific merger efficiencies are achieved or not. Yet, we do not overtly take them into account when deciding merger cases.'[10] A number of others have stressed that the processes that spur innovation, such as knowledge transfers, undergird innovation, which 'provides the greatest potential enhancement of social wealth. [And it is] the single most important factor in the growth of real output in the industrial world, representing over half the total gain in U.S. output over extensive time periods.'[11] Yet predictions of synergies strengthening the likelihood of innovation are among the most speculative undertakings.

Another issue giving rise to additional uncertainty is whether antitrust law should credit efficiencies obtained by the merging parties in markets different from the one in which the merger has an anticompetitive effect. While case law and the language of the Clayton Act seem to preclude such multi-market balancing, changes to the Merger Guidelines in 1997 opened the door slightly, stating the agencies would exercise prosecutorial discretion to take such efficiencies into account where they were 'so inextricably linked' to the market that no remedy could eliminate the anticompetitive harm without sacrificing the efficiencies in the other market.

5.4 Uncertainties in Measurement, Timing, and Balancing

Determining the magnitude of efficiencies necessary to offset anticompetitive harm has long perplexed enforcers and academic commentators. Because efficiencies must offset anticompetitive harms, most agree that a 'sliding scale' approach that would calibrate the magnitude of efficiencies required against the degree of predicted harm is, in theory, desirable.[12] However, enormous measurement and conceptual problems are present on both sides of this equation. As suggested above, many claimed efficiencies do

---

[10] TB Leary, 'Efficiencies and Antitrust: A Story of Ongoing Evolution, Address at the Fall Forum of the ABA Section of Antitrust Law' (8 November 2002), www3.ftc.gov/speecheds/leary/efficienciesandantitrust.htm (accessed 31 January 2008).

[11] JF Brodley, 'Proof of Efficiencies in Mergers and Joint Ventures' (1996) 64 *Antitrust LJ* 575.

[12] *See* US Horizontal Merger Guidelines, 2 April 1992, §4, http://www.usdoj.gov/atr/public/guidelines/hmg.htm (accessed 31 January 2008) ('The greater the potential adverse competitive effect of a merger . . . the greater must be cognizable efficiencies in order for the Agency to conclude that the merger will not have an anticompetitive effect in the relevant market'). The Merger Guidelines include a caveat that would prohibit consideration of efficiencies in extreme cases: Efficiencies must 'not arise out of an anticompetitive reduction in output or service' and will 'almost never justify a merger to monopoly or near-monopoly'. *Id.*

not readily admit to quantitative measurement and are subject to qualifications that make even approximations difficult. Moreover, projected competitive harm is also not subject to precise, or even approximate, ex ante evaluation. Although some suggest using concentration measures as a tool for a crude risk assessment, it would need to be qualified by careful assessment of a host of factors, such as entry conditions, before even the crudest estimation of potential harm could be made. It seems highly doubtful that any form of balancing is feasible. As Professor Hovenkamp's treatise put it: 'Balancing implies an ability to assign a common unit of measurement to the two things being balanced, and determine which outweigh the other. Except in the clearest cases, this is simply not what courts are capable of doing.'[13]

How should antitrust tribunals take into account the pervasive uncertainty described above? In their internal evaluation of claimed efficiencies, the government acknowledges it applies a rather rough discounting approach based on its evaluation of the quality and persuasiveness of the merging parties' substantiation proof:[14]

> The Agencies recognize that assessing a proposed merger's potential efficiency benefits, like its competitive effects, necessarily involves projections about the future. The Agencies do not automatically reject a claim due to minor discrepancies uncovered in the verification process. Nor do the Agencies reject an efficiency claim solely because the efficiency has never before been accomplished. Shortcomings in the substantiation of a particular efficiency claim may cause the Agencies to reduce the magnitude of the efficiencies associated with that claim rather than to reject the claim altogether. Similarly, the fact that one stand-alone efficiency claim cannot be verified does not necessarily result in rejection of other claims.

While this approach understandably seeks to motivate parties to submit reliable information so as to simplify its task, it may have the undesirable effect of further clouding the evaluation process. Parties risk having their claims 'discounted' to some unspecified degree based on the ability of the government to verify the accuracy of their claims.

Another factor introducing uncertainty in evaluating merger-specific efficiencies is the time horizon applicable to the analysis. The Guidelines are not clear as to when the price test is to be applied. For example, where synergies take time to develop, would a temporary increase in price negate an otherwise acceptable efficiencies defence? If not, how long a time lag is

---

[13] Areeda and Hovenkamp, *supra* note 3, at 314.
[14] US Department of Justice and Federal Trade Commission, 'Commentary of the Horizontal Merger Guidelines' (2006) 52, http://www.usdoj.gov/atr/public/guidelines/215247.htm (accessed 31 January 2008).

acceptable? In addition, the Department of Justice states that considerations of a merger's effect on the pace of adoption of innovation will itself constitute a cognizable efficiency factor:[15]

> Claimed cost savings from combining sales and realizing economies of scale . . . might be realized from internal growth. If such unilateral changes are likely without the proposed merger (for example, if they have already been planned), they are not merger-specific. Timing can be an important factor in the consideration of such claims. If a merger can be expected significantly to accelerate the achievement of economies of scale due to increased sales as compared to internal growth, the Agencies credit the merger with merger-specific acceleration of the cost reduction.

Hence, the fact finder is called upon to estimate, in some rough fashion, how quickly efficiencies may be realized and compare that judgment to another (necessarily imprecise) estimate of how quickly the economies of scale might have been achieved by internal growth. The likely compounding effect of imprecision on multiple inquiries here is striking.

6 APPLYING THE EFFICIENCIES ANALYSIS

The government enforcers and the courts have adapted to uncertainty. However they have done so in a manner that is not geared to improving the likelihood of achieving the accuracy hoped for by proponents of the defence. For example, the foregoing analysis suggests that the Agencies themselves have sought to maximize their own flexibility on the efficiencies issue by publishing guidelines that speak in broad and ambiguous terms that provide almost unlimited room for discretion in exercising their prerogative as to whether to bring challenges to mergers. At the same time, they urge narrow readings by courts and insist that their Guidelines are not designed to guide judicial decision making. Faced with the imperatives of reviewing a large number of mergers under time and resource constraints, the Agencies have, perhaps understandably, opted for flexibility over precision.

Courts confronting efficiency issues in litigated cases fare no better. Even where sophisticated econometric data has been put forward, judges seem reluctant to dive in. An example is found in the *Staples* case,[16] in which the District Judge ignored voluminous economic evidence and relied instead

---

[15] Merger Commentary, *supra* note 14, at 'Efficiencies the Agencies Consider. Merger-Specific Efficiencies'.
[16] *FTC v Staples, Inc* 970 F Supp 1066 (D. D.C. 1997).

on internal documents and his own visit to the stores. Triers of fact or those with discretion to prosecute seem reluctant to deal with complex statistics if there are other grounds for decision. While such data is sometimes cited as reinforcing judges' decisions on other issues, according to one FTC commissioner, no court or FTC decision turned on econometric evidence or engineering and accounting studies, standing alone.

In this regard, the experience of the American courts is instructive and discouraging. Faced with the inherent uncertainties and complexities of the efficiency inquiry, courts have resorted to evidentiary shortcuts and other measures that fall far short of a meaningful balancing of efficiencies and harms. In some instances, they have developed tests that make little economic sense (eg a rigid passing on requirement). In others they have resorted to evidentiary sleight of hand (eg relying on findings concerning the 'credibility' of experts or assigning dispositive weight to internal studies). In the end, the results of judicial efficiencies inquiries seem preordained by the courts' conclusions on competitive effects. Most courts finding substantial efficiencies do so only where they also conclude that the merger would not be likely to substantially lessen competition.

Efficiency claims are evaluated by the FTC and DOJ internally when reviewing mergers in a manner that is far less precise than published merger guidelines would suggest. As FTC Commissioner Leary candidly observed:[17]

> Experienced counsel know that in actual practice the vast majority of efficiency claims are resolved internally in the agencies in a much less formal way [than the Guidelines specify]. For mergers that do not involve extreme concentration levels, efficiencies are not analyzed as a 'defence', and rigorously quantified, but rather included in the description of the overall business rationale for the transition. Because there is no need to strike a mathematical balance, the presentation can include not only scale effects on production but also things like improved potential for innovation and managerial efficiencies.

As a general matter, in the case of informal clearances of mergers, antitrust agencies rarely supply enough information to provide an empirical record for appraising the basis for their decision. One reason for this of course may be that the empirical basis for the claim is so slender. Further, as noted above, the lack of information from an adversarial process contributes to the lack of hard information on which to base efficiency evaluations.

Several conclusions flow from the enforcement patterns just discussed. First, the lack of transparency and disregard of standards in the clearance

---

[17]   Leary, *supra* note 10.

process breeds problems besides judicial or administrative error. Where empirical judgments necessary to bring enforcement actions are prone to high rates of error or ambiguity, merging parties may have strong incentives to opportunistically seek out mergers that they would otherwise forego. Second, transparency, though desirable for purposes of ensuring account-ability of public officials, cannot cure many of the problems identified in this chapter. The inadequacy of evidence to provide convincing answers to the several facets of efficiency analysis will not be cured by wider inspection of that evidence. At best, transparency might reveal that the emperor has no clothes, which in turn might spur greater efforts to establish workable presumptions that dispense with factual questions that are impossible to answer.

7 A CAUTIONARY TALE: ANTITRUST EVALUATIONS OF HOSPITAL MERGERS

For better or worse, hospital mergers have become a proving ground in American courts for weighing efficiencies in antitrust cases. These cases are instructive in that they demonstrate the problems antitrust tribunals encounter and spotlight the intractable nature of many of the factual issues. As a result, most courts have employed evidentiary presumptions and relied on the placement of the burden of proof to evade trade-off analyses.

In some respects, the hospital industry in America is well-suited for efficiencies analysis; in others, decidedly not. Clearly, the industry suffers from significant overcapacity attributable to government policies, inefficient reimbursement methodologies and rapid technological change, causing shifts in where many procedures are performed. Moreover, condi-tions on both the demand and supply side are changing rapidly to deal with the new environment. These cataclysmic changes occurring in heath care financing and delivery make it extraordinarily difficult to predict with confidence what kinds of savings are attributable to a given merger and what less restrictive alternatives might exist.

Federal courts have closely examined defendants' efficiencies claims in seven hospital merger cases with a variety of results and approaches.[18]

---

[18] In three of those cases, the district courts made rather cursory findings to the effect that defendants had presented plausible efficiency claims. *FTC v Freeman Hospital* 911 F Supp 1213 (W.D. Mo. 1995), aff'd, 69 F.3d 260 (8th Cir 1995); *United States v Carilion Health Sys* 707 F Supp 840 (W.D. Va.), aff'd, 892 F.2d 1042 (4th Cir 1989); *FTC v University Health, Inc* 1991–1 Trade Cas (CCH) P 69,444 (S.D.

Several observations may be made about the decided cases. First, with one exception, courts have followed a pattern of symmetry between their findings on the merits of the government's merger case and their treatment of efficiencies. That is, courts ruling for defendants on other grounds uphold their efficiency claims, while those concluding that the merger will lessen competition reject efficiencies claims. Courts thus may be taking the easy way out on this complex issue.

While a wide variety of efficiencies have been considered in various cases, those involving economies in scale and scope, as well as savings resulting from combined administrative functions, have proven the most successful. Indeed, in litigation, the government has often conceded the validity of such efficiencies in principle, while vigorously disputing their magnitude or the feasibility of their being implemented. As a general matter, the agencies take the position that preferred efficiencies include better use of fixed cost assets and elimination of duplicative services, while other kinds of efficiencies, such as savings in the cost of capital and shared inputs, are suspect, primarily because they can often be accomplished without merger. Scale economies and other savings, from consolidating programs operated at less than efficient levels, are readily identifiable and estimated. Courts have been sceptical of purported savings resulting from improved information and use of 'best practices' resulting from mergers, contending that such savings readily obtained through other means and were difficult to quantify. However, in one hospital merger case, the appellate court faulted the district court for failing to weigh quality-enhancing aspects of the merger against anticompetitive harms under an efficiency analysis.[19] Thus, the litigated cases have sidestepped many important, but hard-to-quantify efficiencies.

Ga. 1991), rev'd, 938 F.2d 1206 (11th Cir 1991). One other district court relied in part on evidence of efficiencies in finding that the hospitals had rebutted the government's prima facie case, *FTC v Butterworth Health Corp* 946 F Supp 2385 (W.D. Mich. 1996), and another endorsed in dicta the defendants' claim. *United States v Long Island Jewish Hospital* 983 F Supp 121 (E.D.N.Y. 1997). In the only appellate case, *FTC v University Health, Inc* 938 F.2d 1206, 1222 (11th Cir 1991), three district court cases, and several FTC administrative proceedings on the subject, *see eg In Re Evanston Northwestern Healthcare Corporation*, 2007WL4358355 (9 November 2007), defendants' proof on the efficiencies has been found wanting. For their part, the federal enforcement agencies have taken the position that they may weigh efficiencies in deciding whether or not to challenge a merger, while occasionally arguing that efficiencies considerations are not cognizable by federal courts. *See* TL Greaney, 'Chicago's Procrustean Bed: Applying Antitrust in Health Care' (2004) 71 *Antitrust LJ* 857.

[19] *FTC v Tenet Healthcare Corp.* 186 F.3d 1045 (8th Cir 1999).

8 CONCLUSION

This chapter has focused on the dilemmas posed by the efficiency question in antitrust merger analysis. In some respects, the problem is not unique to efficiencies. Antitrust necessarily relies on economic theory to help shape its rules of thumb and presumptions and to inform its analysis of facts. The push to incorporate efficiencies into merger evaluations has been driven by unquestioned economic theory. All that is part of the evolutionary process that has long characterized antitrust doctrinal development. However, matching theory with workable rules of law on the efficiencies issue has generated extensive debate and doctrinal development has failed to isolate critical issues of fact that courts can meaningfully evaluate. Attempts to incorporate efficiencies have been particularly problematic because of the multiple levels of uncertainty that attend the inquiry. The outcome has also been somewhat sui generis among controversial antitrust issues. Courts have taken pains to avoid the issue, while prosecutors have embraced it, but only for purposes of conducting their pre-merger reviews. While this caution is certainly commendable given the problems associated with the defence identified in this chapter, the absence of clear judicial standards may have allowed the defence to flourish behind the scenes without being subject to examination and validation.

13. Efficiency in merger law: appropriateness of efficiency analysis in ex-ante assessment?

Daniel Zimmer*

1 PRESUMPTION OF EFFICIENCY OR INDIVIDUAL ASSESSMENT?

We are aware of not just one way of taking into account efficiency considerations in merger control, but rather of two. We may distinguish a more general concept, sometimes referred to as the 'general-presumption approach', on the one hand, and an individual efficiency assessment on the other hand.

The traditional 'dominant-position' test is often understood as being part of a general-presumption approach. There is, following this line of thought, a general presumption that mergers bring about some efficiency gains. If they did not, the argument goes, firms would not merge. This assumption is, however, highly dubious. It presumes rational conduct by directors in the best interests of their companies, and neglects motives such as personal vanity and management's wish to be among the major firms in the market. According to a study by the consulting firm McKinsey, 70 per cent of mergers fail to achieve expected revenue synergies. In one quarter of the analysed transactions, managers overestimated cost synergies by at least 25 per cent.[1]

The idea of a general-presumption approach is that we take into account presumed efficiency, and thus a welfare-enhancing effect of a merger, by setting a relatively high threshold for prohibition: market dominance. If one does so, it seems logical that one should not recognize efficiency gains for a second time, by taking them into account on an individual basis.[2]

* Prof. Dr., LL.M. (UCLA), Law professor at the University of Bonn.
[1] 'Overestimating Merger Synergies', *The McKinsey Quarterly* (March 2005).
[2] Similarly U Immenga, 'Der SIEC-Test der europäischen Fusionskontrolle als Kompetenzfrage' in C Engel and W Möschel (eds), *Recht und Spontane Ordnung. Festschrift für Ernst-Joachim Mestmäcker zum 80. Geburtstag* (2006) 269, 280.

However, EU law has, by introducing the so-called SIEC test,[3] loosened the link to the dominance criterion, and thus opened the door to prohibition below the level of dominance as well, in order to catch so-called non-coordinated effects in oligopolies.[4] In this setting, one might argue that European scholars and law enforcers now have more reason than prior to the 2004 reform to take into consideration the admittance of an efficiency defence in individual cases.[5]

2   COMPARATIVE ASSESSMENT OF THE APPROACHES

In the following, a comparative assessment of a general-presumption approach on the one hand and an individual-efficiency defence on the other will be carried out, bearing three aspects in mind:

(i)   costs of an individual efficiency assessment;
(ii)   potential welfare gains of an individual efficiency assessment (deriving from the accuracy of results); and
(iii) effects on competition.

---

[3]   SIEC stands for significant impediment to effective competition. Article 2(3) of the EC Merger Regulation 139/2004 provides: 'A concentration which would significantly impede effective competition, in the common market or in a substantial part of it, in particular as a result of the creation or strengthening of a dominant position, shall be deemed incompatible with the common market'.

[4]   *Cf* recital 25 of the Merger Control Regulation 139/2004: 'Under certain circumstances, concentrations involving the elimination of important competitive constraints that the merging parties had exerted upon each other, as well as a reduction of competitive pressure on the remaining competitors, may, even in the absence of a likelihood of coordination between the members of the oligopoly, result in a significant impediment to effective competition. The Community courts have, however, not to date expressly interpreted Regulation (EEC) No. 4064/89 as requiring concentrations giving rise to such non-coordinated effects to be declared incompatible with the common market. Therefore, in the interests of legal certainty, it should be made clear that this Regulation permits effective control of all such concentration by providing that any concentration which would significantly impede effective competition, in the common market or in a substantial part of it, should be declared incompatible with the common market'.

[5]   For this conclusion, *see* D Zimmer, 'Significant Impediment to Effective Competition' (2004) *ZWeR* 250, 262. Decidedly against this reasoning Immenga, *supra* note 2, at 276–83: according to Immenga, the EC Treaty does not allow for an efficiency justification in individual merger cases.

2.1   Costs of an Individual Efficiency Assessment

An individual, case-by-case efficiency analysis is certainly in itself more costly than a general-presumption approach. First there are direct costs, associated with, for example, a detailed examination of the firms involved, their rationalization potential and so forth. If, as is the case under the EU Merger Regulation, a successful efficiency defence requires that the gains will in part be handed over to the next market level (consumer benefit), it also requires a thorough examination of price elasticities and the nature of the competition in the market. These are all direct costs of an individual efficiencies assessment. There are indirect costs, as well: the examination may be time-consuming, retarding the decision on the merger, and thereby retarding the transaction. Moreover, the admissibility of an individual efficiency justification might arguably cause legal uncertainty, at least as long as we have not received a number of reliable judicial decisions on the precise conditions and limits of the defence.

2.2   Potential Welfare Gains of an Individual Efficiency Assessment (Deriving from the Accuracy of Results)

By deciding cases on an individual basis, we may avoid errors. More accurate decisions, meaning fewer errors of one or another kind, may lead to welfare gains. If we want to evaluate the concept of an individual efficiency assessment, we have to weigh its costs against its potential welfare gains. This is, of course, a highly speculative matter. However, we may arrive, at least, at some conclusions.

If we take into account that efficiency defences in real life have hardly ever been recognized and that the requirements posed by the authorities for a successful efficiency justification are extremely high, we may conclude that efficiency defences will only succeed in rare cases.[6] So the potential welfare gains from a 'better' decision being made in cases on the grounds of efficiency analyses will presumably be very limited; there are just too few cases where the defence leads to a different decision.

---

[6]   For this conclusion, *see* the Commission's Horizontal Merger Guidelines: Guidelines on the assessment of horizontal mergers under the Council Regulation on control of concentrations between undertakings, 5 February 2004, [2004] OJ C 31, p 5, para 84: 'It is highly unlikely that a merger leading to a market position approaching that of a monopoly, or leading to a similar level of market power, can be declared compatible with the common market on the ground that efficiency gains would be sufficient to counteract its potential anti-competitive effects'. *See* also the analyses of U Schwalbe and D Zimmer, *Kartellrecht und Ökonomie* (2006) 386–8.

2.3 Effects on Competition

Admitting an efficiency defence means that we accept a certain impediment to competition, in order to achieve a welfare gain. When deciding whether to adopt such an approach we have to know for which legal aspects we are able to make prognoses.

Economists are able to produce more or less accurate statements on the potential of a merger to reduce the merging firms' costs, especially by means of rationalization. A second question causes more uncertainty: Will the merged entity share efficiency gains with its customers? The EU Commission will, according to the Guidelines on the assessment of horizontal mergers, admit an efficiency defence only in cases of consumer benefit.[7] One statement given by economists is that firms will in general share savings only, if at all, on variable costs – not savings on fixed costs.[8] Should this hold true, most of the efficiencies caused by mergers will not be recognized, because most efficiency gains result from savings on fixed costs. Moreover, a prediction on the degree to which a merged entity will pass on advantages to the next market level depends on additional circumstances, including, as already mentioned, the price elasticity of demand and the type and intensity of competition in the market.

We may accordingly conclude: If we discuss an efficiency defence of the consumer-benefit type, requiring participation by consumers in the gains, the predictions become very uncertain. However, admittedly, economists may still be able to come to some conclusions in this respect.

We may now turn to the effects of mergers on market dynamics. The possibilities of integrating dynamic effects in economic predictions are very limited.[9] This assessment has been confirmed by the contribution of Wolfgang Kerber to this conference.[10] Thus, if we admitted an efficiency justification for mergers, we would be running a serious risk that though the parties to the merger would be allowed to present a calculation stating that they would generate short-term savings, we would not be able to seriously address the long-term effects, in particular with respect to innovation.

---

[7] *See* Horizontal Merger Guidelines, *supra* note 6, at paras 79–84.

[8] *See* Schwalbe and Zimmer, *supra* note 6, at 382–3.

[9] *See* already FA von Hayek, *Der Wettbewerb als Entdeckungsverfahren* (1968); E Hoppmann, *Wirtschaftsordnung und Wettbewerb* (1988). More recently, in favour of a reliance on the dynamic effects of market economies, ES Phelps, 'Dynamic Capitalism' (10 October 2006) *Wall Street Journal*.

[10] W Kerber, 'Should competition law promote efficiency? Some reflections of an economist on the normative foundations of competition law', Chapter 6 in this volume.

Since it seems to make an important difference whether two independent firms A and B or just the merged entity AB are exercising research and development, these long-term effects on market dynamics appear to be of vital importance to the competitive process.

After all, it seems to be important to stress that merger control is about market structure. The system has to prevent a market structure that has the potential to significantly impede vivid competition, vivid rivalry among firms. Based on these assumptions, competition law should not admit a justification of a non-competitive market structure by efficiency reasoning. On the contrary, a competitive market structure appears to be a necessary prerequisite for the competitive process, which is the central object of competition law.

14. Efficient and/or effective enforcement

Marie-Anne Frison-Roche*

1 INTRODUCTION

I would like to treat the question of efficient and effective enforcement of competition law not only in technical terms, but also from a systemic perspective. This issue is eminently practical, because it concerns the concretization of legal rules and decisions in real life. It also expresses a sort of positivism, for which only an implemented rule is a real rule. But concrete enforcement depends on the relation between economy and the law, and between theory and practice.

Stated precisely, the question of the efficiency of enforcement is not only a question of practice, such as the coordination between independent authorities or classical states, but also a theoretical question, through a theory of inducement, involving incentives to reveal anticompetitive behaviour for example, or through the conception of public versus private.

The practical necessity of obtaining the most effective implementation of rules is common to all legal rules. Under this condition, it is economic theory that gives specific light to this efficiency in competition law. As such, economic theory transcends legal distinctions between public and private enforcement and helps us to focus our attention on effective implementation more than on the adoption of rules itself. The 'centre of gravity' is moving away from the creation of legal rules (the centre of the legal system) towards the concretization of legal rules and their effects on economic behaviour (the centre of the economic system).

In this sense, economic theory intersects with sociological concerns. In this sense, the Green Paper on damages actions for breach of the European Community antitrust rules[1] is the best expression of the aim to obtain

---

* Professor of Economic Law at Sciences Po (Paris), Director of the Regulatory Chair.
[1] Green Paper – Damage actions for breach of the EC antitrust rules, 19

effective enforcement of competition law by satisfying private interests. I will focus my contribution on these developments.

In the second section of my contribution, I would like to consider the *homo economicus* inside the practice of competition-law enforcement, through its perception as an economic agent that calculates and pursues its own particular interest. The framework of economic conduct is the same for human beings and firms. In the third section, I shall emphasize the legal mechanisms that implement this consideration, namely by using the concept of rivalry between competitors and consequently the status of the victims of anticompetitive conduct, in the attempt to obtain effective market protection. In the fourth section, I shall finish with a remark about the time-frame concerned in the enforcement of competition law, especially regarding remedies, which are more a warning signal for every economic actor than a particular reaction to a particular violation. This makes the future the relevant time-frame for enforcement, and not the past of the violation that is meant to be punished. In these circumstances, the enforcement of competition law, as a signal and as an instrument lending credibility to legal rules, which influences economically rational undertakings, is not the consequence of competition law but competition law itself.

2   THE CONSIDERATION OF THE *HOMO ECONOMICUS* IN THE ADOPTION OF ENFORCEMENT RULES

In general, the enforcement of the law is not only the effective application of remedies, but also, before that, the declaration of the violation. At the end, in a very classical sense, the real enforcement of rules results in the absence of violation.

Why and how should we obtain this compliance with the provisions of these rules, presented as this superior form of efficiency? Is it natural or not? We will see how an approach to this efficiency could be made specific to competition law through the influence of economic analysis.

Classically, before the alliance between law and economy – one could perhaps say their intimacy – the citizen obeyed the law out of love for the law. It is Jean-Jacques Rousseau's conception of the *amour des lois*: everybody loves rules adopted by everybody (in the theory of the social contract, where citizens who express rules express reason), and respect for legal pro-

---

December 2005, COM(2005) 672 final=http://eur-lex.europa.eu/LexUriServ/ LexUriServ.do?uri=COM:2005:0672:FIN:EN:PDF (accessed 31 January 2008).

visions is natural for everyone, even if it is contrary to the particular interest of a person who has the power not to follow the order of the law. Love of law is equivalent to love of reason. This is a sort of natural attitude. It is part of this political philosophy that the use of power by an individual in order to obtain an advantage contrary to legal provisions is considered pathological. From this perspective, the breach of the law as such is a rational surprise and the legal system reacts against this personal and perverse behaviour with detection and sanctions, in the sense of an ex-post reaction.

In the same general line of reasoning, but with corresponding legal and institutional tools, the law empowers public and special organizations, such as competition authorities or more generally administrative bodies, to intervene if, as another sort of 'love of law', a public interest is concerned. The protection of competitive markets belongs to this sort of interest.

In contrast, economic analysis is based on the concept of the firm that seeks its own interest if it has the power to obtain it. Firms 'love' their interest and not the law. If the legislature, the government or courts want firms to comply with the law, the latter must coincide with the individual interest of the market operators.

If this is not the case, the enforcement of competition law becomes the first problem for the system, not just a marginal consideration involving a pathological violation of legal rules. The efficiency of the enforcement needs special tools, essentially the use of private interest to serve general goals. Those who adopt the public-choice theory do not distinguish between state administration and undertakings in this regard. To stay within the less controversial theory of *homo economicus*, one accepts a differentiation between private and public interest and, in consequence, between private and public bodies, between private and public actions. This very well-known theoretical consideration, which transforms the violation of competition law into natural behaviour by firms that have the interest and the power to act in such a way, has significant implications for the enforcement of the law.

If we accept this concept, the correct understanding of legal rules of enforcement is to use this natural economic behaviour with the aim of obtaining its own efficiency. In short, the enforcement system can let the economic rationale and particular interests of the individual operators do the work in its place. This is the same idea as that behind the political *amour des lois* theory, because it is based on the conviction (perhaps it is an illusion) that the system will function naturally through the natural action of the agents.

The concept of a sort of natural enforcement of rules could be presented as a contradiction, because it is a sort of spontaneous enforcement, but it is the concept of new legal rules or reflexions, and this is appropriate to globalization. The evolution of competition law is moving in this direction, giving powers to private victims to seek enforcement against other firms, not because the victims strive for the public and general interest, but on the contrary because they pursue their own particular interest. It is a sort of regulatory arrangement looked at through a liberal glass.

3   THE LEGAL TRANSLATION OF THE ECONOMIC CONCEPT OF BEHAVIOUR INTO COMPETITION-LAW PROVISIONS

In this part of my contribution, I would like to develop an idea of the relationship between enforcement, individual interest and information, and after that I will try to explain the new place of victims in competition law, organized – or able to be organized in the future – in this efficiency perspective.

First of all, it is fundamental to emphasize the crucial place of information in the enforcement of competition law and its connection with the *homo economicus* concept mentioned above. The legal mechanism is very simple: competition law is effectively and naturally enforced if this enforcement is based on the fulfilment of one or several individual interests that will serve to motivate particular firms, at different steps in the enforcement of competition law. These different steps are the detection of anticompetitive behaviour, the transmission of information about mergers, the search for and the treatment of evidence and eventually the decision to sanction or not.

Secrecy and information could be two sides of the same coin in efficient enforcement, and this explains the handling of business secrets and information, without contradiction, by the authorities and courts. At the same time, it explains why competition-law solutions are so different from classical legal concepts of enforcement.

The principle is to obtain information about a violation. In this sense, leniency programmes, for instance, are the right solution for effective implementation of legal rules. The transmission of information to the regulator should be secret. At the same time, information about enforcement action, widely published in newspapers, is an efficient tool to obtain respect for the law by others.

Another point is the use of the individual interest of competitors to activate legal rules through action before competition authorities or courts. It is usual to present this evolution as part of a 'civilizing' of competition law. However, this is not completely true for several reasons.

First, an action before a court, an administration or an agency could be viewed as a simple variation on the transmission of information, hence of the case described before. The goal is not so much to repair damages but to obtain a sanction or to adopt an appropriate solution based on effective information. In this model, the effect of the action of other competitors must be the satisfaction of their particular interests. It could be the refusal of a merger, after their procedural participation in the merger proceeding as potential victims, or an attribution of damages.

This could create a contradiction between economic efficiency and legal principles such as due process, but I shall not develop this issue, because this topic will be dealt with in another chapter of this book.[2]

The European Green Paper on damages actions for breach of the European Community antitrust rules[3] implements the concept of 'civilizing' competition law with several consequences, although, rather than a direct consideration of bilateral relationships between competitors, it is a consideration of global efficiency, obtained through information and action, that can explain this general evolution towards private enforcement. In this sense, individual firms are used by the legal system, and through the legal system, as agents of legality and effectiveness, not only to punish or to repair. This is why the evolution towards private enforcement is closer to public law than private or civil law. The participation of private actors moved by private interests to realize common and systemic interests explains why Bruno Lasserre, president of the French Competition Council, has approved the prospect of class actions in competition law. Class actions appear as a global regulatory tool.

As a first consequence, private and public entities should cooperate, because their goals are the same. For the moment, however, institutional cooperation is organized between administrative bodies, especially through the European Commission and national competition agencies on one side. Civil actions are placed on another side, namely before the private law courts.

But we must consider that private actions contribute to the goal of effective enforcement of the entire system prohibiting anticompetitive behaviour. This is why the 'underdevelopment' of private actions to obtain damages for breach of competition law is a problem for competition law itself, and, in practice, this is why public and private entities must cooperate more with each other.[4] For example, administrative bodies should be able to step into private procedures opened by private actors. Another issue,

---

[2] *See* A Louvaris, 'A brief overview of some conflicts between economic efficiency and effectiveness of the administrative or judicial process in competition law', Chapter 15 in this volume.

[3] *See supra* note 1.

[4] Green Paper: 'Public and private enforcement complement each other and therefore should be coordinated in an optimal way'.

expressed by the European Green Paper, is the difficulty to obtain evidence of the breach of competition law. This opens the prospect of using the disclosure procedure in proceedings before private law courts.

In this sense, this movement of 'civilization' increases the level of enforcement rather than lowering it, because the rationale is to achieve a sort of natural functioning of the legal system by playing with particular interests of competitors and victims. In this sense, this development has adopted a regulatory perspective.

The second consequence could be the attribution to the European Commission of the power to allow damages awards. Perhaps it is not the right political moment to work on this solution, but it would be the logical consequence of the interpenetration between the public and private interest, the protection of competition and the protection of competitors.

On this point precisely, the third consequence is very important and concerns the usual distinction between the protection of competitors through liability for unfair acts, and the protection of competition through a more mechanical and economic implementation of competition rules. The distinction cannot be maintained so easily, because the work of enforcing competition law is now given to competitors and victims as agents of legality. This natural contribution to enforcement by actions, injunctive relief and damages, could be presented as a transmission of information to the regulators in exchange for the satisfaction of individual interests. This leads to a reconciliation between public interest and private interest, competition law and protection of competitors. If we are compelled – but perhaps we are not – to find another division, another *summa divisio*, we may take the distinction between 'simple' markets, which work with their own and sufficient forces, and regulated markets, for instance the energy markets, which need special and strong regulatory rules and legal certainty. For them, the necessity of effective enforcement is more crucial and the reasoning described here is justified even more.

To conclude this third section of my exposé, the greater the consideration of public interest is, the more appropriate is the legal path that seeks the satisfaction of individual interest by liability actions, class actions, damages, leniency programmes and so on. This is so not only because we can think that these sorts of interests are not in contradiction (philosophical point of view), but because the use of them is a way to achieve efficiency (pragmatic point of view). If we disagree with that, it is not necessary to adopt the rules of competition law in the first place (every rule is made to be enforced).

4 THE RELEVANT TIME-FRAME OF EFFICIENT ENFORCEMENT

In the fourth and final section of this contribution, I would like to say some words about another aspect of the topic: the relevant time-frame of efficient enforcement.

According to the classical concept, sanctions are understood as a reaction to a wrong that has occurred in the past. But if we look at them from the perspective of the economic theory of inducement and a theory of signalling, the relevant time is the future, because the goal of public and private enforcement is rather to prevent undertakings from anticompetitive behaviour.

This consideration has many practical consequences. First of all, the reaction to a breach of competition law must be quick and clear. The motivation of individual decisions through incentives has this function, and economic theory recognizes the benefit of this very classical legal rule. Moreover, in this sense, an individual decision is more useful than general rules because it lets each market participant anticipate the future.

In a last conclusion, the practical goal of effective enforcement as promoted by economic theory transcends classical legal distinctions such as public and private procedures, public and private bodies, public and private interest, prohibition of anticompetitive behaviour and prohibition of unfair competition. In a systemic way, it reconstitutes an integral and united concept of competition.

15. A brief overview of some conflicts between economic efficiency and effectiveness of the administrative or judicial process in competition law

Antoine Louvaris*

1 PRELIMINARY OBSERVATIONS

Economic efficiency is a complex notion and its crowning as the linchpin of competition law is controversial. Nonetheless, it is possible to adopt a simple, but sufficiently operational, approach to economic efficiency for the purpose of this chapter. 'In the context of industrial organization economics and competition law and policy, it relates to the most effective manner of utilizing scarce resources.'[1] To suggest that competition law aims at economic efficiency should logically imply, to put it bluntly, that only practices that reduce the well-being of consumers should be forbidden, without prejudice to focal and absolute per se prohibitions as the basis for condemning cartels, 'the supreme evil of antitrust'.[2] Positive competition law is far from reaching this conclusion, supposing that it should.

Undoubtedly, there is still an increasing propensity to promote economic efficiency in the competition law of prominent jurisdictions, such as the EC, at least since the Guidelines on Vertical Restraints[3] and, later on, since the

---

* Professor of Public Law at the University of Paris Dauphine.
[1] OECD, 'Glossary of Industrial Organisation Economics and Competition Law', http://www.oecd.org/dataoecd/8/61/2376087.pdf (accessed 31 January 2008), p 41.
[2] *Verizon Communications Inc v Law Offices of Curtis V Trinko LLP* 540 US 398, 408 (2004).
[3] *See* Commission Notice – Guidelines on vertical restraints, 13 October 2000, [2000] OJ C 291, p 1, para 7: 'The protection of competition is the primary objective of EC competition policy, as this enhances consumer welfare and

reform of EU merger control in 2004.[4] This orientation was again recently illustrated by the discussions launched by the European Commission regarding a 'more economic approach' in the application of Article 82 EC prohibiting abuse of dominant positions.[5] As a result of this evolution, among the classical triad of objectives of the Community competition policy – that is, the ordoliberal concept of defence of competition deemed as an objective of law to be protected in itself, the common market integration, initially predominant, and economic efficiency – the third one

---

creates an efficient allocation of resources. In applying the EC competition rules, the Commission will adopt an economic approach which is based on the effects on the market'. These guidelines are set in the framework of Commission Regulation (EC) No 2790/1999 of 22 December 1999 on the application of Article 81(3) of the Treaty to categories of vertical agreements and concerted practices, [1999] OJ L 336, p 21, the sixth recital of which reads: 'Vertical agreements of the category defined in this Regulation can improve economic efficiency'.

4   Council Regulation (EC) No 139/2004 of 20 January 2004 on the control of concentrations between undertakings (the EC Merger Regulation), [2004] OJ L 24, p 1; Guidelines on the assessment of horizontal mergers under the Council Regulation on the control of concentrations between undertakings, 5 February 2004, [2004] OJ C 31, p 3.

5   Para 88 of the European Commission DG Competition Discussion Paper on the application of Article 82 of the Treaty to exclusionary abuses, December 2005, http://ec.europa.eu/comm/competition/antitrust/art82/discpaper 2005.pdf (accessed 31 January 2008): 'The Community competition rules protect competition on the market as a means of enhancing consumer welfare and of ensuring an efficient allocation of resources. This requires that the pass-on of benefits must at least compensate consumers for any actual or likely negative impact caused to them by the conduct concerned. If consumers in an affected relevant market are worse off following the exclusionary conduct, that conduct cannot be justified on efficiency grounds'. The Report by the EAGCP, 'An economic approach to Article 82', July 2005, http://ec.europa.eu/comm/competition/publications/studies/eagcp_ july_21_ 05.pdf (accessed 31 January 2008), p 2, also states that: 'An economic approach to Article 82 focuses on improved consumer welfare'. *See* also D Geradin, 'Efficiency Claims in EC Competition Law and Sector-specific Regulation' in: H Ulrich (ed), *The Evolution of Competition Law* (2006) 313. This new 'economic approach', which is not yet laid down in a global and final official EC act or document, will, if achieved, in any case have to be validated by EC and Member States' courts, a process that will take some years, given the average timing of litigation, from competition authorities and trial courts to supreme courts, including of course the first of them in these matters, the ECJ. For some recent examples of this EC 'new approach': Commission Guidelines on the application of Article 81(3) of the Treaty, 27 April 2004, [2004] OJ C 101, p 97, paras 11 and 30; Case T328/03 *Germany v Commission* [2006] ECR II-1231, para 69 and the quoted case-law.

tends, in an approximation to US competition law enforcement,[6] to acquire more importance.[7]

---

[6]   According to the US Supreme Court in *Northern Pacific Railway Co v United States* 356 US 1, 4 (1958), '[t]he Sherman Act was designed to be a comprehensive charter of economic liberty aimed at preserving free and unfettered competition as the rule of trade. It rests on the premise that the unrestrained interaction of competitive forces will yield the best allocation of our economic resources, the lowest prices, the highest quality and the greatest material progress, while at the same time providing an environment conducive to the preservation of our democratic political and social institutions.' This statement was noticeably quoted by the Congress-established Antitrust Modernization Commission (AMC), 'Report and Recommendations', April 2007, http://govinfo.library.unt.edu/amc/report_recommendation/amc_final_report.pdf (accessed 31 January 2008), p 2, which adds (*id*, at 3), that '[a]ntitrust law prohibits anticompetitive conduct that harms consumer welfare . . .. Antitrust law in the United States is not industrial policy; the law does not authorize the government (or any private party) to seek to "improve" competition. Instead, antitrust enforcement seeks to deter or eliminate anticompetitive restraints. Rather than create a regulatory scheme, antitrust laws establish a law enforcement framework that prohibits private (and, sometimes, governmental) restraints that frustrate the operation of free-market competition'. However, the report (*id*, at 24 note 22) cautiously goes on to warn: 'Debate continues about the precise definition of "consumer welfare.". . . The Supreme Court has not ruled specifically on this issue. The Commission's use of the term "consumer welfare" does not imply a choice of a particular definition.'

[7]   That is not to say that this goal has become the only own accepted, even in the US, which can be shown through the ordoliberal finding closing the quotation of the above decision of the Supreme Court, and surely not in Community law or in many national competition laws, *eg* French law. More generally, it may be asserted that two models of competition law and policy are referential in the globalization of competition issues: those of the US and the EC, essentially for two reasons: 'First, as a practical matter, the lion's share of global antitrust enforcement is done by the US and EC. Second, as a conceptual matter, nations outside those jurisdictions by and large borrow the basic statutory frameworks of either the US or EC and employ similar methods of antitrust analysis. Knowing how the US and EC jurisdictions have grappled with the standard set of antitrust problems thus goes a long way to understanding how antitrust analysis is done in the rest of the world too.' (E Elhauge and D Geradin, *Global Competition Law and Economics* (2007) p VI). Their differences remain noticeable; compare the European system, with its supposed conciliation between core competition objectives and other public-interest goals, to its US homologue, with its theoretically exclusive combination of economic efficiency and promotion and protection of the competitive process. This conclusion should be somewhat qualified, as the EC competition policy is getting closer to its US counterpart, so that the discrepancy between the two systems is diminishing. The intensity, and moreover the opportuneness, of this 'harmonization' is disputed: among many, *see* CA Jones, 'Foundations of Competition Policy in the EU and USA: Conflict, Convergence and Beyond' in H Ullrich (ed), *The Evolution of European Competition Law – whose Regulation, which Competition?* (2006) 17; L Boy, 'Abuse of market power: controlling dominance or protecting

This stressing of the necessary closeness between economic efficiency and competition law should naturally render this branch of law one of the most pacified, so to speak, regarding potential or actual conflicts between economic efficiency and procedural and substantive law.

It can indeed be deduced from the above that the administrative and judicial process (hereafter 'the process') in competition law, that is to say, the sum of the competence, form and procedural rules that are the formal framework of the decision-making process in public enforcement of competition law, and in private enforcement of the same law,[8] must necessarily enable public competition authorities and judges to target the substantial goal of economic efficiency of competition law, in so far as no other goals, indifferent or contrary to the efficiency target, imply other ways of developing procedural rules. The procedural system is naturally made to correctly perform the substantial duties fixed by law.

To stress the instrumental character of procedure is not to ignore the fact that, in competition law, procedure and substance are intermingled. Thus the trade-off between private enforcement and public enforcement, the former privileged in the United States, the latter preferred in the EC,[9]

competition' in H Ullrich (ed), *The Evolution of European Competition Law – whose Regulation, which Competition?* (2006) 201; P Behrens, 'Comments' in H Ullrich (ed), *The Evolution of European Competition Law – whose Regulation, which Competition?* p 224; EM Fox, 'Comments' in H Ullrich (ed), *The Evolution of European Competition Law – whose Regulation, which Competition?* (2006) 233.

[8] In public enforcement, a decision is generally made by a specialized competition authority that is liable to judicial review and/or more or less intricate procedures by which competition authorities may apply to the courts for enforcement, the US public enforcement system being peculiar because the administrative enforcement does not entail the same scope of final decisions ordinarily and directly granted to competition authorities in many jurisdictions, including the EC and EC Member States, in particular administrative fines for misconduct. On the other hand, criminal enforcement is an important province of US public enforcement, in contrast to the EC's one level of enforcement. In the US, public enforcers act in cooperation with courts in bringing civil actions or criminal charges or in requesting courts to uphold their decisions or to enact them. In private enforcement, the first-instance decision is a judgment, appeal against which can be heard by a superior court, whose judgment may, in turn, be impugned before the Supreme Court.

[9] This assertion should be qualified, in so far as the frontier between private enforcement and public enforcement is rather porous: private enforcement, in relation to public enforcement, may be either de novo, or independently initiated, or a follow-on case lodged during or after public enforcement proceedings. It seems that in the United States, 'many (if not most) of the civil antitrust cases . . . follow government cartel prosecutions, and allege the same conspiracy against the same defendants as does the government' (*see* LB Greenfield and DF Olsky, 'Treble Damages: To What Purpose and to What Effect?', British Institute of International and Comparative Law, *International Cartels – Comparative Perspectives on Practice,*

obviously reflects a public-policy choice between two kinds of proceedings, which relies on different substantial orientations concerning the role of undertakings and consumers in enforcing and legitimizing competition law.[10] Another example can be given from the evolution of Community

---

Procedure and Substance, 2 February 2007, http://www.wilmerhale.com/files/ Publication/dc8754ff-a713-459e-80aa-f8e5cf50cf12/Presentation/Publication Attachment/98011e52-2e46-41c1-ae26-019292035734/Treble%20Damages%20 Article_%20BIICL%20conference.pdf (accessed 31 January 2008), p 9. JC Coffee, Jr, *Rescuing the Private Attorney General* (1983) 42 Md L Rev 215 at 222 *et seq*, describes the US private antitrust litigant as follows: 'a recurring pattern is evident under which the private attorney general simply piggybacks on the efforts of public agencies . . . in order to reap the gains from the investigation undertaken by these agencies'. On the other hand, recent surveys submit that the level of private antitrust litigation does not seem to be strongly related to the level of US government cases, although the number of government cases may be an imperfect measure of enforcement, because government action does not necessarily involve the filing of a case (*see* AE Abere, *Trends in Private Antitrust Litigation: 1980–2004, 2003–2005*, Princeton Economics Group). One may also observe that '[i]n the US, *follow-on* cases typically start well before the competition authority has reached its decision. The reason for this can be found in the incentive provided by class actions. Being the first law firm to bring a suit puts the firm in a strong position to be in charge of the class action. Thus there may be a race between law firms to initiate the case as soon as possible. In an EU context where class actions are not generally available, we would expect the competition authority to have scrutinised the case and reached a decision before any potential *follow-on* case by the plaintiff is initiated against the defendant.' (M Harker and M Hviid, 'Competition Law Enforcement: the "Free-riding" Plaintiff and Incentives for the Revelation of Private Information', ESRC Centre for Competition Policy and Norwich Law School, University of East Anglia, CCP Working Paper 06-9 April 2006, http://papers.ssrn.com/sol3/papers.cfm?abstract_ id=912180#PaperDownload, accessed 31 January 2008, p 1 note 2). In the US, there is also the half-public, half-private *parens patriae* proceeding, which enables state attorneys general to bring civil lawsuits claiming damages from antitrust law violators. One can also note that private parties, by complaining to administrative competition authorities, or as third parties, trigger or boost public enforcement, which obviously cannot be an exclusive ex-officio enforcement.

[10]   As stated by the European Commission Green Paper on damages actions for breach of the EC antitrust rules, 19 December 2005, COM(2005) 672 final, p 4: 'Damages actions for infringement of antitrust law serve several purposes, namely to compensate those who have suffered a loss as a consequence of anti-competitive behaviour and to ensure the full effectiveness of the antitrust rules of the Treaty by discouraging anti-competitive behaviour, thus contributing significantly to the maintenance of effective competition in the Community (deterrence). By being able effectively to bring a damages claim, individual firms or consumers in Europe are brought closer to competition rules and will be more actively involved in enforcement of the rules. The Court of Justice . . . has ruled that effective protection of the rights granted by the Treaty requires that individuals who have suffered a loss arising from an infringement of Articles 81 or 82 have the right to claim damages.'

competition law. Regulation 1/2003 is essentially a reform of procedure, but it is this procedural reform that has to carry the burden of the 'modernization' of EC competition law,[11] that is to say, the more or less radical transition from a form-based approach to an effects-based approach, considered as being the economic approach. This structurally interactive situation of process and substance appears when one considers, for instance, the replacement, in the control of anticompetitive agreements (Article 81 EC), of the previous system of notification by a system of exemption that provokes discussions on whether the first (prohibition) and the third (legal exemption) paragraphs of Article 81 EC should be construed in isolation from one another or combined by using a rule of reason,[12] which also has important consequences for the determination of the burden of proof.

Furthermore, one must not underestimate the fact that the process can develop autonomous or semi-autonomous effects, expected or not, on the very substance of competition law. For instance, the role assigned to courts, whether in a common-law or Roman-like law system, in the implementation of competition law is a paramount parameter of the evolution of its content.[13] Thus, the rule of reason is a judicial creation born of the methods used by generalist common-law courts in charge of settling

---

[11] L Idot, *Le nouveau système communautaire de mise en oeuvre des articles 81 et 82 CE* (2004).

[12] AP Komninos, 'Non-competition Concerns: Resolution of Conflicts in the Integrated Article 81 EC', The University of Oxford Centre for Competition Law and Policy, Working Paper (L) 08/05; L Idot, 'La qualification de la restriction de concurrence: à propos des lignes directrices de la Commission concernant l'application de l'article 81, §3 CE' in G Canivet (ed), *La modernisation du droit de la concurrence* (2006) 85. As for Article 82 EC, the abovementioned report of the EAGCP, *supra* note 5, at 4, affirms: 'In terms of procedure, the economic approach implies that there is no need to establish a preliminary and separate assessment of dominance. Rather, the emphasis is on the establishment of a verifiable and consistent account of significant competitive harm, since such an anti-competitive effect is what really matters and is already proof of dominance. In an effects-based approach, the focus is on the use of well-established economic analysis. Such a conceptual framework provides a benchmark for the detailed assessment of the key ingredients that have to be present in a case, whether one tries to check the presence of significant competitive harm, or the achievement of relevant economic efficiencies. This approach has also natural implications in terms of the burden of proof in specific cases. Competition authorities have to show the presence of significant anti-competitive harm, while the dominant firm should bear the burden of establishing credible efficiency arguments.'

[13] OECD, 'Judicial Enforcement of Competition Law', OCDE/GD (97)200 (1997), http://www.oecd.org/dataoecd/34/41/1919985.pdf (accessed 31 January 2008).

competition litigation in the US jurisdiction. On the other hand, the allocation of adjudication to independent non-governmental, yet administrative, bodies is also an eloquent example: this type of public authority is supposed to guarantee a 'pure' enforcement of competition law, without distortion of policy choices that could produce market malfunctioning at the expense of economic efficiency.[14]

In this chapter, which can be but a modest overview, considering the Byzantine complexity and the infinite variations of potential and actual processes in international, regional or domestic legal systems,[15] it will be supposed that respect for economic efficiency is granted, totally or partially, because if this were not the case, the problem would be the risk or the emergence of a conflict not between procedure and economic efficiency, but between the substance of competition law and this efficiency. This hypothesis is put forward while acknowledging the fact that lawyers are indeed entitled to note that economists do not necessarily agree on the meaning of efficiency and that, in a given proceeding, it is not rare that the economic analyses of the private parties, or of the public competition authority or agency, in the case of public enforcement, diverge over the efficiency or inefficiency of an impugned practice or behaviour.[16] One also cannot deny that competition law, for example, EC law, does not provide undertakings with a defined and precise description of economic efficiency, even if, as in its merger guidelines, the European Commission has moved towards a more sophisticated approach, by introducing the appraisal of 'dynamic efficiency' (innovation efficiency) into the ex-ante control of mergers.[17]

Having made these preliminary observations, one may now propose a definition of the effectiveness of an administrative or judicial process as its *ability to produce real effects on the players on the markets*, or, more precisely, *to be operative regarding the subjects of law entailed in the scope of the administrative or judicial decision in the making of the process.* Theoretically, there should not be any conflict between procedural effectiveness and economic efficiency (hereafter 'efficiency'), because the latter is a goal aimed at

---

[14]   Which, by the way, raises the question of the political, and not mere administrative, nature of the European Commission as the Community public enforcer of competition law.

[15]   Not to mention the fecundity, the richness and the frequent contradictory lessons of the related economic theories.

[16]   *See* Geradin, *supra* note 5. The 'Post-Chicago synthesis' is an illustration of the continuous evolution of economics-dominant doctrine in the field of competition problems (*see* D Encaoua and R Guesnene, *Politiques de la concurrence*, Conseil d'analyse économique, Documentation française (2006) 274). There is also the phenomenon of 'ad hoc' models fitted to special competition cases (*id*, at 275).

[17]   Horizontal Merger Guidelines, *supra* note 4, para 81.

by the very substance of competition law, whereas procedure is but a legal tool at the service of this law.

But this optimistic description does not represent the reality of dealing face-to-face with efficiency or with administrative or judicial effectiveness. One must take into account another parameter: efficacy. The efficacy of the process is the quality of the process that makes it fit to attain the expected results for which it has been set out by the public authorities, the competition agency or the judiciary. But the fitness of the process, from the point of view of law, depends also on constraints, which may be, in some cases, independent from or even at odds with efficiency. These constraints express the autonomy of law vis-à-vis economics or other social artefacts and originate in one hard-core requirement: the respect for due process of law, which obliges public authorities to respect or make respected the fundamental rights of natural and legal persons. The efficacy of fundamental-rights protection is a major component of procedural efficacy.

At this stage of the reasoning, one can then describe the delicate and unstable equilibrium that an ideal and perfectly efficacious process would permanently achieve. On the one hand, its efficacy should be efficiency-oriented in order to enable the competition agency or the court to, ultimately, deliver a decision compatible with economic efficiency without disturbing the management and strategy of the undertakings beyond what is necessary to control the alleged infringement of competition law and to remedy it, or to prevent such an infringement. The process should be, in more practical terms, quick, fair, predictable, certain and at a reasonable cost, both for the public budget and for private agents.[18]

On the other hand, the process should be based on sufficient powers given to competition agencies and courts, whose aptitude to solve competition cases should be ascertained. But these efficacious powers should produce their effects within the strict observance of fundamental rights, too.

In striking this balance, and following an elementary taxonomy, two kinds of conflicts between efficiency and effectiveness of the process may come to light, if efficacy is also taken into account.

The first conflict category comprises what can be called *failure conflicts*. In this configuration, the process is effective, but it is not efficacious, that is to say, the way it is performed or the tools it uses does not provide for good results in the case of decisions favouring economic efficiency. There are flaws in the process. The effects do not match the purposes. Of course, these

---

[18]   As summarized in R Posner, *Antitrust Law* (2nd edn, 2001) 266: 'It is not enough to have good doctrine, it is also necessary to have enforcement mechanisms that ensure, at reasonable cost, a reasonable degree of compliance to the law'.

flaws must be suppressed or their probability of occurring must be drastically reduced. This requires that the competent authority be aware of them, if necessary through an ex-post evaluation, and that remedies be found irrespective of legal, institutional, budgetary or any other objective limitations.

The second series of conflicts encompasses *structural conflicts*. These occur when the process is both effective and efficacious, but its efficacy opposes efficiency, because of its own autonomous logic, essentially the protection of fundamental rights and the necessity of compliance with law in respect of the Kelsenian hierarchy of norms. Then, even if it is possible to attenuate the clash to some extent, there will always remain an irreducible zone of opposition, though this conclusion must at once be qualified, as the respect for fundamental rights is a powerful means to legitimize the competition-regulation process and to render it acceptable to society.[19]

2   FAILURE CONFLICTS

2.1   The Gauging of Failure Conflicts: Assessment and Awareness

Two cumulative parameters condition the finding of failure conflicts. First, normative assessments of flaws in the process must be justified by use of sound economic theories, or at least those broadly accepted as referential, and/or by balancing the effects of the process on efficiency, which must appear to be negative, after a full and diachronic cross-examination.[20] Second, the competent public authorities (legislature, government, competition agencies and courts) must be aware and con-

---

[19]   M-A Frison-Roche, 'L'efficacité des décisions en matière de concurrence: notions, critères, typologie, Les ateliers de la concurrence', DGCCRF (2003), http://www.finances.gouv.fr/fonds_documentaire/dgccrf/02_actualite/ateliers_conc u/decisions 2.htm (accessed 31 January 2008).

[20]   This cross-examination ends up of necessity with a policy choice by the competent authority using its margin of discretion, because, except on unknown planets, one will never reach an agreement based on an incontestable balance-sheet on how best to balance the advantages and inconveniences of a new solution. For example, a cross-reading of some important institutional comments on the abovementioned Green Paper of the EU Commission on damages, *supra* note 10, shows a variety of responses, from globally positive (Observations de la Cour de cassation française sur le livre vert, http://ec.europa.eu/comm/competition/antitrust/actions damages/green_paper_comments.html, accessed 31 January 2008) to rather cautious and even somewhat reluctant reactions (Comments of the German Federal Ministry of Economics and Technology and the Federal Cartel Office on the Green Paper of the EU Commission, http://ec.europa.eu/comm/competition/antitrust/ actionsdamages/green_paper_comments.html, accessed 31 January 2008; Rapport d'information déposé par la délégation de l'Assemblée nationale pour l'Union

vinced of the existence of a failure conflict. This awareness is legitimately dependent on the legal culture concerned.

This means that there is no failure conflict when paramount inherent qualities of the process are at stake, such as the constitutional allocation of competence (separation of powers), fundamental forms and procedures (natural-law rules) that are indubitable keystones of a given jurisdiction. If there is any conflict, then it is a structural conflict (see section 3 below).

More broadly, law is a general and autonomous system of regulation of society that cannot be fragmented into separate areas (such as competition law), subject to the domination of other social and economic instances, whatever reasons of efficiency are advanced. The process of competition law enforcement is not to be captured by economic-efficiencies claims, but is to integrate them into its assessment, in so far as this is possible. It is the determination of these limits that can be the focus of more or less severe or durable failure conflicts.

Next, there is no failure conflict as long as economic analysis provides no better and sufficiently uncontested solution than the present impugned scheme. In this perspective, there is no failure conflict that can really be predicted by law enforcers.[21]

To be sure, there is an irreducible amount of imperfection in the system that cannot be assimilated to a failure conflict. As the AMC appositely observed:

> Of course, antitrust compliance and enforcement will always impose some costs on companies, regardless of the number of enforcers. It is important, however, to ensure that those costs do not overwhelm the benefits of antitrust enforcement

---

européenne (1), sur le livre vert sur les actions en dommages et intérêts pour infraction aux règles communautaires sur les ententes et les abus de position dominante, http://www.assemblee-nationale.fr/12/europe/index-rapinfo.asp, accessed 31 January 2008), and approval with some qualifications (British Office of Fair Trading, Response to the European Commission's Green Paper, http://ec.euro pa. eu/comm/competition/antitrust/actionsdamages/green_paper_comments.html, accessed 31 January 2008).

21   An example can be given regarding treble damages. The AMC, *supra* note 6, at 246, underlines that '[t]reble damages serve five related and important goals: (i) deterring anticompetitive conduct; (ii) punishing violators of the antitrust laws; (iii) forcing disgorgement of the benefits of anticompetitive conduct from those violators; (iv) providing full compensation to victims of anticompetitive conduct; and (v) providing an incentive to victims to act as "private attorneys general". . . . Although it has been argued that, in certain circumstances, something more or less than treble damages would better advance one or more of these goals, . . . the Commission concludes that an insufficient case has been made for changing the treble damages rule, either universally or in specified instances. . . . The Commission concludes that, on balance, the treble damages rule well serves the defined goals.'

or undermine consensus about the value of a strong antitrust enforcement regime. Enforcers should strive to avoid the imposition of unreasonable costs – for example, costs not reasonably justified by legitimate needs to gather further evidence or that could be avoided by coordination with, or deference to, other antitrust enforcers.[22]

One can also stress that the resources of public enforcers and private litigants are scarce, absolutely or relatively, whatever their budgetary or financial efforts,[23] which also explains a residual threshold of inefficiency. It should also be borne in mind that antitrust agencies suffer from information asymmetries that constrain their ability to detect anticompetitive market malfunctioning.

Yet in their constant quest for optimal enforcement, jurisdictions should organize independent, periodic and deeply penetrating assessment proceedings of the process, in order to facilitate its compatibility with efficiency, and to effect practical solutions to put an end to a conflict failure, if one is revealed after the cross-examining operation. This is a vital condition for a correct and enduring resolution of failure conflicts and of an efficacious search for possibly hidden defects of the process.

This kind of highly advisable periodic assessment already exists in some legal orders,[24] but it seems that it has to be strengthened, and that many efforts are still to be made.[25] Ex-post review of past remedies aims at providing guidance for future ex-ante remedies.

---

[22]   *Id*, at 127.

[23]   Efforts are, alas, not always duly performed, as in the case of the French Competition Council, whose budget is clearly insufficient; *see* M-A Frison-Roche, 'Étude dressant un bilan des autorités administratives indépendantes. Rapport sur les autorités administratives indépendantes' in *Office parlementaire d'évaluation de la législation* (2006) Vol II, chapter 1.1.11. In this kind of situation, there is a failure conflict, because the capacity for expertise of the CA, whatever the quality of its intervention, is limited.

[24]   The AMC is a good example of the institutionalization of assessment proceedings, set by law, at a high level, in terms of both administration hierarchy and intensity of technical scrutiny. Merger remedies have also been a field of such assessment at the initiative of competition agencies both in the US (*see* the pioneering study carried out by the FTC, '*A Study of the Commission's Divestiture Process*' (1999), http://www.ftc.gov/os/1999/08/divestiture.pdf, accessed 31 January 2008) and in the EC (DG Competition, 'Merger Remedies Study' (2005), http://ec. europa.eu/comm/competition/mergers/others/remedies_study.pdf (accessed 31 January 2008); Laboratorio di economia, antitrust, regolamentazione (Lear), 'Ex-Post Review of Merger Control Decisions', A study for the European Commission prepared by Lear (2006), http://ec.europa.eu/comm/competition/mergers/studies _reports/lear.pdf, accessed 31 January 2008).

[25]   OECD, 'Evaluation of the Actions and Resources of Competition Authorities', DAF/COMP (2005)30, 2005, pp 7–10. This report correctly and

2.2 Types of Failure Conflicts

First, as enforcement of competition law is intrinsically pluralistic, failure conflicts can occur in addressing this pluralism, which is expressed through its goals, its territorial scope and its organs and procedures.

The monitoring of competition policies gravitates around a couple of dual and interdependent central goals that consider its unceasing struggle against anticompetitive conduct: prevention and deterrence, on the one hand, and prosecution and reparation, on the other.

The pluralistic territorial scope can be expressed thus: 'First, markets (not to mention legal practices) generally span regions far larger than any state. Second, antitrust analysis has a common methodology applicable across the states, and thus does not benefit from a state-centric focus. Modern antitrust law is global antitrust law.'[26]

---

successively holds that '[t]here is a general consensus that competition agencies should regard evaluation programs as necessary, integral elements of good public administration. . . .. There are growing demands from outside competition agencies to develop and apply measures to test the effectiveness of competition policy. In an increasing number of jurisdictions, legislatures and other public bodies are initiating projects to evaluate the effects of competition policy programs or to analyse the efficiency of competition agency organisation and procedures. . . . Evaluation should be a routine ingredient of the competition agency's annual agenda and should be incorporated into the formulation of budgets and operational plans . . . Over the past decade competition agencies have responded to their own awareness of the importance of ex post evaluation and external demands for performance measurement by devoting increasing attention to analysing the effectiveness of existing institutional arrangements and specific initiatives, such as cases and advocacy measures. Useful insights can be derived from a variety of evaluation methods, using resources within and external to the competition authority. . . . One of the most fruitful areas of evaluation to date has been the field of merger control. Studies of the results achieved with merger remedies have yielded important insights about improvements in the design and implementation of merger enforcement policy. . . . Evaluations of existing institutional arrangements, including organisation, management methods and operational procedures, have proven useful in identifying areas for improvement and motivating adjustments. . . . The organisation assessment and development framework shows genuine promise as a means for competition authorities to improve the quality of their institutional arrangements. . . . Considerable work remains to be done to refine the methodologies used to evaluate the effectiveness of completed competition policy interventions. . . . Systematic efforts to collect information on evaluation methodologies and the substantive reserves of individual evaluation exercises would facilitate useful comparative analyses of competition policy and improve the pursuit of evaluation efforts within individual jurisdictions. Authorities would benefit from continuing to develop a repository of information on evaluation issues'.

26 Elhauge and Geradin, *supra* note 7, at p v. This triggers the problem of jurisdictional conflicts in competition law and the need for international cooperation, whether formal or not.

Antitrust enforcement encompasses public and private enforcement, civil, penal or administrative litigation, ministries and independent public agencies, generalist or specialized courts, supranational, national, local enforcers, inquiring, prosecuting, adjudicating, punishing, advocating, repairing proceedings, ex-ante and ex-post actions or remedies, unilateral public enactment and cooperation with private parties. Legal monitoring of this manifold entity is undeniably complex and flaws in the process are not infrequent. These failures express excessive complexity, inconsistency and redundancy in the system, which cripple legal certainty, predictability and efficacious and timely intervention, at the expense of the good functioning of markets.[27]

The resolution of the conflicts is to be found in constant readjustment of the communicating vessels of enforcement[28] via institutional cooperation and harmonization,[29] if simplification by unification or suppression of some enforcing organs is not possible,[30] and in optimal trade-offs between different ways of enforcing and in the balance of the judicial review between sufficient control of public enforcement and the necessary margin of discretion that must be conceded to competition authorities.

Second, failure conflicts may arise in a single enforcement process. Here the issue is the search for optimal use of a given legal resource of the enforcement system. For instance, the process timing should approximate the economic timing, which is not always the case, both in the prosecution of anti-competitive practices and in merger control. Choices also have to be made between ex-ante or ex-post intervention by the Competition Authority.

Another instance can be given with the quest for predictability, which is affected by an inherent paradox: certainty is indeed necessary for promoting efficiency, but too much predictability kills flexibility, fosters complexity and increases insecurity.

---

[27]   There can be excessive 'competition among procedures in competition law'; *see* N Dorandeau, 'La concurrence des procédures en droit de la concurrence' in *Mélanges en l'honneur d'Yves Serra* (2006) 133.

[28]   As the enforcement system is divided into interactive components, a change in one component necessarily alters other sections. Thus the pressure for a 'recriminalization' of European competition law comes from the lessening of ex-ante monitoring (by the suppression of previous exemption notification), which creates new demands for more deterrence and harsh punishment ex-post.

[29]   The creation of the European competition network is a good example of this evolution. There is a powerful trend towards harmonization of competition law in the Northern Atlantic zone, both between the US and the EC, and inside the EC.

[30]   *Eg*, in the case of two national competition authorities, the General Direction for Competition, a ministerial central service, and the Competition Council, an independent administrative authority.

A last example concerns the administration of proof in competition litigation. The monitoring of the standard of proof has to be performed with caution. If too demanding, it can weaken the efficiency of public enforcement when the enforcer has to make complex economic assessments and when undertakings are ever keener to hide relevant information,[31] or it can render private enforcement unattractive, if the proof of the infringement and of the link between the alleged infringement and damage is too difficult for private plaintiffs to bring. If the monitoring is too lax, it can induce false assessment, and in criminal cases especially, such errors can be highly nefarious.[32] The search for the grail of information is also the main reason for the increasing success of leniency programmes, notwithstanding some debates concerning their ethical basis.

3 STRUCTURAL CONFLICTS

3.1 Efficiency versus Legitimacy through the Protection of Fundamental Rights

3.1.1 The scope of these conflicts: the dilemma of an efficient enforcement fully respecting protective procedural rules

The efficiency of the process is inseparable from its legitimacy, because it needs to be accepted by society and by economic actors, be it only to foster

---

[31] OECD, 'Roundtable on Prosecuting Cartels Without Direct Evidence of Agreement Proceedings', DAF/COMP/GF/WD(2006)2, http://www.olis.oecd. org/olis/2006doc.nsf/LinkTo/NT00000DBE/$FILE/JT00200658.PDF (accessed 31 January 2008, p 2, contains this observation: '*Circumstantial evidence is employed in cartel cases in all countries.* Competition law enforcement officials always strive to obtain direct evidence of agreement in prosecuting cartel cases, but sometimes it is not available. Cartel operators conceal their activities and usually they do not co-operate with an investigation of their conduct, unless they perceive that it is to their advantage to participate in a leniency programme. In this context, circumstantial evidence can be important. Almost every country making a written or oral contribution to the roundtable described at least one case in which circumstantial evidence was used to significant effect. At the same time, there are limits to the use of circumstantial evidence. Such evidence, especially economic evidence, can be ambiguous. It must be interpreted correctly by investigators, competition agencies and courts. Importantly, circumstantial evidence can be, and often is, used together with direct evidence.'

[32] One cannot but approve of this warning of the OECD, *supra* note 13, at 13: 'Regardless of how these specific evidentiary questions are answered in a given system, the trend toward civil and administrative treatment of competition violations, and hence toward more liberal and subjective judicial standards in these cases, can conflict with the need for protection of due process for the citizens of a country. Courts must not sacrifice due process requirements in their quest for more accuracy in competition cases.'

the development of a culture of competition. Its legitimacy is twofold: first, general competition rules must have been adopted by democratically chosen and controlled legislative and governmental bodies, and second, proceedings must abide by fundamental rights, especially procedural fundamental rights.

This requirement is all the more demanding as enforcement of competition law is based on the use of penal and quasi-penal measures, such as administrative fines, and because, in most jurisdictions, especially in the EU, competition authorities are administrative bodies that have been endowed with quasi-judicial powers of investigation, prosecution and punishment, which, contrary to the judiciary, they can use ex officio and not only following a complaint, or with powers of authorization or opposition, which limits business freedom and the right of property. If all these competencies are obviously submitted to judicial review by courts, their deep potential or effective impact on natural and legal persons has to be checked and balanced by appropriate formal and procedural guarantees.[33]

In other words, a core dilemma is at stake here: on the one hand, public enforcement of competition law must deal with the imperatives of flexibility, quickness and efficiency, but enforcement authorities have to cope with a procedural feedback protecting fundamental rights of market operators, which tends ineluctably to make their intervention slower, less adaptable and less efficacious in terms of monitoring, preventing, deterring, punishing, and repairing antitrust-law violations.[34] Striking an optimal balance between these two vital organs of competition law enforcement is not easy.

Yet the protection of fundamental rights is rendered all the more necessary as, following the trend of fulfilling economic efficiency, competition law is becoming, if one may say so, more and more economic, and thus more and more unpredictable, at least from a lawyer's point of view. Competition regulation addresses from a strictly economic standpoint the effects on the market rather than the behaviour in the market. This is typical in the control of abuses of dominant position, but the same evolution can be seen in anti-cartel prosecution, where the finding of a dysfunction of the market precedes the proving of an anticompetitive practice. In the name of efficiency, the market distortion prevails on supposed agreement, so that the graver the distortion is, the more readily the existence of an agreement

---

[33] L Vogel, 'Droits de l'homme et droit de la concurrence' in *Mélanges en l'honneur d'Yves Serra* (2006) 443.

[34] This problem exists in economic regulatory law application in general, of which competition law is one of the main components: A Louvaris, 'Lois techniciennes et droit à un procès équitable. Le cas des lois de régulation économique', 2007 *Les Petites Affiches* no 134, p 60.

will be admitted. Similarly, fines must be set in a proportionate way, but, beyond the prosecution of individual culpable behaviour, the assessment of the gravity of the infringement aims at optimal deterrence by taking account, implicitly or explicitly, at various stages, of the harm done to the market and by neutralizing the amount of gain improperly made.[35] It is thus important to endow the process with procedural stabilizers, protecting the fundamental rights of natural and legal persons, which are impugned, whatever the objectively economic purposes of competition law enforcers.

3.1.1 Illustrations of the Dilemma

The requirements of fundamental rights have provoked, noticeably in EC and Member States' competition law, a real institutional and procedural reshaping of the enforcement system.

It is beyond the scope of this limited survey to describe this phenomenon in its entirety. It can be summarized as follows: first, the European Commission and the national competition agencies, though executive or administrative bodies, have become 'judiciaries' by bearing the burden of procedural rules normally designed only for courts; second, the judicial review of these national competition agencies has been strengthened, both by the control of the respect for procedural law by the competition authorities,[36] and by the more intense scrutiny of the assessment of facts and law by the courts, the control on the merits having a propensity to nibble away at the discretion of the public competition enforcer.[37]

The result of this evolution is a kind of cat-and-mouse game between the development of intervention by public enforcers with powerful competencies of investigation, even by dawn raids in professional as well as private settings, and adjudication, including quasi-penal fines and injunctions to cease and divestiture orders (in the field of merger control) and the limitation of this administrative pro-competitive imperium by the courts.

---

[35]   Goals which are also those of civil punitive damages.

[36]   The recent judgment of the EC Court of First Instance in Case T-351/03 *Schneider Electric SA v Commission* [2007] ECR II-0000 (not yet officially reported), holding that Schneider Electric must be partially compensated for loss sustained as a result of the illegal prohibition of its merger with Legrand because of the grave and manifest failure of the Commission to have regard to Schneider's rights of defence, which constitutes a sufficiently serious breach of Community law to confer such a right, shows that respect for procedure is a paramount requirement of competition law enforcement.

[37]   H Legal, 'Standards of Proof and Standards of Judicial Review in EU Competition Law' in B Hawk (ed), *International Antitrust Law & Policy: Fordham Corporate Law 2005* (2006) chapter 5.

The paradox is that this situation is not fully compatible with respect for legal certainty, because of the not always easily predictable character of the sinuosities of case-law regarding for example to what extent the competition agency, though an administrative body, should abide by the requirements of fair trial resulting from Article 6 of the European Convention for the Protection of Human Rights and Fundamental Freedoms.

3.2   Structural Conflicts can only be Partially Resolved

3.2.1   An unstable modus vivendi
To avoid a reduction in the efficiency of competition law enforcement, courts have developed a case-law that accepts reasonable limitations on fundamental rights in view of the prominent, or deemed as such, public interest governing respect for competition law.

Thus the courts validate some adaptations of fundamental rights requirements.[38] Some are unsatisfactory; one thinks especially of the insufficient control of the power of inspection of the European Commission in professional as well as private premises.[39]

3.2.2   The irreducible amount of conflict
The existence of a certain irreducible level of conflict stems from the preeminence of fundamental rights in jurisdictions obedient to the due process of law. This implies that grave breaches of procedural rights can only lead to the quashing of the impugned enforcement decision, without any possibility of overhaul at a later stage of the proceedings, or of remitting the case for a fresh decision, even if the decision is basically grounded and serves economic efficiency. Various examples of this conflictive configuration can be given. This is the case when the structural impartiality of the enforcer is contested.[40]

The control of proportionality of fines may also lead to fines being set aside whose amount depends on the method of calculation and which

---

[38]   *See* OECD, *supra* note 13, at 10: 'Courts ensure that fundamental procedural rights, including rights of privacy, the right to a fair and impartial hearing, and confidentiality of business information, are protected. Procedural safeguards are a prerequisite for an effective competition policy. Procedural due process makes certain that antitrust policy is implemented in an objective fashion and that the competition agency is accountable, thereby enhancing its credibility with the public. But procedural due process is not absolute. Courts must make allowance for the imperatives of economic policy in implementing competition laws.'

[39]   B Hatoux, 'Visites domiciliaires: une triste histoire communautaire ou le naufrage d'une liberté', (2004) *Bulletin fiscal Francis Lefebvre*, No 4, Chronique, p 223.

[40]   Cass. com, 23 June 2004, Bulletin civil, IV no 132.

would be economically efficient, but disproportionate to the financial situation of the punished undertaking.[41] The presumption of innocence and the rights of defence bar the use of some economic standards of proof considered as too lax. The protection of business secrecy, and more generally of private secrecy, by law also appears to be a strong limitation on public enforcement, especially in the coordination and cooperation of the different internal and foreign public enforcers.

To briefly conclude, one may wonder if one could not escape reasoning in terms of conflicts between economic efficiency and judicial and administrative process in competition law. In the last analysis, does not legal efficacy strengthen the legitimacy of competition enforcement and thus the culture of competition and its acceptance by undertakings as a sound and regular parameter of their commercial strategy? If one reckons that economic efficiency must be inscribed in a wider concept of *social efficiency*, grounded on fundamental rights, might not one pass, though avoiding a naïve irenism, from a perspective of conflict to a notion of common cooperation in the building of social efficiency, as put forward, for example, by Article 2 EC, while keeping in mind that competition is not a goal per se, but a tool, however essential, that contributes to the achievement of social welfare through efficient working markets.

---

[41]   E Combe, 'Quelle sanction contre les cartels? Une perspective économique', (2006) *RIDE* 45.

16. Conflicts between economic efficiency and effective judicial process

Muriel Chagny*

1 INTRODUCTION

How can economic efficiency, so dear to competition law, and the effectiveness of the administrative or judicial process enter into conflict, or opposition, with each other? At first sight, there can be no conflict between economic efficiency and process effectiveness, since the latter is devised as a means to reach the ends of competition law, one of which is precisely economic efficiency. However, in reality, not only does it appear that a conflict can arise, but also that it can take various forms, as the plural chosen for the title of this contribution foreshadows. This will lead us to try to identify the different types of conflicts.

Paradoxically, the position of a commentator prompts us, on the one hand, to adopt the vocabulary chosen by the main speaker and to remain in line with his expressed views, and, on the other hand, to set ourselves apart from those views, in particular by choosing a different framework for our study. Consequently, the definitions of the various words in the heading are exactly the same as those given by Professor Louvaris,[1] though the 'effectiveness–efficiency' duo of our topic becomes a trio in his contribution, efficacy being introduced into the reasoning following the method suggested by the main speaker.

We will hereafter consider the two types of conflict identified by Mr Louvaris, namely 'failure conflicts' and structural conflicts. However, they will be studied in the light of French private law, and with a prospective

---

* Professor of Private Law, University of Versailles-Saint-Quentin-en-Yvelines, France.

[1] A Louvaris, 'A brief overview of some conflicts between economic efficiency and effectiveness of the administrative or judicial process in competition law', Chapter 15 in this volume.

dimension. This implies taking into account the legal actions brought before civil courts for the application of both competition and restrictive-practices law. It must be mentioned that the latter is a French specificity. These rules, which can only be applied by the judicial judge,[2] actually fall within the scope of contract law rather than competition law. They are thus often referred to as 'little' or 'false' competition law.[3]

The scope of this study leads us to treat with care the assumption that economic efficiency is at least partially reached. Indeed, the place for economic efficiency within competition law depends on the provisions in question: while competition law gives it an increasingly warm welcome, the law on restrictive practices does not seem to take it into account.

Moreover, a serious difficulty arises from the fact that victims often do not dare complain about competition-law violations when these violations are not the act of competitors, but rather of contracting partners (except, of course, when their relationship has ended and they therefore do not have anything to lose). It is then truly a problem of effectiveness that arises, since the rules are not used by those who are in the best position to know of the illegal practices. This phenomenon has led to allowing people other than the victim, and in particular the Minister for the Economy, to take action.

In accordance with the double dimension – positive and prospective – we will consider failure conflicts (*infra* 2) and structural conflicts (*infra* 3) between economic efficiency and the effectiveness of the judicial process in competition law. While doing so, we will try to identify those conflicts and to suggest some paths of evolution.

2   FAILURE CONFLICTS BETWEEN ECONOMIC EFFICIENCY AND THE EFFECTIVENESS OF THE JUDICIAL PROCESS

The enforcement of competition law reveals that the implementation of the judicial process does not necessarily produce the expected result and that it

---

[2]   The French judiciary system is divided into two main branches. The first is called the judicial branch (*ordre judiciaire*) and encompasses the criminal and civil courts. The second branch is referred to as the administrative branch. Besides those two branches there are several regulatory authorities (*autorités administratives indépendantes*), such as the *Conseil de la concurrence*, in charge of applying competition law.

[3]   *Eg*, L Idot, 'L'empiètement du droit de la concurrence sur le droit du contrat' (2004) *Revue des contrats* 882; M Chagny, 'L'empiètement du droit de la concurrence sur le droit des contrats' (2004) *Revue des contrats* 861.

may, as a result, come into conflict with economic efficiency, a situation which cannot be considered satisfactory. Hence, after having underlined the manifestations of failure conflicts between economic efficiency and the effectiveness of the judicial process (*infra* 2.1), we will suggest ways to resolve those conflicts (*infra* 2.2).

2.1 Manifestations of Failure Conflicts between Economic Efficiency and the Effectiveness of the Judicial Process

Saying that the judicial path sometimes seems to suffer, in the case of competition law, from a lack of effectiveness is an understatement. This insufficient result of the civil proceedings has several sources; it stems, on the one hand, from difficulties in the characterization of infringements and, on the other hand, from the deficiencies of civil-law sanctions.

Difficulties of characterization appear particularly – but not exclusively – when parties refer to anti-competitive practices before the private law judge. It is important to recall that when victims of such behaviour intend to obtain civil remedies – nullity of a contract and/or damages – they must refer the matter to a private law court. However, their action is likely to be hindered by obstacles such as the legal definition and the proof of the practices, especially since the burden of proof rests on the plaintiff. The difficulties are all the more important as the characterization of a cartel or of an abuse of dominant position requires an economic appraisal and, therefore, some form of economic expertise, which the private law judge may not have.

This is why victims may prefer first to refer their case to the *Conseil de la concurrence* in order to benefit from its economic expertise, its means of investigation and *in fine* its judgment. This usually then makes it easier to prove the violation of a competition rule before the judicial judge. However, the civil judge before whom the matter will later be laid is not bound by the decision of the *Conseil de la concurrence*, which does not have the authority of res judicata. In addition, even if the decisions of this specialized authority do have some influence on private law courts, 'follow on' actions significantly increase the length of proceedings, even though 'economic time' calls for speedy solutions. In addition, this difficulty is notably exacerbated in the case of civil liability suits. Even if the problem of characterizing the infringement is resolved, a second problem arises in the evaluation of compensatory damages. The judge may be tempted to ask for an expert opinion in order to overcome this difficulty. Though such a course of action may slow down the proceedings while increasing their cost, it does allow for more efficient civil remedies.

One of the main flaws of civil remedies is their lack of efficiency. Not only are past offenders not properly penalized, but potential offenders are not sufficiently deterred. That is particularly true in the case of liability suits, which can be brought by the victim of anti-competitive or restrictive practices. As a result of the difficulties in establishing and evaluating the loss caused by an infringement of the competition rule, the amount of damages awarded will often be low, leaving the victim unsatisfied and allowing the offending company to make a profit through the violation of the competition rule. If this failure is alarming in view of the victim's situation and, more widely, of private interests in competition law, it is even more so in the case of restrictive practices, since the *Conseil de la concurrence* is not entitled to order fines.

Consequently, it is not surprising that French lawmakers have provided, especially in the case of restrictive practices, for other civil remedies and have significantly extended the powers bestowed upon the Economy Minister. Following a statute of 15 May 2001, not only can he ask for 'a civil fine the amount of which cannot exceed 2 million euros', but he can also 'have illicit clauses or contracts declared void and request that restitutions be made'.[4] Yet even though these prerogatives are implemented by the Economy Minister, until now they have been of limited efficacy.

On the one hand, the civil fines ordered by judicial courts are of a rather limited amount, since the judge does not have to justify his decision on this point. Though the legislature has set a ceiling on fines, it has given no guidance as to how their amount is to be determined. On the other hand, although the restitutions following the annulment of a contract can add up to large amounts,[5] many victims – who according to the law are to be the sole recipients of these damages – do not wish to receive them. Also the terseness of the current provisions does not bring any sure solution to this problem.[6] Yet if the insufficiencies and deficiencies we have set forth are genuine, they can most likely be overcome.

2.2   The Resolution of Failure Conflicts between Economic Efficiency and the Effectiveness of the Judicial Process

My point is to suggest, in view of a competition-law reform, and with no claim to be exhaustive, some remedies likely to reinforce the efficiency of the judicial process.

---

[4]   Article L. 442-6-III C. com.
[5]   T. Com. Créteil, 24 October 2006, *min. Eco c/ SAS Systeme U*, (2007) *Revue Lamy de la concurrence*, No 11, 87, comments by M Chagny.
[6]   Cour d'appel de Versailles, 12th chambre, section 2, 3 May 2007, *Galec contre min. Eco*, Case No RG 05/09223.

To some extent, EU competition law shows the way when it compels internal procedural legal provisions to meet the requirements of full effectiveness (*'effet utile'*) and tries, in the name of economic efficiency, to safeguard the rights of victims of anti-competitive practices. To do so, it goes as far as excluding putting aside the application of national rules on the basis of which damages could not be awarded or contracts could not be annulled in competition law cases, if these rules contravene the principles of equivalence and effectiveness.[7]

Actually, some forms of remedy have already been tested and new ones can be added, both in order to make the characterization of those practices easier and to reinforce the efficacy of civil sanctions. Two main paths can be taken in order to facilitate the proof of infringements, depending on whether we focus on the necessary economic expertise or on the problems of proof. As far as economic expertise is concerned, it is possible to strengthen the role of private law judges and to take advantage of the specialized authority. The will to reinforce the economic expertise of judges applying competition law has undoubtedly played a role in the fact that the 2001 reform has limited the number of private law courts having jurisdiction over these matters.[8] As desirable as it can seem, this specialization raises some as yet unresolved difficulties. Moreover, it appears excessive considering the very limited list drawn up by the decree,[9] which identifies the law courts empowered to apply competition law.

In order to benefit from the undeniable economic expertise of the *Conseil de la concurrence*, it might be advisable to grant its decisions the authority of res judicata. However, in order not to excessively lengthen proceedings, the creation of some sort of speedy procedure could be a solution when the case brought before the private law judge is a 'follow on'. It would also be conceivable to allow the Paris *Cour d'appel* (Court of Appeals),[10] to grant civil remedies and in particular damages, when reviewing a decision rendered by the *Conseil de la concurrence*.

As far as the problem of evidence is concerned, it is possible to impose some type of burden-sharing or, more radically, to invert the burden of proof. The latter has been the option taken by the French legislature. A law of 2 August 2005 provides that 'in all the cases, the provider of services,

---

[7]   Case C-453/99, *Courage v Crehan*, [2001] ECR I-6297; Joined Cases C-295/04 to C-298/04, *Manfredi and others*, [2006] ECR I-6619.

[8]   Article L. 420-7 C. com.

[9]   Décret No 2005–1756, 30 December 2005, JO 31 December. 2005, p 20831.

[10]   The Paris Court of Appeal is the only court of appeal having jurisdiction to hear appeals against the *Conseil de la concurrence's* decisions.

the producer, the seller, the manufacturer or the person registered on the roll of craftsmen who pretends to be released from his obligations must prove the fact which released him'.[11] This seems to be a rather effective course of action, since evidentiary questions are often tricky. Yet if acting upon the burden of proof is undoubtedly effective, it is not always fair. In any case, it is too early to draw a conclusion about the real effectiveness of this device.

Although we can imagine some less constraining courses of action, such as setting guidelines to facilitate the evaluation of damages by judges, these do not seem sufficient to reinforce the efficacy of civil remedies in competition-law cases. On the one hand, with regard to the prerogatives given to the Minister for the Economy in cases of restrictive practices, if it is true that the mechanism of restitutions can lead to the award of large amounts of damages, it remains necessary to find a way to overcome the disinterest or even opposition of victims who do not want to receive those damages. If no satisfactory solution can be found to this problem, the deterrent and penalizing effects of the civil fines provided by Article L 442-6-III of the *Code de commerce* could still be increased by replacing the absolute value ceiling with a relative value ceiling and by including guidelines to help judges evaluate damages. The illicit profit made by the offender could thus be one of the elements taken into account.

On the other hand, the search for effective civil remedies should, in our opinion, lead to judicial courts being allowed to award punitive damages. Without going into excessive detail on what is a matter of deep controversy in France, it is important to mention the existence of a preliminary draft of reform of the law of obligations, which provides for punitive damages.[12] We wish to stress the fact that allowing such damages to be awarded can be done without necessarily copying the American model and that measures can be taken to curtail some frequently criticized abuses.[13]

The will to reinforce the effectiveness of the judicial process, for the purpose of solving failure conflicts, is sometimes in opposition to economic efficiency. This leads to another type of conflict, which I will now address.

---

[11]   Article L 442-6-III C. com.

[12]   Avant-projet de réforme du droit des obligations, 22 September. 2005, Article 1371.

[13]   *See* L Idot, 'Rapport de synthèse' (2007) *Concurrences*, No 2, 91, and M Chagny, 'Faut-il prendre en compte les objectifs du droit de la concurrence dans les actions en dommages-intérêts?' in 'Les sanctions civiles des pratiques anticoncurrentielles: compléments ou substituts des sanctions du droit de la concurrence?',

3   STRUCTURAL CONFLICTS BETWEEN ECONOMIC EFFICIENCY AND THE EFFECTIVENESS OF THE JUDICIAL PROCESS

The judicial process sometimes produces the awaited result while challenging economic efficiency. Professor Louvaris refers to this type of conflict as structural.

If it is true that the conflict between economic efficiency and the procedural rights of economic actors appears difficult to overcome (*infra* 3.1), the same cannot be said of the conflict between economic efficiency and legal proof of the violations of competition regulations (*infra* 3.2).

3.1   The Truly Structural Conflict between Economic Efficiency and the Procedural Rights of Economic Actors

Rather than stress the procedural guarantees given to those suspected of having violated competition regulations, I have chosen, as a complement to the main speaker's lecture, to focus on the victims' rights. Conflicts appear with regard to both the law of restrictive practices and antitrust law.

The quest for efficacy, which lies at the heart of the statute of 2 August 2005, has given rise to several procedural reforms. In the case of the offences provided for by title IV, book IV of the Commercial Code, several exceptional solutions have been created in order to reinforce sanctions and to speed up the dispute resolution.

It is however possible to wonder if a mechanism such as reaching a settlement with the administration outside a courtroom[14] does not deprive the prosecuted company of the guarantees that are necessary to legitimate the process. It is therefore important to surround these practices with enough guarantees to preserve due process, even if it were to reduce economic efficiency. Moreover, we must deplore the fact that these practices leave victims on one side and do not in any way reinforce their rights.

Competition law also faces such a problem. It can even be increased by the development of new negotiated procedures to which competition authorities resort in the name of economic efficiency. In the absence of legal provisions, one may wonder when an economic actor who has suffered loss as a result of some antitrust behaviour can claim compensation for this loss, especially if the procedure ends with each party taking on new obligations

---

Colloque Le Mans, 5 December 2006 (2007), *Concurrences en ligne*, p 3, http://www.concurrences.com/IMG/pdf/Concurrences_2–2007_Colloque_Le_Mans_051 206–3.pdf (accessed 31 January 2008).

[14]   Article L. 470-4-1 C. com.

or when the leniency program is implemented. If commitments are made by the defendant,[15] we may wonder whether the concerns about competition expressed in the decision of the *Conseil de la concurrence* allow the finding of a violation of competition law, since the *Conseil* does not pronounce any sentence against the defendant(s). It is true that a civil court can take into account concerns about competition when assessing a defendant's behaviour. Yet the victim can never be sure of succeeding, all the more so when the decision recording the commitments does not contain much information that could be of help to the civil judge.

The conflict may be even more direct in the case of the leniency program.[16] Its implementation obviously supposes the violation of antitrust law, and, as a consequence, the victim could seem to be in a comfortable position. However, he or she can have trouble gaining access to the evidence collected by the specialized authority. It is therefore particularly important to make sure that the determination to preserve economic efficiency by making the leniency program attractive does not result in sacrificing the victim's rights. From this point of view, and in conformity with the French constitutional principles, the victim of a cartel thus revealed must be able to be compensated by the offender, whoever he may be. The applicant to the leniency program must not be allowed to shirk his obligation to compensate the loss caused by the prohibited practice. However, as far as sanctions are concerned, one might imagine excluding punitive damages – if they ever were to be adopted by French law.

Even if partial solutions may be found, the opposition between economic efficiency and procedural rights seems to give rise to an unsolvable conflict. We must now see if the same can be said of other structural conflicts.

3.2   The Apparent Structural Conflict between Economic Efficiency and Legal Proof of the Infringement of Competition Law

The effectiveness of the judicial process is likely to be hindered by evidentiary difficulties, especially as far as economic matters are concerned. That has led the French Parliament to adopt per-se prohibitions in the case of restrictive practices. Their implementation does not require the judge to ensure that the practices at hand are in fact harmful to competition. These provisions undoubtedly have real advantages: they are foreseeable, simple and effective. However, they also have a major disadvantage: they are

---

[15]   Article L. 464-2-I(2) C. com.
[16]   Article L. 464-2-IV C. com.

applied in a general way and automatically, without any consideration for the configuration of the market or for the situation of the companies concerned. These rules do not allow for an economic analysis of the impact of the infringement on competition and can therefore condemn practices that are actually economically efficient. Consequently, if implementation of these rules is clearly facilitated, it is only at the cost of a conflict with economic efficiency.

Yet this conflict is perhaps not as insurmountable as it seems, at least if one accepts contemplating an evolution of the law of restrictive practices and questioning the merits of per-se prohibitions. Furthermore, besides the fact that the number of per-se prohibitions could be reduced, it seems possible to reconcile the effectiveness of the judicial process and economic efficiency by favouring 'quasi per se' prohibitions. These prohibitions would rest upon the assumption that the practice at hand is harmful to competition, but that assumption could be rebutted by the alleged offender.

This shows us that although it is indeed difficult to reconcile economic efficiency and legal certainty, and, more generally, economics and law, the mission is not impossible.

PART IV

Guest speech

17. Efficiency in the enforcement policy of the French *Conseil de la concurrence*

Bruno Lasserre*

1 INTRODUCTION

1.1 Defining Efficiency

I would like to open with a couple of thoughts on the meaning of the word 'efficiency'. What does it mean to be efficient? Certainly, being 'efficient' is more than merely being 'effective'. Being 'effective', or *'effectif'* in French, means being capable of producing effects. Being 'efficient' goes further than that. On the one hand, it means being capable of bringing about the desired effects, of performing a predefined task. In that sense, 'efficient' corresponds to the French word *'efficace'*. Yet, on the other hand, it also relates to how well one brings about these desired effects, to how well one performs that task. In that sense, 'efficient' corresponds to another French term: *'efficient'*.

This definition is reflected in economics. A basic economic view of efficiency is that a certain allocation is more efficient when it increases the net value of resources. Now, I will not delve into the subtleties of Pareto or Kaldor-Hicks types of efficiency – it is not my place and I would not want to offend serious economists. However, I would like to use the following basic definition of efficiency: one's aptitude to perform one's task with the least waste. And I would submit that this notion is the driving force of an antitrust authority such as the French *Conseil de la concurrence* (hereafter: 'the *Conseil*').

The performance of an antitrust agency is constrained by three main factors:

(i) the scarcity of its own resources;
(ii) the limitation of its legal powers; and

---

*   President of the *Conseil de la concurrence* (French Competition Council).

(iii)   information asymmetries which cripple the agency's ability to detect
         anticompetitive practices.

Still we are expected (and rightfully so) to conduct our action efficiently.
That means four things:

- first, we must implement a credible fining policy in order to send the
  right signals to the market;
- second, we need to make use of the full range of measures available
  in order to deter anticompetitive practices and correct market conditions;
- third, we must issue our decisions in a timely manner, that is, matching market-based time constraints; and
- fourth, ideally, we should be selective and focus our efforts on the
  most harmful practices, and we should also evaluate our action *ex
  post*.

1.2   Towards Efficiency: The Development of Legal Means in the Hands of the *Conseil*

Recent reforms have increased the range of tools available to the *Conseil* in
France. The diversity of the means that are now at our disposal has contributed to improving our performance. And I say 'diversity' because the
new powers at the hands of the *Conseil* differ in nature from the ones it was
initially endowed with.

Our traditional tools are fines and injunctions. Such remedies are
imposed by the *Conseil* in order to put an end to a given practice, punish
infringers and deter anticompetitive behaviour.

New types of measures have been introduced in 2001 and 2004. They
allow the *Conseil* to: (1) accept commitments offered by parties in antitrust
proceedings; (2) acknowledge a defendant's decision not to challenge
charges notified to it; (3) grant total or partial immunity to leniency applicants. All of these measures are alternative or accessory measures, insofar
as they offer to both, the authority and the defendant, a choice between full
punishment, on the one hand, and limited punishment or even no punishment at all if other means of achieving our goal of restoring competition
in the marketplace seems more efficient. In addition, all of these measures
entail a new type of relationship between the authority and the defendant.
However, this relationship is different in all three cases. It goes from fully
fledged negotiation in the case of commitments, to circumscribed cooperation in the case of settlement, and to unilateral cooperation on the part of
the undertaking in the case of leniency.

Analysing these tools under the perspective of efficiency amounts to asking three questions:

(1)   Are these tools efficient in and out of themselves?
(2)   Are these tools efficiently coordinated?
(3)   Are these tools implemented in a time-efficient fashion?

Finally, if efficiency amounts to the best allocation of resources, I will say a few words about case prioritization.

2   THE EFFICIENCY OF MEASURES ADOPTED BY THE *CONSEIL*

2.1   Greater Efficiency for Traditional Legal Tools

Legal reform and French antitrust policy combine in a movement towards greater efficiency for the traditional tools used by the *Conseil* to punish anticompetitive conduct:

● the scope of fines has been broadened;
● we seek to increase their punitive and deterrent effects; and
● we are being given the means to make injunctions effective.

First, 'injunctions' are orders to cease or engage in certain behaviour (for example, to stop a practice, to grant access to an infrastructure, or to publish a decision). Their goal is to safeguard or re-establish conditions of competition in the market, and to put an end to anticompetitive behaviour. Injunctions seek to repair and/or prevent illegal practices. They can also be designed to deter future anticompetitive practice through orders to publish a decision.

It goes without saying that the efficiency of such measures only goes as far as defendants are willing to implement them. And willingness is not always there! In which case the Conseil is, of course, watchful. For example, France Telecom was fined €20 million in May 2004 because it had not complied with an injunction to allow third parties to gain access to the circuit for the provision of Internet via ADSL. That fine was doubled by the Paris Court of Appeals in January 2005.

Yet it is not enough to be able to fine defendants severely after they have failed to comply with our injunctions, since that does not solve the fact that the orders' main purpose (the immediate re-establishment of a competitive marketplace) is defeated by non-compliance. Therefore, since the end of the

year 2004, we have been able to accompany injunctions with penalty payments in case of non-compliance. We have thus been given the tools for
making injunctions effective.

This tendency towards greater efficiency can also be seen in the area of
fines. Fines are not just punitive: they should also be a deterrent against
anticompetitive practices. Now the question is how much is enough to
deter, given the limits set by the law?

First of all, the limits imposed by the law have recently been dramatically
broadened since we may now impose fines of up to 10 per cent of a
company's worldwide turnover, instead of just 5 per cent of the French
turnover under the previous system.

Second, and perhaps more significantly, the level of fines is now increasing. Total fines imposed by the *Conseil* in the years 2001 to 2004 were in the
region of €40 to 60 million per year. In 2005, we imposed a total amount
of over €750 million, that was partially due to a high fine on a mobile
phone cartel. The total amount imposed by mid-2006 already exceeded
€120 million. So fines are increasing, a fact that has been widely publicized
in the French press. We are thus sending a strong signal that the market
regulator is a force to be reckoned with. In economic terms, what higher
fines achieve to show *ex ante* that the financial risk of entering into anti-
competitive practices may make them unprofitable at the end of the day.
And this is not a simple 'catch-me-if-you-can' situation, because higher
fines and increased awareness of the antitrust risk in the marketplace have
fringe benefits: higher deterrent effects mean that companies will take compliance programs more seriously, that they will exercise tighter control of
executives or commercial people in positions to implement cartels and that
they will factor-in leniency programs when discovering that illegal practices
are ongoing.

That was a brief overview of our traditional means of action. These tools
have been recently complemented by a series of new powers, which I
referred to earlier as 'alternative measures' that contribute to improving our
performance.

2.2 New Tools for Greater Efficiency

New tools give us alternative ways to deal with situations falling under our
control. These tools also allow for faster proceedings and remedies that are
crafted to match every situation.

First, defendants may forgo the possibility of contesting charges that
were notified and of committing to adopt certain behaviour in the future.
Defendants can thus benefit from a lower maximum penalty (the ceiling is
reduced by 50 per cent), a potentially reduced fine, and faster proceedings.

Up to now, this settlement procedure has been applied ten times. A first series of lessons may therefore be drawn. From the authority's perspective, having recourse to the settlement procedure increases certainty of the appropriateness of its remedies, since commitments are negotiated and must be deemed credible and suitable for solving competition issues. In addition, it enables the *Conseil* to deal with cases promptly, and thereby to free up resources for other proceedings, since the second round of exchange with the undertaking (Report) is waived, while the first (Statement of Objections) is kept. In practice, the time gain ranges between two and six months, to which one must add the fact that there is generally no appeal.

Second, companies may propose commitments, even without settling. Commitment proposals must intervene before a Statement of Objections is issued; if accepted, the authority will close proceedings. The impact of these new powers should not be under-estimated: through the negotiation of commitments, what the *Conseil* is actually doing is evaluating the competitive situation in a given market and closing cases under conditions that credibly restore competition. Up to now, this procedure has been applied 13 times, mainly in order to adjudicate on issues relating to the articulation of antitrust law and intellectual property rights, to solve a range of market-access problems, especially in recently liberalized sectors such as telecoms, and to regulate new or recent sales methods such as Internet sale.

Third, cartel participants may apply for leniency. Leniency programs have been designed to cover the participation in hardcore cartels (for example, horizontal price-fixing agreements). Such practices have become increasingly sophisticated in time, in the sense that they are durable practices, designed to be concealed from antitrust enforcers. Their concealed nature makes them hard to detect. The absence of a direct paper trail makes them hard to prove. Hence the emergence of leniency programs, which afford immunity or reductions from fines to applicants who disclose the existence of cartels, stop their participation in them, explain their workings, and provide evidence of their existence to antitrust agencies.

3   THE EFFICIENT COORDINATION OF THE *CONSEIL'S* LEGAL POWERS

The workings of antitrust regulation can be considered as a system of incentives: the question is how to efficiently deter anticompetitive conduct and install desirable incentives (incentives to innovate, to improve productivity, to compete on prices, etc). The regulator, through powers conferred by law, manipulates market incentives in order to align them with antitrust policy and consumer welfare. The notion is quite simple: our goal is to deter anticompetitive practices, given our limited resources and imperfect information on market behaviour.

In that context, fines and alternative measures cannot be considered in isolation. All of our tools are interdependent and mutually contribute to the efficiency of the overall system.

3.1 Efficient Fines: Improving the Authority's Ability to Detect Anticompetitive Behaviour

Economists agree that the efficiency of fines is a function of an antitrust authority's ability to detect anticompetitive behaviour. In order for our fines to have deterrent effects, companies must consider *ex ante* that the future profits that they will generate from anticompetitive conduct cannot exceed profits generated from competitive behaviour in the event they are fined. Fines induce a trade-off between, on the one hand, competitive behaviour, and on the other, anticompetitive profits minus the potential fine.

But the 'potential fine' itself is not certain: it is the level of the fine multiplied by the probability of detection. Therefore, the efficiency of our fining policy largely depends on how efficient we are in detecting illegal practices.

This, in turn, depends on how well an antitrust authority is informed on market behaviour.

If we leave aside the possibility of intervening *proprio motu* in a given case or of opening sectoral enquiries, the traditional path for information on anticompetitive behaviour reaching the *Conseil* is through complaints. But at a time when the most harmful cartels tend to cover wide markets, for a long period of time, and are operated by sophisticated authors that leave no paper trail, this traditional path is insufficient. Hence the adoption, in 2001, of a leniency program, that has been creating an incentive for cartel participants to report and provide evidence of infringements in exchange for immunity from fines. Leniency programs create an incentive to 'defect' and increase an authority's ability to detect anticompetitive behaviour.

Leniency has been criticized – for certain critics, it is immoral to 'reward' infringers, while for others, leniency is 'pro-collusive'. Quite true since there is a moral dilemma in deciding whether infringers should benefit from cooperating with the authorities. But in view of hard-core, concealed behaviour, the trade-off tips in favour of the efficiency of leniency programs, for several reasons. First, granting immunity also means penalizing several co-infringers, and the better the evidence, the harsher the penalty. Second, in more cases than we would like to admit, leniency is the only, or the most reliable, means of detection. Third, critics also omit the notion that immunity recipients do not go unpunished: first, because their reputation is tarnished, and second, because they remain liable under our civil and commercial laws. Even though the relationship between leniency and private litigation raises complex issues beyond the scope of this speech, it suffices to say that the existence of a decision punishing a cartel does not help defendants in civil lawsuits. Authorities like the European Commission go further, by suggesting that potential plaintiffs engage in litigation in its recent press releases on cartel decisions.

Then there is the notion that leniency is pro-collusive, in other words that leniency creates an incentive to conceal and secure cartels even more. But this is only one term in another balancing act: the trade-off between leniency's destabilizing effects and its pro-collusive effects. In reality, leniency provides a constant 'way out' to cartel participants, with an incentive to be the first to apply for leniency. Therefore, I would submit that to the extent that a leniency program is clear and provides predictable outcomes, it is likely that leniency's destabilizing effects will prevail.

3.2 Efficient Alternative Measures: High Fines

As I noted before, all of our tools are *inter*dependent. Meaningful incentives to apply for leniency can only exist if operators feel that lack of cooperation is risky, if they foresee a credible risk of a significant fine being imposed (should their behaviour be detected). Thus a harsh fining policy is a prerequisite for an efficient leniency program. Leniency programs should, in turn, reduce information asymmetries and, eventually, lead antitrust agencies to impose *more* fines on *more* secret cartelists.

It is no accident, therefore, that the emergence of the French leniency program happened at the same time that the legal ceiling on antitrust fines was increased. And it is no accident that we receive a higher number of leniency applications at the same time that the level of our fines increases. As of today, that number has reached 20, which is by no means a small figure given the recent incorporation of leniency into French antitrust law.

The same goes for negotiated measures, which would not be a success if companies were not otherwise faced with burdensome fines.

4   TIME CONSTRAINT

Yet there are cases where the main issue facing an antitrust authority is not to decide whether to punish or to favour alternative ways of restoring competition in the market. There are situations where, whatever instrument is chosen, there is a risk that it will be applied too late, for example because an undertaking has already been driven out of the market or because a given technological or commercial standard has already prevailed on the market, by anticompetitive means. In these cases, the time bell has rung and cannot be unrung. In other words, the question is not 'what', but 'when'.

It is obvious, in such situations, that an antitrust authority cannot be fully efficient if it cannot intervene before time has elapsed. It will be asked to rule on a set of facts, will take the time needed to build a careful analysis and will render an impeccable decision . . . a few years too late. Of course, I am not saying that these years indicate that antitrust regulation is inefficient. On the contrary, an efficient regulator will take the time necessary to bring together sufficient proof of anticompetitive behaviour, to analyse its effects on the market instead of jumping to conclusions, to hear the defendant and assess its defence, and so on, before making a decision. What I am saying is that there may be a conflict between quality and time.

Fortunately, the *Conseil* is equipped with a tool specifically crafted for the purpose of reconciling the regulation time with the business time: interim measures. They give the *Conseil* the possibility of preventing a possible harm to the market where it appears necessary to do so in order to preserve a chance of maintaining competition once a fully fledged analysis has been carried out.

But the existence of interim measures only tells us that the *Conseil may* be efficient in theory. If one wants to know if the *Conseil is* efficient in practice, one must still take a look at how interim measures actually work. Do they allow the *Conseil* to detect which antitrust issues must be dealt with swiftly? Do they also allow the *Conseil* to deal with these issues?

Regarding the first point, I think that the answer is 'yes' in great part because the *Conseil* has gradually eased the two conditions needed in order to grant interim measures. Roughly speaking, these conditions relate, first, to the existence of an illegality and, second, to the existence of a prejudice. Historically, the first condition was met only in the case of a 'manifestly illicit trouble'. The *Conseil* subsequently decided to ease this criterion by allowing interim measures where 'it could not be excluded' that there was an anticompetitive practice. The formula has now settled in between these extremes: interim measures can be granted where it appears that the practices under examination 'may, at the present stage of the investigation' fall within the scope of the rules prohibiting anticompetitive behaviour. As for the second condition, its text remains unchanged: it is met where a 'serious and immediate prejudice' may be caused. However, it is also interpreted with more leniency than was the case in the past. Consequently, we are able to take care of an increasing number of situations calling for swift action on our part.

Regarding the second point, I will also say that the *Conseil* is able to deal efficiently with the issues calling for urgent action, mainly because it is not bound by the interim measures requested by the applicant and may instead order whichever interim measure it deems appropriate.

I will take a recent example of how interim measures can operate. On 18 September 2006, the *Conseil* was asked to rule on an alleged abuse of dominant position committed by Société Nationale Corse Méditerranée (SNCM) and to grant interim measures pending the adoption of a decision on the merits. After only a couple of weeks, on 11 December 2006, the *Conseil* granted such measures.

First, the *Conseil* considered that SNCM might evict its competitors by making a global offer in response to a bid launched by public authorities regarding the routes between Corsica and the mainland, and that the signature of a public service delegation contract in such conditions might directly prejudice both consumers and the sector. Second, the *Conseil* took note of the fact that the existing contract was due to expire on 31 December 2006, that its renewal was pending and that allowing such a renewal through a distorted bid did not guarantee an appropriate economic choice for public authorities and would produce hard-to-reverse effects.

In these conditions, swift action was needed to guarantee competitive bidding conditions within the planned time-frame. That is why the *Conseil* ordered SNCM to accept, with a 48 hour delay, an examination of its offer on a line-by-line basis if public authorities so requested.

But this is only one aspect of a multi-faceted story: a few days later, on 15 December 2006, the supreme administrative judge, the *Conseil d'Etat*, judged that the administrative part of the process, that is, the procedure set up for the attribution of the public service delegation contract, was to be annulled and reinitiated in a way that ensured that a competitive bid took place. This is therefore a story where both regulators and judges showed their capacity to act swiftly and efficiently in order to restore competition on the market.

5   CASE PRIORITIZATION

A final effort towards improving an antitrust agency's efficiency consists in allowing the agency to 'prioritize' certain cases, and thereby direct its resources to detecting, investigating and litigating cases deemed more worthy of its action than others.

Prioritization and the notion that certain cases are more worthy than others is controversial, and not fully reflected in French Law – the *Conseil* cannot decide that it wishes to pursue certain cases and not others, although the law imposes deadlines that mean that some types of cases – mergers, opinions requested by the government or by the courts – must be treated as priorities.

Yet this does not mean that priorities cannot be set, and that more resources cannot be allocated to them. There is a European-wide movement in recognition of the fact that hard-core cartels are among the most harmful conduct under the antitrust laws, and that priority should be given to these cases. The *Conseil* itself has said that hard-core cartels are priority. Yet opponents of prioritization argue that the 'potential harm' should not be the only criterion for pursuing certain practices, that it is difficult to assign gravity to cases and that even small cases merit attention because they can raise interesting legal issues.

In that debate, we should not lose sight of the fact that consumer welfare is the ultimate goal of antitrust enforcement. Therefore, efficiency must be considered in relation to consumer welfare. This leads me to three remarks.

The first one relates to the criterion for prioritization. The criterion should be the gravity of the conduct at issue: the potential harm the practice can inflict on consumer welfare. Prioritizing cases on that basis is possible. I do not mean to say that we should adopt a clear-cut sliding scale of potential anticompetitive conducts' gravity. That is not possible given the variety of practices that fall under our jurisdiction or the way they are implemented. What we understand well, however, is that certain categories of practices are more harmful than others: for example, conduct leading to market foreclosure, market partitioning, cartels and certain unilateral behaviour are more harmful than certain vertical restraints limited in scope.

Second, there is little question, at this point, that hard-core cartels should be an enforcement priority, at both European and national level. In this respect, the *Conseil* is working in continuance of both EC antitrust policy, and national legislation. In 2001, the legislature gave us a leniency program; in 2005, we accompanied our first leniency decision with the publication of leniency guidelines. We are thus working towards more transparency, more predictability and, therefore, more efficiency for our leniency program and overall antitrust system.

Third, it must be borne in mind that criteria other than consumer welfare are *not* a benchmark for efficiency. If targeting our resources at the most harmful conduct means that less harmful conduct will be marginally neglected, then let it be so. Some will be concerned by the fact that, sometimes, small cases bring big innovations. Yet legal innovation is not our goal. If the antitrust literature suffers from less variety of practices to comment on, I can live with that.

This is all the more true since the *Conseil* cannot ignore any complaint submitted to its review. The *Conseil* cannot reject a case on the basis of opportunity. So we do review even 'small cases'. Yet, if the *Conseil* is free to allocate its resources, it should do so in furtherance of its basic mandate for the consumer.

6.   CONCLUSION

The few thoughts that I have developed above clearly show that 'efficiency' structures the entire thinking and action of the *Conseil*, from our priorities to our schedule, from the way we use our resources to the way we implement our legal powers, and from the way we apply and interpret the concepts of competition law to the way we frame our objective, and, indeed, we perceive the very philosophy of antitrust. This is the result of a drastic evolution, which had barely started when I took over the presidency of the French antitrust enforcer, but which has deeply remodelled our institution, as well as the way it is perceived by consumers and society as a whole, in only a few years.

Index

Printed and bound by CPI Group (UK) Ltd, Croydon, CR0 4YY

23/04/2025

14660987-0005